Invi
Dad

INCLUDES JOURNAL

Candice Crear

To order products, or for any other correspondence:

Candice Crear
Email: CandiceCrear@gmail.com
www.CandiceCrear.com

Chief Editors: Gord Dormer & Grace Kerina
Book cover design: John Matthews
Final Layout Design: Phil Coles Independent Design
Layout & logos: Exousia Marketing Group www.exousiamg.com
Author's photo courtesy of AP2 Photography

ISBN: 978-0-9989306-2-6
Printed in the United States of America.

Dedication

To all the children who have less than a father,
this is for you.

Acknowledgments

I have so many people to acknowledge and thank for helping me on my journey, but first and foremost, I want to acknowledge God. He's been with me through this entire journey. I'm so thankful He used me to write this book for you, His Baby Girls. I am forever grateful that He loves me so much and never gave up on me. He is the light unto my path. By His grace, I will bring girls back to Him.

Thanks to my cousin and my sister. This book is for you. I hope you will take this journey.

Thanks to my mother who taught me so much, who pushed me to be better, and who never settled for anything less than taking care of her family (including adopting other little girls like me). I love you and thank you for praying me through my toughest times.

Thanks to my dad for coming back into my life. I truly love you. Through our path together, I hope we can mentor others to never give up.

Thanks to my husband. I appreciate your support of me throughout my journey. I'm grateful to you for just being here. Love you always.

Thanks to my uncles for being examples. You didn't know it then, but I sure looked to you to help me understand a man's role in a child's life.

Thanks to my grandmother and aunts for every sleepover, pick up, drop off, and everything else – for helping to raise me.

Thanks to Dr. Jasmin Sculark for sharing her story. Now, I have the freedom to tell mine.

And, last but not least, thanks to Mrs. Joni Parsley, for being so real. You are a beautiful light.

Table of Contents

Introduction

I was fatherless, but I had dreams. Big dreams. But my dreams would be tossed in the wind with the weight of my reality. In the United States, forty-three percent of children live without a father, and I was one of them. And while there was plenty of negative information on the Internet that could tell me what I had the potential of becoming, I stuck to my own aspirations. I wanted so much more for myself. I wanted to enjoy life and all that it had for me.

I was a perfectionist; at least you would think so. I would put on a show that my life was going great. Everything on the outside was perfect. I had a newer car, was leaving to go to college, I'd graduated at the top of the class and I was having fun! I even told my high school classmates to vote for me as the "Most Likely to Succeed," just so I could hide behind another title. Plus, I went to church every Sunday, and sometimes to Bible study, too. I tried to control people's perceptions of me, because it was much easier than revealing the truth.

That was me, good ol' Candice. Every day would be a new day of over-trying and over-delivering. People called me the "good" girl. You wouldn't even know I was bleeding inside from the gaping wounds of my pain. I had everyone fooled, even the closest person to me, my mother. Everything was a secret that I was happy to hold if no one could tell that I was dying inside. Every breath I took was another breath of defiance. I was angry, belligerent, mean and tired. I needed help… I needed my father.

I was just like you. My scar wasn't visible from the outside, but it was there – a gaping wound ready to bleed out at any moment. No matter how much I tried to fix it, my fatherless nightmares followed me everywhere I went: the grocery store, the restaurant and even my Aunt's house. What could I do to make it all stop?

I would have to embark on a new journey – no holds barred.

The journey would not be easy; in fact, it has been the most challenging trip I've ever had to face.

You can spend every day of your life pretending your life is perfect, or you can work through your problems and take a piece of your power back every day to become free. That's what I did, and that's what you'll need to do, too.

I know not having your dad in your life is not fair, but how long do you think you can hold on to this façade? It's okay not to be okay. I know that if you could magically change it all, you would. But you can't. The painful reality is that he wasn't there for your first day of kindergarten, he missed your elementary school performances and he had the nerve to miss your high school graduation. There were no father-daughter dances, no basketball games, and no Father's Day dinners. He wasn't there, and the sooner you try to face that reality, the sooner you will know that you've had what you needed all along. You can receive the peace you've always longed for and the love you've always desired.

This book may not be what you expect, but it's real. You'll see the entire picture of my fatherless daughter story. I will show you each journey I had to take to find peace about my invisible dad. The very emotions I tried so desperately to hide from everyone would turn out to be the same emotions that would get me through this journey. I would need to re-engage with my true self, be shaken to my core and finally find my way back to the Lover of my soul.

So, before I get too far ahead of myself, here's my story.

Chapter 1
Without a Father

"Let your father and mother be glad; let her who bore you rejoice."
Proverbs 23:25, English Standard Version

My dad left me at the age of two, but the story doesn't begin there. My father was a hairdresser; yes, a hairdresser (that's what they called them back then, instead of hair stylists). He was premier back in the day, with his family doing the hair of celebrities like Chaka Kahn and Oprah. When my dad was twenty-four, the salon was at the peak of its performance and he was at the height of his career. By 1982, he met my mother, who came to the salon with her sister to get her hair done. Everything was going very well. He was a genuinely nice, easy-going guy. He enjoyed karate and joked all the time – so I was told.

With love in the air, the two continued dating for three years. At the age of twenty-eight, my mother became pregnant out of wedlock. It was a disappointment to her family and a burden to her. She was young and considered a "good" girl. With a baby girl on the way, she would have to face her challenges head on, but my dad loved her to no end. He wanted to get married, but only after he fulfilled his dream of making a million dollars. She was the one.

Two years after I was born, my dad's life hit rock bottom. His mother died, leaving him, his sister and brother alone. His mother had been the strong glue that held the family together (his dad died a few years before), but she didn't have life insurance or insurance policies on her home or businesses. My dad and his siblings would end up selling the salon building to Burger King. Soon after, the money from the sale would disappear due to a faulty investment. That was all my dad had left.

"Many are the plans in the mind of a man, but it is the purpose of the Lord that will stand."
Proverbs 19:21, English Standard Version

My dad was without money, without a plan, and without any hope for tomorrow. He was raised in church, but he didn't understand God had a purpose for his life. He was between a rock and a hard place. He immediately turned to drugs to cope with the enduring pain of loss and being lost. That mask would only conceal his troubles for the interim. His visits and phone calls happened less and less frequently. He couldn't handle the weight of his depression. His hopelessness would end up costing him far more than he could pay – a relationship with his daughter. He didn't know what else to do… so he left.

Something Missing

I was a church kid. Every Sunday, my mom took me to church. She would listen to the preacher and I would go to sleep. The best part for me was the Sunday dinners. We'd finally have time to be together after a whirlwind of a week. Just us: me and my mom.

Invisible Dad

I was always ready for some action when I was a kid. I was excited to just go, play, and do! And, of course, I was bossy. I was always ready to tell someone what to do.

I used to go to daycare in the early mornings, elementary school through the afternoon, and then daycare again in the evenings. It was a long day, but it had to be that way. With my dad gone and my mom getting no child support, money was definitely tight.

One day, my mom received bad news for any single parent: "We're letting you go." She had worked for GM for several years and in one fell swoop, it was all taken away. No job, no help, nothing but bills and responsibility. She was doing her best to raise a child. She was holding onto God, but she was fighting in the trenches, just trying to get through.

My mom told me the story that one day, we were home and she broke down crying. I went up to her with a big smile on my face and said, "What's wrong, Mommy? Don't worry, be happy!" She believed God was telling her, through me, to hold on. From that day forward, my mom never worried about where her next dollar or our next meal would come from. She trusted Him, because that's all she had.

"Commit your way to the Lord, trust also in Him, and He shall bring it to pass."
Psalm 37:5, New King James Version

Soon enough, my mom was employed again. She would end up working three jobs to make ends meet. My mom had five sisters, and all five of my aunts played a role in taking care of me. They picked me up, dropped me off, and sometimes, I slept over at their houses. My grandmother helped, too. I would go over to her house where she'd let me eat my favorite treats.

At five years old, I played on the swing set, hung on the monkey bars and worked my math problems like there was no tomorrow. I was good at math, among other subjects. I was a good kid, a great student. I thought kindergarten was the life. I could interact with other kids and no longer be alone so much, since I was an only child. But one day, I felt that something wasn't quite right. I noticed there were men picking their children up from daycare and the kids were yelling out, "*Daddy!*" with excitement. That was the first time I realized something was different about me. I paid more attention to what was happening around me. I didn't have a dad to pick me up. I wanted a dad, too. Why couldn't I have one? Why was I different?

Although I was not mature enough to ask those questions, my family was also not the most talkative. We really didn't share our feelings much, so I continued to keep my feelings hidden. I was missing something, but I couldn't define it beyond the realization that I didn't have a dad. I couldn't hold it, and I couldn't ask for it. Therefore, I accepted things as they were.

By the time I was in third grade, I was part of the popular crowd, which got me in trouble more than a few times; however,

I still came home with honor roll certificates, perfect attendance awards, and A's on my report cards. I was a kid trying to fit in with everyone else. However much I tried to fit in, I didn't. I was selected for an advanced class called *Spectrum*. I was pulled out of class once a week for this advanced curriculum. *Spectrum* was fine until the other kids made fun of me for being "smart." I couldn't catch a break.

I coasted through school. Because of all the rewards I received, I also got rewarded at home. Going to McDonald's was my favorite treat. I looked forward to it on the weekends. My uncle would visit from Kentucky and take me and my cousin on shopping sprees. He would buy us anything we wanted, because we were doing so well in school – toys, games, clothes – you name it, we could have it. I remember one particular Christmas when we were over at my grandmother's house opening gifts. That year, my uncle gave me and my cousin a Game Boy, a case, and plenty of games. I was so excited! Later, after all the excitement died down, I thought about my father. Why didn't he buy me gifts and take me out shopping?

All those questions I had were valid, but I was just too young to ask them. Really, I wanted to be like everyone else. If it wasn't me being without a father, then it was me being pulled out of class to go to *Spectrum* – I just wanted to be "normal."

I decided if I never exposed my feelings that would be fine. Instead, I would try to look and act like everything was okay. At least, that's what I thought I was doing. Hiding behind "perfect" is what I did, but that could only last for so long.

What I had on the inside would soon come out on the outside.

Self-Reflection

1. What is your story? Why did your father leave your life?

_____

_____

_____

_____

_____

_____

_____

_____

_____

_____

_____

_____

2. When did you realize there was something missing in your life?

_____

_____

_____

_____

_____

_____

_____

_____

Chapter 2
Trials & Tribulations: Broken, But Not Hopeless

*"… come to Me, all of you who are weary and carry heavy burdens, and
I will give you rest."*
Matthew 11:28, New Living Translation

I was growing up… but in pain and anger. Every day, I was
trying to overcome the cards that I had been dealt, but the anger
and bitterness overshadowed my heart, which was full of love
and power. I was yearning for something more, but it seemed out
of my control to find it. I guess knowing something was missing
was better than never knowing what I missed.

Everyone around me thought I had it good, that I didn't have
problems. I was still going to church and even singing in the
school talent shows. So why did I think about suicide when I was
twelve years old? I knew exactly how and where I would do it. I
imagined going into my room, slitting my wrist, and bleeding out.
It wasn't that I wanted to die; I just didn't want to live with the
same heartache every day. I needed relief from the pain. I needed
relief from myself.

Girl, by the time I was in middle school, my mom and I
finally had a long talk about my dad. In the past, she told me little
things here and there, but that day, she told me everything that

happened – everything about my dad's drug addiction, his family's hair salon business and his pursuit of money. She also said I was fortunate to not have him in my life, since he was on drugs. She explained that my life could've been so much worse if he'd stayed around with his addiction.

That message was not what I wanted to hear. I wanted my dad there, without the drug addiction. I needed him, but did he need me? My mom didn't seem to quite understand the huge missing piece of my puzzle, since she grew up with both of her parents. My parents were supposed to be my foundation. I was supposed to be standing on two stones, but with my father missing, I was left standing on one foot the rest of my life. From that day forward, in-depth conversations with my mom about my dad were kept to a minimum. I wanted someone to truly understand and, to no fault of her own, my mom couldn't.

Dreaming of What Could've Been

My mom and I were close, really close. We still are – I talk to her on the phone several times a day. Even though she showed me every day how strong she was and how strong I could be, I was tired, tired of the disadvantage of not having a father. She never said anything bad about my dad, but the pain of his absence still remained. I was mad, very mad. Every day, I thought about what we could have been as a family. We could've had a white picket fence, I could've had a few brothers and sisters, and we could've had a couple of dogs. Everything in my mind would have been just fine if only my dad had stayed. Why couldn't he stay?

By the time I was thirteen, my mom and I were having the usual mother-daughter issues. I wanted to be the boss, but she was already the head honcho. It was the battle of the strong-minded women. My feeling of being abandoned by my dad continued to dampen our relationship. I took it out on her, because I was mad at the world. I was disappointed. I was his only child, *so how could he leave me?*

My dad, who was supposed to be my hero, my first knight in shining armor, was not a knight at all. He was a villain. In fact, he was nowhere to be found. He'd left me, and in my eyes, had never looked back. Why couldn't I have been what he needed to keep going in life? I could have given him strength to carry on. I would have loved him unconditionally. I would never have turned my back on him.

With all of the emptiness inside, the girl who'd been a "good" kid became a broken child and her worst enemy.

Screaming, but No One Can Hear

I was developing into a young woman. I had done very well in middle school; I even graduated as the valedictorian of my eighth-grade class. I was well on my way to pulling off this perfection streak. I thought it was far easier than talking about my true feelings. Exposing myself would only leave my heart on the table for someone else to trample upon. So, I guarded my heart like it was the only thing I had left.

High school was here before I could blink my eyes, and I was a little scared. I quickly realized that I wasn't a kid anymore. Not to mention, there were now three buildings I'd have to walk to for different classes. I heard stories about how upperclassmen didn't make high school such a great time for freshmen – and that worry made things far worse. I was maturing as the young woman my mom had taught me to be, and I was definitely going to attack high school head-on. I was fourteen years old, ready to start my new adventure.

I was never a "sports" type of girl. Throughout all my years of schooling, I would definitely join any indoor organization – student council, yearbook committee, National Honor Society, etc. My aunt told me to join as many organizations as I could, so that I could get my picture in the yearbook. Ha, ha! So, that's what I did. You name an organization, I was in it. High school was a little different. I decided to join the color guard. Even though I was not athletic, I could definitely twirl a flag. The color guard traveled with the band to perform at the high school football games. It turned out to be something I was good at – all of us on the color guard team were good at it.

One day, after an away game, I was riding on the bus back to our high school. It was late, so it was pitch black outside. I was so tired. I wanted to sleep, but the kids in the back of the bus kept making so much noise. I was annoyed, so I asked the assistant band director if I could move up front. I sat in the seat next to a guy I knew, hoping to catch some zzzzzz's. His father and my mother had worked together for quite a long time. What ended up happening next is hard to put into words.

He put a blanket over me and started to touch me. I was being molested, but I couldn't move. I was in shock and I wanted to scream, but it was like I was paralyzed. My mouth was glued shut and I couldn't say or do anything. I needed help, but no one was there, but everyone was there. All these people on this bus – the band members and the color guard – and no one to help me. I prayed so hard for the lights to come on, because I knew when they came on, he would stop. After a few minutes, which seemed like eternity, we pulled into the high school and the bus driver turned the inside lights on. He pulled his hand from under the cover so that no one would see him. And I never spoke a word, not even when I saw him in the hallways. We never talked, and I never forgot. I had been an innocent little girl, but now I was broken. I was damaged. The girl who got on the bus that day was completely different from the girl who got off the bus. I tried to pretend that it didn't happen, that I was not molested on the bus that day. I blamed myself for not speaking up. I blamed him for being a molester. And I blamed my dad for never being there to protect me.

You're only the second person I've told what happened that day. However much I'd like to forget it ever happened, I can't be silent any longer. I really need to give you my truth. I was hurting. Things were taking a turn for the worse. Every time I tried to start fresh, something would pull me back into my devastation. I had a choice every day to either hide behind perfection or to let all my truth out. Even when I thought perfection was the way to go, I couldn't help but show my wounds in other ways.

Where Were You?

"A father of the fatherless and a judge and protector of the widows is God in His holy habitation."
Psalm 68:5, Amplified Version

I was finally sixteen years old, which meant I could drive. I was so excited! My mom taught me and I also went to driving school. By early February, I had passed my driver's test and my mom gave me a newer, 1999 Caramel Beige Pearl Mitsubishi Galant. I loved it! That car was mine, all mine. That was, until my friend and I got into an accident on the way back to her house. We were supposed to be at church that evening. She and I were taken to the hospital, and the car was counted as a total loss. Every time I tried to climb to the top, I was slammed to the ground.

School was also getting harder and harder. I tried to over-succeed like I had in middle school, but girl, that wasn't happening. My goal was to get done with high school, but getting done meant distractions along the way: boys, or should I say young men. My choice of men would soon reflect what I knew – brokenness. I attracted what I was inside. The men would typically be older, so that I could feel like someone was taking care of me, when, in actuality, I took care of them. I knew my mom would not be fond of me being with an older man, so I decided to hide it for a while. I was hoping that a relationship would somehow fill the void, but who was I fooling? Their lack of maturity would unite with my lack of wisdom. We were two broken people clinging to each other for wholeness. So, to keep myself from drowning and leave myself some sanity, I would break up with each of them.

I needed my dad, and it showed. I would often wonder where he was. There was no rejection like the rejection I received from him. I was him. We shared the same blood. I had his nose and his allergies! I wanted him to be my example, to show me all about life and to keep me from falling. I knew everyone had their trials and tribulations, but to know that this picture-perfect girl was bleeding on the inside wasn't so evident. I was a ticking time bomb, but I couldn't hide behind the curtain if my feet were still showing.

Self-Reflection

1. Feeling alone can be the most painful experience. Who are you hoping will understand you better?

_____
_____
_____
_____
_____
_____
_____
_____
_____
_____

2. Have you ever been broken? Describe how you felt.

_____
_____
_____
_____
_____
_____
_____
_____
_____
_____

Chapter 3
Fighting Depression

"...casting all your care upon Him, for He cares for you."
1 Peter 5:7, New King James Version

College bound! Yes, this girl started college in June at the age of eighteen, just two weeks after graduating from high school. I had gone on a college tour during my junior year of high school, so I knew exactly where I wanted to go. I also knew I wanted to go *far, far away*. I was ready to embark upon a new journey. This could be a clean slate for me. A new start. A new me. I could easily leave behind everything in my past. I thought that if I wasn't staring my despair in the face, I wouldn't have to deal with it. My thinking was completely wrong, but you couldn't have told me that. I had to experience it for myself.

I went to Hampton University, my home by the sea. The campus was beautiful! Church was right on campus, so I didn't have to worry about that. I was finally on my own and in my own. I was independent and loving it! No one knew me, so I created my own reputation. Instead of packing on the "freshman fifteen" (pounds), I lost the freshman fifteen. I was a Computer Science major, following in my mother's footsteps. In fact, Hampton gave me a scholarship to their Computer Science program. I had no idea what I was signing up for. College turned out to be tough, but I was having fun, at least at first.

It was great to know that I was not the only one who didn't know anyone. I met people from all over the world. Soon enough, I had my core group of friends. We were the trio. We fought like sisters, but that didn't tear us apart. To this day, we still talk occasionally. In school, we decided to be more active, doing things besides the typical parties. We signed up to be ball girls for the football team, so we went to the football games every Saturday.

I was finally making my own way.

Used and Abused

By December that same year, I was sent right back to my mother's house. I never had enough money to attend college, but I believed God would make a way for me to continue my education. With school loans maxed and my mom out of money, I was out of time and I was sent right back to where it all began. I was knocked down again. I felt like I was a disappointment. Everything was going so well in college. I'd been getting the fresh start I thought I needed.

As soon as I got back to my mom's, I applied for a job as a teller at PNC Bank. I started working immediately. Feeling dazed and confused, I bided my time while I still had the chance.

"God is our refuge and strength, a very present help in trouble."
Psalm 46:1, New King James Version

I had no idea what I was going to do next. I just knew the independence my mom taught me. The bounce-back of coming home shifted me back onto the highway to hell. I started dating an older man, ten years my senior. He had been in jail for quite some time, but had been out for a few years. I don't know exactly what I was looking for – maybe for hope, maybe for love, maybe for a male to bond with. Whatever it was, I was definitely looking in the wrong direction. He was emotionally abusive and used me. Our arguments would take me to my knees, crying hysterically. The name calling, the yelling and screaming would leave me hurt to my core. What was left of me, he would crumble into pieces. I faked that I was happy, but I was dying inside, trying to escape the prison that, in some ways, I'd formed. This was not how I thought life would be. I thought I would actually *be* happy, instead of just acting. After several months, I got up the courage to end the relationship.

I had worked so much at PNC that I could finally pay Hampton University the money I owed them. I immediately thought I could try college again. I called Winston-Salem State University, my second choice, and got all the information on how to get in. My mom and I visited the college again and mapped out a plan of how I could get into college and *stay* in college this time. The only way I would be able to go to school was if I lived off campus and worked. Then, I wouldn't have to pay for room and board. I applied for a job at Circuit City while I was down there visiting. I also looked into apartments. It was time to tackle the world again. In August, I left for college, again, but this time, I was so depressed that I was running to get there.

This "different" me would be different alright. I was all in. I was going to work my way through college if it was the last thing I did. I was going to graduate on time and, yes, I was going to go to church every Sunday to sit on those pews and listen to the Word of God, whether I understood it or not, whether I thought I needed it or not and whether I wanted to change or not. I was finally *really* changing, coming into something promising, it seemed. But, like I said, just because you're not looking at the problem, doesn't mean it's not there.

The Breakdown

"Let all bitterness, wrath, anger, clamor, and evil speaking be put away from you, with all malice."
Ephesians 4:31, New King James Version

I was trying hard to make ends meet. I was being responsible, or so I thought. Then, my depression began to bare its true colors. I began reliving all of my pain: the molestation on the bus, the emotional abuse from my former boyfriend and, most of all, the abandonment of my father. Living by myself, it had all finally caught up with me. I was mean and over it. Now, instead of being used by men, I was using them. I was getting them back for what they had done to me. Sure, I would go to dinner with them just for some free food. Yep, they would buy me things and I wouldn't bat an eye. That was the game I played because my heart was so broken… but that wasn't who I was supposed to be.

Hell was patiently waiting for me to get there. I found a new so-called friend and she introduced me to a new way of drowning my pain away – alcohol. It was easy for me. It didn't take any extra effort, I didn't have to think about it and I wasn't really hurting anyone, or so I thought. Alcohol was my newfound love. I started off slow, but soon, I was going out and purposely drinking to get drunk. My goal was to make all of my hurt disappear. The easiest way to do that turned out to be the exact thing that took me to my lowest point in life. I was bitter, I was angry and I was becoming an alcoholic.

"Wine is a mocker, strong drink is a brawler, and whoever is led astray by it is not wise."
Proverbs 20:1, New King James Version

I was drowning in my sorrows and wisdom had left a long time ago. I shouldn't have driven after I'd been drinking, but God spared my life (and the lives of others) every time. Alcoholism and God would end up meeting me at a crossroads. I was still going to church every Sunday to make sure my cover wasn't blown. Perfection was success to me, so I continued to play the role. There was only One who was not eating what I was serving: God. The preacher's sermons and the Bible scriptures could only penetrate my ears for so long before the conviction set in. I was set back so much in life that I was just trying to make it to the finish line without having to take a break. I didn't want to work on myself, because I knew how painful it would be.

One day, I finally had a breakdown. I knew sooner or later something would have to give. I fell to my knees crying at the intersection of hell and heaven. I couldn't keep going to church knowing that God was the answer, but not letting Him solve the problem. I needed to choose life or death, peace or perfection, love or abuse. I finally needed to choose me. And although I went to church every Sunday *hoping* my life would magically change, I would need to choose God so my life *would* change. Going through the motions at church would not make my problems disappear. I chose to let God control my life through His perfect and steadfast love. His presence would take me to a place of submission. I admit I tried to fix it all and make it all perfect, but my perfection was not perfect at all. I was not capable of changing my own life. It was such a mess, but He gave me the strength to stop drinking and start living.

Having a mother who had rooted me in what mattered would be the thing that freed me from death. She trained me up, which showed me God's Word is true.

"Train up a child in the way he should go, and when he is old he will not depart from it."
Proverbs 22:6, New King James Version

Although my mom never truly knew what was going on in my life, she always prayed for me. So, after eighteen years of devastation, defeat, bitterness, betrayal and abuse, I made the ultimate decision: I could no longer carry that burden alone; it was way too heavy. It was so much to carry that it made me sick… sick enough to wither away in my own guilt and shame. I guess that's why David said,

"Cast your burden on the Lord, And He shall sustain you…"
Psalm 55:22, New King James Version

I couldn't sustain myself any longer. I was failing at that process. So, on that day, I chose *life*.

That choice would be a process for me. I would turn to God to help me every step of the way. I was on my way back. The Lord was with me and I knew that. There were so many times when I could have died, but I was still alive. He kept me through all those years of pain. I fought for peace, and He was there to give it to me. My life was not a fairy tale, but it was mine and that's all I had. My truth and God. God and my truth.

Self-Reflection

1. Fighting your feelings does not make them disappear. Not showing your feelings doesn't make them affect you any less. How do you truly feel about being fatherless?

   _____

   _____

   _____

   _____

   _____

   _____

   _____

   _____

   _____

   _____

2. Even though you can run, you can't hide. Has life caught up with you? What are you running from?

   _____

   _____

   _____

   _____

   _____

   _____

   _____

   _____

   _____

Chapter 4
Finding the Solution

"The Lord is near to the brokenhearted and saves the crushed in spirit."
Psalm 34:18, English Standard Version

This Was Me, Back Then

My story may be your story, but you don't have to stay broken. I didn't have it all figured out either, even though I thought I did. I thought perfection would be the life for me. I could live in that perfect position forever, but no one ever told me that trying to be perfect was bondage. I was the leading character in my life, but I was playing someone else. Before I could ever know who I was, I had to first know who God was. No more playing on pews, singing to the melodies and pretending to listen to the pastor. I had to be honest with myself. If I wanted to truly be at peace with everything I'd been through and was going through in my life, and to wash my hands of the pain, I had to conquer three journeys: redemption, forgiveness and restoration.

Your life may not have been what you wanted it to be, but you can still feel at peace with the life you were given. You sit in church every day hoping that someone will see you. Well, I see you. I know you are dying in that seat waiting for someone to say, "I get it" or "I'll talk about it, I'll tell the truth." I know you hope to go from just sitting in the church pew to actually knowing the God people talk about. You've been to church all your life, and still it's the same story over and over again. The victory you are supposed to have, you don't have the capacity to handle. You want to feel presence and harmony with the most important Father you could ever have, God, but the earthly father you long for is invisible. You ask yourself, "Why me?" Every day, you deal with this inner voice saying that you're not loved, you were never worth it; you messed up.

"Another person's pain gives us perspective. Regardless of what we go through, God still has a plan."
Mrs. Joni Parsley

I know you're angry and scared and feel like no one understands. I am writing this book for you. For the girl who wants to be loved, but was rejected before she even had a chance. For the girl who feels like a new journey is on the horizon, but her inner journey is just beginning. For the girl whose feelings are screaming from her soul, yet she is as quiet as a mouse. The little girl in you is fighting to stay alive, while the young woman in you is fighting to breathe. You're thinking this can't be life, but it is only if you want it to be. You have a voice. Stand up and tell your truth. You may have feelings that even your own mother does not understand, and that's okay. But that does not mean you don't need to share them with someone, somehow. You need to be able to feel vulnerable. No, everything is not perfect. But you are a treasure, a young woman of integrity, strength and power. Have the courage to show your light, and to start your journey.

"Fear not, for I am with you; be not dismayed for I am your God. I will strengthen you, yes, I will help you, I will uphold you with My righteous right hand."
Isaiah 41:10, New King James Version

The three journeys I took to heal my wounds of fatherlessness would be my stepping stones to living the life God wanted me to live as His child. Here's the life-changing process I conquered.

Journey 1: Redemption

At church, I learned how God gave redemption to His only Son, Jesus Christ, knowing that His Creation was in desperate need of saving. I accepted Jesus as my Savior when I was a little girl, but I didn't know this would ultimately lead to my first journey. In order for Jesus to redeem us, He had to go through a process of brokenness. He is our Redeemer, but He wasn't granted a right to fast-forward His journey to the end. His patience would equate to our deliverance.

"Rise up; come to our help! Redeem us for the sake of Your steadfast love!"
Psalm 44:26, English Standard Version

Redemption is real. It is one of the most profound journeys of the healing process. God was not looking for me to be too righteous or to forget all about the events of my life. Just like He gave Jesus redemption, He gave it to me too. I didn't need to lie about my feelings or my story. I also didn't need to consider my dad innocent – he wasn't innocent. I just needed to stop pointing the finger at him and calling him guilty. Even though he was guilty as charged, so was I. I was guilty of alcoholism, bitterness and a whole host of other things. Jesus redeemed me before I was born. He knew there would come a time of redemption where I would be guilty as charged, but His love would set me free. So, that's what I did for my dad: he was free to go.

Journey 2: Forgiveness

At that stage in my life, I would have fought you tooth and nail to make you understand that I should not be the one forgiving anyone. I hadn't done anything wrong. *He* left me. And if I could put my life back together as I thought it should have been, I would, and it would look like a perfect park scene, with my dad and I walking hand in hand. Just like we were supposed to do. I loved him, even though I didn't know him. And I thought that was enough to move on, but it wasn't.

I was bitter and at war in my mind. I needed help, but didn't yet realize it was right in front of me. I could have the peace I wanted, but I had to take the first step. I had to walk into my new season, the season of forgiveness. And although I could name every color guard performance, every graduation and every father-daughter dance he missed, I could not keep dragging my past into my future. Reliving my past contaminated everything in my present, ultimately manifesting in my attitude, my happiness and my outlook on life. Holding my dad to the fire was far easier than trusting God and letting it go. But trusting God was far better than any other solution I'd ever tried. I had to relieve myself of the pain and the anger to make the peaceful decision to live a life that was free.

"Trust in Him at all times, you people; pour out your heart before Him. God is a refuge for us."
Psalm 62:8, New King James Version

Journey 3: Restoration

Every day, I relinquish my control to let God restore me. Every day is a new day of grace, mercy, peace and love. I am embraced with the light of God's rays, praying that He will keep me in His perfect will, leading me to be who He wants me to be.

I have to come to accept that I won't have the picture-perfect life I wanted, the one with the white picket fence. But I can finally meet my dad where he is in his life without judgment, condemnation and ridicule. He's my dad. We have something new and fresh that we can create together. And, all the while, I am looking to God to be the anchor in this relationship.

"Be anxious for nothing, but in everything by prayer and supplication, with thanksgiving, let your requests be made known to God; and the peace of God, which surpasses all understanding, will guard your hearts and minds through Christ Jesus."
Philippians 4:6-7, New King James Version

* * *

And that's exactly what I keep doing: looking to God to be my steadfast foundation.

These three journeys revealed my true character, challenged what I had known for so long and pieced together the broken parts of my life. Redemption, forgiveness and restoration – none of those journeys would be easy, but they all would be necessary. The process wasn't pretty – that's not what it was about. It was about how I came out when the process was finished. For God says,

"Behold, I have refined you, but not as silver; I have tested you in the furnace of affliction."
Isaiah 48:10, New King James Version

My setback was a set-up for my comeback. When I came out, I was refined, but not as silver. I'd become the best me I could be. The best me is the one that God made me.

Chapter 5
Redemption:
Taking Him Off Your Hook

Understanding Redemption for Myself

So, here I was on Redemption Drive. God was transforming my life and altering my destination, so that I could be free from the heavy bondage of guilt, anger and rejection. I had finally made the choice to be free. I chose life, and now life was choosing me. God was showing me what a father was. He was teaching me that being a parent is a lot of responsibility, and in order for Him to bless me, He would have to chastise me, too. Being chastised was not punishment; it was correction. It would lead me in the direction of living a better life, because it showed me that God was mine and I was His. When I set out on Redemption Drive, I wasn't sure where God would lead me, but I was willing to go.

In order for me to continue down that path, I needed to grasp redemption and what it meant for me. Soon enough, on Redemption Drive, I would face one of the hardest steps in the process. It would make me evaluate who was right and who was actually wrong. It would make me look fear in the eye and say, "Today, I will conquer you."

While sitting in church, I sang songs like "My Redeemer Lives" and read Bible verses like:

"Let the redeemed of the Lord say so, whom He has redeemed from the hand of the enemy..."
Psalm 107:2, New King James Version

It wasn't for twenty years that the message of redemption became as real to me as my right hand. That revelation was the first journey of my process. I had heard so much about redemption, but it wasn't until I actually learned who God truly was that I understood what it even meant. It was very possible to sit there in church Sunday after Sunday and still not be present. I did it for years. I had the answers, but I was still asking the same questions.

Redemption is defined as the act of redeeming or atoning for a fault or mistake. I had made so many mistakes in my life, and I was guilty of every single one of them. As a mortal human, I would sin, but as a child of God, I was His own. What would you do if someone who was your own disappointed you every single time? Your answer may not be God's answer, but He decided to protect His own, help His own and love His own. That was what a true father did. He protected His kids like their lives depended upon it...because they did. Experiencing His ocean of love was the deciding factor between me being given my rightful sentence or being redeemed for my mistakes.

"For all have sinned and come short of the glory of God..."
Romans 3:23, King James Version

Although His redemption would cover both my past and my future, it would be necessary, because He was my father. He would prevent the preventable, while still loving me unconditionally. If I could have protected myself, I would have, but I needed something greater than myself. I could not do it for myself, so the responsibility went to the Holy One who made me. God sent a Redeemer to earth to fix it all. He would be an example for me to live by. The Redeemer would not be His brother, His uncle, or His cousin. God would send the closest person to Him – the blood of His blood, the flesh of His flesh: Jesus Christ.

Jesus was born of a virgin named Mary and a stepfather named Joseph. Jesus was both flesh and spirit. He could cry like me and bleed like me, but He could also remain holy and foresee the future, something I could not do. Jesus would not step into His purpose until He was thirty-three years old. Then, He walked the earth professing the love of His father, God. His great journey of healing the sick, casting out demons and remaining blameless is a perfect example of living by God's love. At the end of His physical life, Jesus would be condemned, beaten and nailed to a cross to die for everyone's sins. Three days later, Jesus' tomb would be empty, because He'd been resurrected to join God in Heaven.

The death of Jesus Christ was enough to redeem me from my present sins, but it wasn't enough to redeem me from my future ones. When God resurrected Jesus from the tomb, He overcame death and redeemed me for all my sins once and for all. When the tombstone was rolled back and Jesus' body was no longer there, people knew the ultimate victory had been won. God's redemption was afforded to everyone who wanted it. Every feeling I had of guilt, shame, depression, loneliness and blame should have died on that day, because Jesus stood in the gap for me. It wasn't until I understood this divine message that I could actually let it all go.

"In Him we have redemption through His blood, the forgiveness of sins, according to the riches of His grace."
Ephesians 1:7, New King James Version

So, there it was: the truth. All that time, I'd been trying to fix things and it hadn't worked. Sometimes, we can't change ourselves even if we want to. We need someone to make it right once and for all. We need a redeemer – someone to free us from destruction. When I understood this, I saw that redemption wasn't just a Bible story anymore. It finally became my life. Peter said it best:

"But you are a chosen generation, a royal priesthood, a holy nation, His own special people, that you may proclaim the praises of Him who called you out of darkness into His marvelous light."
1 Peter 2:9, New King James Version

I was special. Special enough to be bought with an expensive price I could never afford to pay. Jesus paid it all for me. When God sent His Son to die for my sins, it didn't matter who was right and who was wrong. The love of His Creation shined through it all. God's true love turned His Creation back to His holy presence.

The Gift

This newfound gift I held so close was mine, all mine. I held it tight like a new pair of shoes (my fave). This gift had always been there, but I hadn't recognized it as the foundation for my entire being. It was my newfound hope in life to let God handle situations in my life. I wanted to be everything God wanted me to be. I would finally begin what would later be known as the *great exchange.*

"To console those who mourn in Zion, to give them beauty for ashes, the oil of joy for mourning, the garment of praise for the spirit of heaviness...."
Isaiah 61:3, New King James Version

I released my spirit of heaviness, so God gave me the garment of praise. I had been sitting in church and lifting my hands and singing songs, but until true redemption was my song, my heaviness would leave the words empty. I was finally on the way to a new beginning.

I knew this personal gift of God's redemption was for me, but I didn't particularly think about others. God would soon correct my selfish view, because not only was this relationship with God and Jesus for me, but it was given to everyone. Jesus died just as much for me as He did for my father, who was shown mercy just as much as I was. So why was it so hard for me to forget my dad's sin, then? Because it's easier to point out someone else's sin than to look at your own.

I finally understood the meaning of redemption. I finally understood that I didn't have to let my dad off the hook; I just had to let him off *my* hook. I didn't have to excuse him for what he did; I just had to trust God to handle things. It didn't matter who was wrong and who was right. My role wasn't to play judge and convict my dad of the same sin I had committed. If I pointed the finger at him, then, in turn, God's finger would be pointed at me. I realized that the love I still had for an *invisible* man, my dad, was far greater than the crime he'd committed by leaving me. The truth was that I was just as guilty as he was, because I had sinned too. We are all guilty.

Peace finally began filtering into my life and I felt like I could breathe again. My dad had done what he did, and I couldn't change the past, but I could change the future.

Finding Grace

"... being justified freely by His grace through the redemption that is in Christ Jesus"
Romans 3:24, New King James Version

When I think about grace, it makes me smile. God gives us grace even when we least deserve it. He favors us by giving us the honor of living another day to do His will, even when we continue to sin in this race called life. His favor and amazing love surrounds us, as though we are without blemish. That's how much love He has for us.

We may take His grace for granted, because he extends it daily. We are the apple of His eye, His children. Every day I sat in church, God was granting me the grace, over and over again, to choose life. He gave me so many chances that I didn't understand, not until I looked back over my life. I know the term *grace* can be overused, but it is very evident that it's there, even when we least expect it.

"And if by grace, then it is no longer of works; otherwise grace is no longer grace."
Romans 11:6, New King James Version

Even during this time that I'm writing to you, God is giving me immeasurable amounts of favor to be His light. I am not the only one who is called, but I am the one who has been chosen for this purpose, the purpose of helping you.

41

Grace is not reserved for anyone, except those who believe. You have grace just like I do — you just have to realize it. Every day, God puts His hand upon us to anoint us for His calling. If you can breathe, walk, see, reach, run, or if you woke up this morning, that's God's grace manifesting in your life. You are the living testimony that grace is still available for anyone who looks to find it. It's not hard to find, you just need to open your eyes.

When I could finally see how grace had affected my life, I could give grace to the dad I never had. God had given me a gift, which I could, in turn, give to my dad. The best thing about grace is that you don't have to be *right* to give or receive it; you just have to be willing.

Trust God

"Trust in the Lord with all your heart, and lean not on your own understanding."
Proverbs 3:5, New King James Version

So, that's what I did. I trusted Him to lead me through life. Whatever He wanted me to do to be whole again, I was willing to try it, step by step.

It feels good to know that my story just might change the way you view yours. I truly want to help another woman, another daughter, another sister and another best friend. If it were up to me, I probably would have kept my container of feelings on a shelf in my heart that only God and I could get to. But today, right now, I am getting out that container, putting it on the table, dumping it all out and letting everyone see how the puzzle pieces of my life have come together. You may laugh and you may cry, but you will know that I am praying for a girl who is just like me, who wants to reveal her truth, but doesn't have confidence in her own voice to do so.

"Blessed is the man who trusts in the Lord, and whose hope is the Lord."
Jeremiah 17:7, New King James Version

Being someone who trusts God was no longer just words on a page for me. I was coming face-to-face with the preacher's sermons and the Bible scriptures.

Chapter 6
Forgiveness:
Receiving Beauty

"For if you forgive men their trespasses, your heavenly Father will also forgive you. But if you do not forgive men their trespasses, neither will your Father forgive your trespasses."
Matthew 6:14-15, New King James Version

Forgiveness is for You

I was at the end of Redemption Drive, and it turned into Forgiveness Road. Forgiveness is a hard, steep road to climb. Saying the words "I forgive" is not enough to get you to a place of restitution. What you want when you are trying to forgive are not words of wisdom or words of encouragement. You are looking for empathy, a path to wholeness. You are longing for more than the two words "I'm sorry." Forgiving is about so much more than cleaning up a mess. Your heart is at stake. You're close to losing your sanity, but you have one last plea inside.

How can you get to a place of peace? The person who folds their cards first loses, right? Or do they? You feel like you'd be taking responsibility for what he did if you took the first step, if you folded your cards first, if you made the first phone call... but what if your life depended on forgiving? Is it easier to be pained and reluctant than to be exposed and peaceful?

One of the hardest things to do is accept pain that you didn't cause. Forgiving someone is not easy, but it is necessary if you're going to trust God and have complete serenity in your life. He gave us forgiveness for our sins many years ago. God knew what we needed when He sent His Son to die for our sins. The gift of sacrifice did not come at a fair price. When I understood that I was forgiven and took that walk down Redemption Drive, then I could forgive my dad for the mistakes he made in the past, and even for the mistakes he may make in the future. I couldn't carry unforgiveness in my heart anymore. God freed me from myself by opening my eyes to what He, my heavenly Father, had given me so that I could pass that same gift on to my earthly father.

I know you're saying there's no way you can forgive your dad. It's been way too long and he's done way too much. Well, Girl, I completely understand, because that's exactly how I felt. I cried struggling to understand why I had to accept his actions, but I was misunderstanding the true meaning of forgiveness. Forgiveness is not about what he did or did not do, it is about what I was able to do. I thought that if I forgave him, he would win, but I failed to realize this was not a contest. This was our lives we were talking about, not some Monopoly game. I had filled the hole in my heart with anger, bitterness and depression. God was willing to take it all away, to exchange ashes for beauty.

The little girl who longed to have a picture-perfect life was not able to fathom a life without rejection and anger. But what if you could give away your pain, and get beauty instead? You've wanted joy for so long, so why not give up mourning every day? You have tried to hide your true feelings for so long that you're actually starting to believe they're not there, but they are.

It's okay not to be okay... but it's not okay not to do anything about it. Dreams only come true when you take the first step. And, just like your dreams, healing only comes to fruition when you take the first step. So, give it up. Release your pain. In order for you to receive, you first have to give. In order for you to be at peace, you have to trade the ashes of your pain for something beautiful. Even though you may not see the beauty of letting your pain go, believe that God will send you beauty when you do.

Make the ultimate trade with God. That death-grip you have on anger and rejection is hurting you – and hurt people hurt people. You have tried to be the best person you could be – going to church every Sunday, taking notes, singing in the choir – but you can put on your greatest mask and you will still be seen by the One who knows all, sees all and hears all. God can renew anything, but you need to be honest, and you can't be honest with anyone else, until you first get real with yourself.

* * *

So, that day... the day of my last cry, my last scream, my last illusion, I finally let it all go. I finally forgave my dad for everything he was and everything I wanted him to be. I also forgave the other men for hurting me. I finally accepted that I am who God made me to be and my truth is all I have. God's Word says,

"And we know that all things work together for good to those who love God, to those who are called according to His purpose."
Romans 8:28, New King James Version

I knew I was His, so this journey would have to work out for my good. Somehow, someway. All the guilt, all the shame, all the sleepless nights, the cries and the depression were no longer ruling my life. I finally asked Jesus to cleanse my heart. I'm crying now as I write this, remembering when I washed my hands of the "what if we could's" and the "I wish we would have's." I'm crying, because I am finally free.

"Before I formed you in the womb I knew you…"
Jeremiah 1:5, New King James Version

When I made the decision to forgive my dad, I knew I would need to take it one day at a time, not knowing what might lie ahead. Whether my dad came back into my life or not, I could heal. My healing was not based on his happenstance. I moved forward and let God lead the way. The process was slow and it took everything I had to move forward, but everything I didn't have, God gave me.

I decided to forgive my dad, so that I could have my own life again. And I did it. I completed the second exchange. I gave my ashes to God, and He gave me beauty in return.

Parallel Paths

Forgiveness is never tangible, until you come face-to-face with the person you need to forgive. They say everything happens for a reason and, by all means, I definitely believe that. But nothing could've prepared me for what happened next. My life would completely change, forever.

I was twenty-one years old. In six months, I would graduate from Winston-Salem State University, which, of course, was a big victory. I was excited and just ready to get done! I was working two jobs and taking twenty-one credit hours. I was very determined to graduate on time, which took extra work, since I'd taken a semester off during my freshman year due to my financial trouble. One of my jobs was being a night auditor at a hotel, working the graveyard shift. Almost every week, I woke up on Monday and couldn't go to sleep until Wednesday. When I think about that time, I can only credit God for getting me through.

One chilly December evening, I pulled into the parking lot to get my nails done and I received a call that made my heart drop.

"Hello, this is Keith, your dad... I'm sorry."

With tears streaming down my face, something I'd longed for happened. My dad had come back to find me.

That phone call began a new era in a relationship I wanted desperately to unbreak. I used to be so wrapped up in my emotions that I failed to wonder who my dad had become after all these years. Or what would lie ahead. I wish he could have put his trust in God at that time, but if he didn't know who God truly was, then how could he trust Him?

My dad explained that for twenty years he had been on drugs. Drugs had taken over his mind and his actions. He had been in and out of jail, crack houses and group homes. He'd tried time and time again to get clean, but every time, something would push him back down again. He was poisoned by his own actions, his own heartache and the devil's antics. He was chasing money, instead of chasing He who created money – God.

While my dad was fighting God and demons at the same time, I was... angry, bitter, mean and depressed. I was fighting my own demons. "How could you?" and "Why did you?" were running through my mind. With no one to truly understand how I was feeling, every Sunday I was in church with pain that kept getting deeper. My friendship pool shrank.

Over those same twenty years, I had contemplated suicide, gravitated toward alcohol, sought out acceptance from men and was physically and emotionally abused. I wanted more than that for myself, but I could not figure out how to obtain it. I needed help. So, I decided to go through the motions every day, until I figured out that I could not truly be transformed until I renewed my mind.

"And do not be conformed to this world, but be transformed by the renewing of your mind, that you may prove what is that good and acceptable and perfect will of God."
Romans 12:2, New King James Version

My dad ended up not coming to my college graduation, because he was still in a battle between his old life and freedom. His decision not to attend my graduation left me wondering: If I did let him back into my life, would he leave me again? The various over-promising and under-delivering experiences I'd had in my life had let me down so much, I wasn't sure if I could take anymore disappointment.

God had to remind me that He was the One who placed my dad back in my life for a reason, and all my work on Redemption Drive and my climb up Forgiveness Road would not be in vain. I held steadfast to the journey. I would need God more than I could have ever imagined.

Relationships Don't Define Your Purpose

Relationships don't define your purpose. They never have. Relationships are your position. I always defined my purpose around what did or did not happen in my life, but that was giving other people way too much power. My *position* is that I am a daughter, but my purpose was decided by God before the foundation of the earth.

"In him we have obtained an inheritance, having been predestined according to the purpose of him who works all things according to the counsel of his will."
Ephesians 1:11, English Standard Version

You might be having a misunderstanding about your purpose. Maybe no one has ever asked you how you felt about being a fatherless daughter. Even so, it's time to push past the pain and the loneliness and pursue peace. God is your healer. His amazing love is like a warm coat wrapping around you again and again. His peace is your inner freedom to choose life and to choose it more abundantly.

You don't have to regret the past in order to strive for the future. God can remove the guilt and the shame if you release it to Him. Girl, it's that easy! Just surrender it all and never pick it back up again. Your sense of purpose only comes from God who created you. Be you. You will change just by understanding that you belong to God. Your being is not based on your father's absent love for you or whether he's there for you. You have been loved endlessly since before you were born. From your first movement to your first smile and ever since, God loves you because of whose you are, not who you are. Do what's in the depths of your heart – open up. Your earthly father may have abandoned you years ago, but there is One far greater who has never left your side: God.

Pursuing Patience

Patience is one of the most important keys in life you don't want to be without. But telling people to have patience is so much easier than practicing it yourself. Patience makes the heart grow fonder. It also makes you face the truth. I was longing for spiritual fulfillment, while seeking an earthly desire. I had images in my head of myself as a daddy's girl. I was waiting for my dad to say, "Where's my baby girl?" And then I would run to him when he picked me up at school. We would have so much fun. He would spoil me and I would love him unconditionally. That's all that I wanted, and all I thought I needed and what I'd hoped for. That was the illusion I breathed daily.

An earthly father should resemble your heavenly One. But it didn't for me. So, what happens when it doesn't? How was I supposed to truly understand what a heavenly Father was until I first got a glimpse of an earthly one in real life? How was I supposed to make that connection?

The answer is love. This is the only answer. When you read the Bible, God shows you His perfect ways of being a father. He not only gives blessings, peace, increase and hope, but he also gives rest, food, healing and correction. There's no one like Him. Although I had uncles who were great examples, God is the only perfect example. Before I could understand what an earthly father was supposed to be, I had to first read His words so He could show me. He taught me through His scriptures exactly who He will always be: *love*.

It will never be enough to try to change your life – actually changing your life is what truly matters. What you need in order to do that is something only God can give you. I can now pin the truth on my heart and look at it every day. My truth is that I have finally made the ultimate trade: "Here are my ashes. Please, God, please give me beauty."

The Bible says in Psalm 119 that testimonies are our counselor, which is why we can conquer battles in the midst of mayhem; yet few people want to discuss how they got to their testimony. I couldn't tell you about how I talked to my dad when I was twenty-one years old (after he was absent for twenty years) without being mad, screaming, or bitter... until I first got over those mountains. We can do anything and everything through God who strengthens us, but it's the process we're at war with. Your passion to be supported through your life of climbing mountains and tripping over mole hills will only lead you to healing if you pursue patience.

The key to beauty is easily accessible, but you have to know how to use that key. Being free from bondage will only help you if your mind is also willing to be free. Forgiveness is a choice. It will help you regain the power you always had, but stopped believing in.

If I asked you, "Would you choose life or death today?" you would most likely say, "Life," but in order to have life, you have to take it back from the depths of destruction. Live in God's given purpose and forgive.

Chapter 7
Restoration:
Walking Hand in Hand

"Restore to me the joy of Your salvation, and uphold me by Your generous Spirit"
Psalm 51:12, New King James Version

I finally was able to maneuver off Forgiveness Road. I had redeemed my dad by letting him off my hook, I had forgiven him and received beauty for my ashes and I was well on my way to healing. I thought I had changed everything I needed to about how I felt towards my dad. My vision of him was no longer distorted. But who was I? What I'd known was gone, my perfect façade had been cast away, and all I had left was... me. The journey could end right there, but I couldn't give myself to God and not receive greater in return. He never works that way. Greater is what He knew, and greater is what I received.

So, here I am, on Restoration Highway – and it feels good, like walking in a fresh blowing wind. Every day, I am one step closer to understanding who I am and what I am to be. I am being renewed, revived and refreshed. I am finally free from the guilt, the pain and the anger – well on my way to fully restoring the beauty of my testimony.

"So we do not lose heart. Though our outer self is wasting away, our inner self is being renewed day by day."
2 Corinthians 4:16, English Standard Version

I trusted God to restore me, ultimately letting Him mend my heart. I had to be open and willing to do the work. I had to be willing to change.

Sitting in church was no longer just a tradition, but a delight. Sermons became the thick coat of protection I needed to cover me from future woes. The Bible was no longer a magical mystery, but an instruction manual on how to handle life's struggles. God was restoring my joy, and it wasn't just regular joy, He gave me the oil of joy. Oil saturates your skin so that it is rich and glistening. Your skin becomes soft and smooth, and even though you may have scars, oil still enriches them with pure brightness. That brightness is the reflective light that allows others to see my scars and still be drawn to the connection of my heart. God and I could do this. We had been to hell and back. I was finally following His refreshing path.

The Road to a Relationship: The Ultimate Battle

While God was restoring me, He was also restoring my dad. Within a few years after that surprising phone call, my dad had cleaned up his life and given his life to God. He is now a minister! I thought that everything I had imagined and wanted was staring me right in my face. My dad was pursuing God and so was I. I thought we could be just like that picture in my mind, but that wasn't how it worked. Even if God had told me that my dad would return, it still wouldn't have prepared me for the work I would need to do.

Although I wanted this relationship with my dad, I didn't know I was going to have to fight for it. He showed up, and it all hit me. My mind went back to the past and I thought again about what he hadn't done, all that he'd missed out on and what he was guilty of. I succeeded at the journeys along Redemption Drive and Forgiveness Road when it was just me and God, but the real test came when the person I was redeeming and forgiving looked me right in the eyes.

My dad tried to give me advice about men and relationships, but I'd already learned them from first-hand experience. And how could I take advice from a man who couldn't follow through with his own relationships? I couldn't take his advice seriously, even though what he was saying was true. His subjective judgment had no impact on my personal preferences. It was too late for that. It was too late for him to be talking to my boyfriends and wondering who they were. He didn't get that privilege; I didn't allow him that honor. God would quickly remind me of redemption. If my dad was off my hook, then why did I still have the hook in my hand, ready to nab him at my first instinct?

My dad also tried to talk to me about business and real estate. Although his suggestions may not have been bad and some of his stories were hilarious, I still wanted to say *"Hello!* You've been missing for twenty years! Don't you want to talk about something else?"

It took some time, but God finally helped me realize that my dad didn't know how to be a father. In order to know what a father truly is, you have to first be one. We could talk on the phone and chitchat a little bit. We could talk about his long-lost love for my mom and how he did hair, back in the day, but we couldn't talk about how I was doing or what I needed from him. He had never been a father, so he didn't know what the next step was after "I'm sorry."

"Commit your way to the Lord, trust also in Him, and He shall bring it to pass."
Psalm 37:5, New King James Version

I had to trust God. He met me on Redemption Drive and has been with me for the entire journey. Why would He fail me now? So, here I am teaching my dad how to be a father. Or, really, here is God, restoring me and my dad back to each other. As much as he needs to be shown how to be a dad, I need to be shown how to be daddy's little girl. As I write this, it'll soon be nine years since I received that first phone call from my dad that left me shaken. Nine years of transformation. Nine years of restoration and forgiveness. We are in the midst of creating our own bond. He has to learn me, and I have to learn him. No, we're not perfect, but who is?

Every time my dad sees me, he stares at me like it's the first time he's laid eyes on me. Maybe, for him, he's just happy to finally have a relationship with his daughter. It feels weird to me, because I am finally looking into his eyes. I always knew he existed, but didn't know how to reach him. In my mind, he was always there, even if I couldn't touch him.

I am happy to have my dad back in my life. Although he has every opportunity to hurt me and leave again, I can be vulnerable, because I trust God. I made a trade with God quite some time ago. With all the ashes gone, I was basking in beauty.

The beauty I've received is not for my dad coming back into my life. In fact, if he never came back, I would still receive beauty. You may not see your father in the future, but you have a heavenly Father that you can experience every day.

"And let the beauty of the Lord our God be upon us, and establish the work of our hands for us; Yes establish the work of our hands."
Psalm 90:17, New King James Version

Walking Hand in Hand

Every day it's me, my dad and God. Today may have been a good day, but tomorrow may not be… and I am okay with that. I am walking with them hand-in-hand. My father and I don't need perfection, we need rest. We need to be able to rest in God's love. That is enough. God is the peace we need to survive the new challenges we face.

Candice Ragland

"I have seen his ways, and will heal him; I will also lead him, and restore comforts to him and to his mourners."
Isaiah 57:18, New King James Version

Even when I didn't see God during my trials and tribulations, He was always there. I finally can grasp the love of God. God loved me enough not to leave me. And He never will. God was preparing me to accept change. Even when it is uncomfortable, it is always better to grow. I leaned on Him for my strength, day after day. Even when He corrected me, I knew I was His. He loves me beyond anything I can understand.

God will restore my picture of a life with my dad to a greater beauty than ever before. My journey is not over – it's just beginning!

Chapter 8
Living in Your Testimony: Finishing the Healing Process

"God cannot heal what we conceal."
Dr. Jasmine Sculark

I was at a Dominion Camp meeting recently and heard Dr. Jazz say those words: "God cannot heal what we conceal." I felt like I had been called out in a room full of people. Ten thousand people heard the same sentence, but she was talking directly to me. I had been down Redemption Drive, turned onto Forgiveness Road and maneuvered my way to Restoration Highway. I thought I was done with the process. I thought God had transformed my life, and that I was a better person. I knew that restoration would be an ongoing journey, but I didn't know that restoration was not the last phase.

I had hid my feelings about my father leaving when I was two years old for so long that I completely missed finishing the healing process. I was still concealing myself from others – only God and I knew the full story. I would tell people here and there parts of my story, but I'd never discussed all one-hundred percent with anyone but God. I'd forgiven my dad for what had happened, but the wound was not fully healed.

Even though my healing started long ago with redemption, it didn't stop at restoration. I remained shadowed with the truth until I found out that healing is not given to us, we have to take it. God heals, but God heals when you take the first step. Believing is the first step. Without faith, mountains cannot move – I could never be whole, until I first was healed.

"And they overcame him by the blood of the Lamb, and by the word of their testimony"
Revelation 12:11, King James Version

It was not enough to go through the journeys; I also had to tell my testimony. It was the only way to fully overcome. It was the only way to completely heal.

Being Free of Perfect

"Beauty is not in the face; beauty is a light in the heart."
Kahlil Gibran

Telling the truth is necessary. My vulnerability about my truth was a weakness of my heart. There are so many fatherless daughters like me, but I never heard anyone who could relate to my feelings…I matter, too. I had to choose the life of a flower bud or the life of a perfect canvas painting. I thought beauty was the picture I had that seemed perfect, but true beauty would be the unveiling of the innermost sanctum – my heart.

Chapter 9
Start Your Journey

Well, if you're like me, this book has made you laugh, made you mad and made you cry. I'm emotionally drained just thinking about it. Ha! But it was my life – it is my life. And as much as I wanted to alter this imperfect picture, now I wouldn't change it. Perfection was the illusion in my mind that I tried to put together on my own. But that dream could never compare to my new relationship with God. It is stronger than it has ever been, and growing every day.

Although my dad is back in my life, he will never be able to take the place of my heavenly Father. And, come to think about it, a relationship with God was what I was missing all these years. Until I understood who He was personally through my journeys of redemption, forgiveness, and restoration, I tried to fill that void with anything I could get my hands on. I wanted fulfillment, but the emptiness was still prevalent. If I hadn't gone through my trials and tribulations, I would still be sitting in church every Sunday morning going through the motions. I wouldn't even remotely understand who God truly is.

"For in the midst of an ordeal of severe tribulation, their abundance of joy and their depth of poverty [together] have overflowed in wealth of lavish generosity on their part"
2 Corinthians 8:2, Amplified Version

Maybe you're not at the "I'm glad this happened to me" phase about your dad. That's okay. Take it one step at a time. Nothing will be fixed overnight. Pursue patience and that will help you conquer the *great exchange*. God will show you the way. Just take the first step. God is right there with you. He never leaves your side, and He will walk with you every step of the way.

My hope for you is that you come face-to-face with yourself, that you reflect over your life as a fatherless daughter and are finally honest about all of it. Take it from me, it will be challenging, but it will also be worth it.

Your journey of healing might take a while and you will have some bumps. Girl, I'm happy to help you on your journey. Bring your tissues, your Bible, and your true self. It's time to take those first steps and head down Redemption Drive. Come on! With God, you can do this. I know you can.

Start Your Journey
21-Day Kick Off Journal

Do you want to start your journey, but are unsure about where to begin? I completely understand. Sometimes, you just don't know where to start after so many years of heartache and pain. There's no need to worry. I want to help you overcome your past.

For the next 21 days, you and I will walk down Redemption Drive, turn onto Forgiveness Road and end up on Restoration Highway. Here's your roadmap:

- ❖ Week 1 – Redemption Journey: Taking Him Off Your Hook
- ❖ Week 2 – Forgiveness Journey: Receiving Beauty
- ❖ Week 3 – Restoration Journey: Walking Hand in Hand

Every day you'll focus on a new lesson to conquer. You'll also journal through your journey. Your goal is to begin the healing process, which is filled with more peace than you could ever imagine. Let's get started!

Day 1

Surrender to the Process Face-to Face

Today is a fresh start and a brand new beginning. Let's start down Redemption Drive.

Becoming numb to your past does not help you to advance to your future. You can accomplish your journey, but in order to do so, you'll have to look at yourself in the mirror and surrender to the process face-to-face. BELIEVE that you can do it!

Release your thoughts. Write them down.

Day 1

Being numb to your past does not help you to advance to your future.

_____
_____
_____
_____
_____
_____
_____
_____
_____
_____
_____
_____
_____
_____
_____
_____
_____
_____
_____
_____
_____
_____
_____
_____
_____

Day 2

Foreseeing the End

You must always start with the end in mind to celebrate your achievement.

Write one goal you will accomplish for each of your journeys. How do you plan to accomplish it?

- ❖ Redemption_____

- ❖ Forgiveness_____

- ❖ Restoration_____

Day 2

You must always start with the end in mind to celebrate your achievement.

_____
_____
_____
_____
_____
_____
_____
_____
_____
_____
_____
_____
_____
_____
_____
_____
_____
_____
_____
_____
_____
_____
_____
_____

Day 3

Understanding Redemption

A clear depiction of what redemption means for you personally is the only way to advance to the next journey. Jesus came to bear all of our burdens. He loves you beyond what you could ever imagine. Through Him, your healing begins. Understanding how you're forgiven leads to an open road for you to forgive others.

Read chapter five today. Write your reflections.

Day 3

Understanding how you're forgiven leads to an open road for you to forgive others.

_____
_____
_____
_____
_____
_____
_____
_____
_____
_____
_____
_____
_____
_____
_____
_____
_____
_____
_____
_____
_____
_____
_____
_____
_____
_____
_____
_____

Day 4

It's All Washed Away

Jesus came so that we could all have life, and have it more abundantly. He carried the burden of our sin upon His shoulders so that we can live eternally with Him in Heaven.

Get a pencil and write down every single thing you've ever done wrong.

> ### Day 4
>
> **H**e carried the burden of our sin upon His shoulders so that we can live eternally with Him in Heaven.

_____
_____
_____
_____
_____
_____
_____
_____
_____
_____
_____
_____
_____
_____
_____
_____
_____
_____

Now erase it. It's that easy.

Ask Jesus to come into your heart, forgive you for all of your shortfalls and change your life.

Day 5

Grace

I know the journey to healing is challenging. Put a stake in the ground and refuse to turn back.

Grace has been given to you by God. You continually walk in His grace, and so does your father. The amount of grace is not measured by how much "good" you do. In fact, it is measured by the depth of God's love. He loves all of His children, which grants you and your father the privilege of grace.

Meditate on these Bible verses today:

"In him we have redemption through his blood, the forgiveness of our trespasses, according to the riches of his grace..."
Ephesians 1:7 English Standard Version

"For from his fullness we have all received, grace upon grace."
John 1:16 English Standard Version

"But we believe that we will be saved through the grace of the Lord Jesus, just as they will."
Acts 15:11 English Standard Version

Day 5

He loves all His children,
which grants you and your
father the privilege of grace.

_____
_____
_____
_____
_____
_____
_____
_____
_____
_____
_____
_____
_____
_____
_____
_____
_____
_____
_____
_____
_____
_____

Day 6

Taking Him Off Your Hook

Everyone has heard the saying "the truth shall set you free". Well today, we are going to have a standoff with the truth – it's time to take your father off your hook. You can't continue the healing process if you continue to nab him for everything in your future. Having a painful past, does not allow you to continue using it as an excuse for your future. I know you're scared, but taking him off your hook does not mean that he's "won"; it means that you no longer have to carry that burden.

From this day forward, you will have to take responsibility for your own actions. Today is the day you stop blaming your father for every situation that may arise, and begin stepping into every decision you make.

You are loved. You are worth the fight.

You are a conqueror!

Write and reflect upon today's lesson.

Day 6

Having a painful past, does not allow you to continue using it as an excuse for your future.

_____
_____
_____
_____
_____
_____
_____
_____
_____
_____
_____
_____
_____
_____
_____
_____
_____
_____
_____
_____
_____
_____

Day 7

Trust God

Trusting God can be challenging, especially if you like to be in control. But the heavy load you may carry of stress, pain, anger, resentment, depression and abandonment will always warrant relief. The secret desire of your heart is freedom. The freedom to strive, breath, release and LIVE!

Whether it is a tainted relationship, a stressful job, a daunting past or a fixed failure, surviving can compromise your future. Release the heavy load. God is ready to take the lead in your life. He is waiting for you to release the spirit of heaviness, so that He can give you the garment of praise.

Write down everything that is weighing you down. God will not only take the heavy load from you; His love will guide you through life, one day at a time.

Day 7

God is ready to take the lead
in your life.

_____
_____
_____
_____
_____
_____
_____
_____
_____
_____
_____
_____
_____
_____
_____
_____
_____
_____
_____
_____
_____
_____
_____
_____

Day 8

Pursue Patience and Leave the Rest Behind

Whew! You're here, Forgiveness Road. We're going to kick this journey off by focusing on patience. This is truly a process. And as with any process, it takes time. This journey is not a race for speed or endurance, or for power or resilience. The medal cannot be seen, and the cheers cannot be heard. This journey is to heal. This journey is to have peace. This journey is to take your life back. This journey is for you. You have one goal: make it to the finish line.

Today, take a long look at the people around you. If they are not supporting you on your journey to healing, then they are hindering you. This includes family, friends and anyone else you interact with on a regular basis. Remove the hindrances, so that you can focus on making it to the finish line. Think about the serious affect this is having on your life. Take the step – cut the fruit and leave the rest behind.

Write down who you are taking with you on your journey and ways they have supported you. Reflect on how you will pursue patience.

Day 8

Remove the hindrances, so that you can focus on making it to the finish line.

_____

_____

_____

_____

_____

_____

_____

_____

_____

_____

_____

_____

_____

_____

_____

_____

_____

_____

_____

_____

_____

_____

_____

_____

_____

Day 9

Forgiveness

The journey of Forgiveness is the hardest journey, but will be the greatest fear you've ever conquered. You may be thinking that forgiveness is not a fear – but what about when you've done nothing wrong? You have every right to be raging with anger. Whether you have conveniently forgotten your fatherless troubles or if you are reminded of your past daily, we all have the same thing in common – fear. Fear binds us into thinking that if we forgive, we are no longer holding our fathers accountable for their actions. God does not want us to act as if nothing ever happened. The truth will always remain just that, the truth.

God wants the opposite. He wants you to realize that the same redeeming power He has afforded you has also been afforded to your father. Your father will always be held accountable for his actions, but it is not your responsibility to point the finger or deliver the punishment. Forgiveness does not require you to forget; however, it does require you to release judgment.

Read chapter six today. Write a list of everything your father ever did wrong. It's time to put it all on paper.

Day 9

He wants you to realize that the same redeeming power He has afforded you has also been afforded to your father.

Day 10

Relationships Don't Define Your Purpose

Purpose is defined in the dictionary as the reason for which something is done or created, or for which something exists. People may come in and out of your life, but that will never define who you are or who you were created to be. Being rejected by your father is quite a blow, but God, the Heavenly Father, created you with a purpose from the very beginning. You are made in His image. He possesses your purpose. Seek Him and He will show you.

Write a letter to God asking Him to lead you to His purpose.

Day 10

People may come in and out of your life, but that will never define who you are or who you were created to be.

_____

_____
_____
_____
_____
_____
_____
_____
_____
_____
_____
_____
_____
_____
_____
_____
_____
_____
_____
_____
_____
_____
_____
_____

Day 11

Parallel Paths

You're half way there. You can't stop now!

Alter your view today. What if your father feels pain like you do? What if he wanted to be with you, but just couldn't? What if he wanted to reach out, but the voices in his head told him that you would never speak to him? What if?

Your story is important, but your father has a story too. His story could help bring clarity to your past or explain his disappointing actions. Whatever the case may be, the parallel paths of your stories could open your eyes to something much bigger.

Meditate upon this Bible verse:

> *"...for all have sinned and fall short of the glory of God."*
> Romans 3:23 English Standard Version

Write and reflect on how you feel about today's lesson.

Day 11

Your story is important, but
your father has a story too.

_____

_____

_____

_____

_____

_____

_____

_____

_____

_____

_____

_____

_____

_____

_____

_____

_____

_____

_____

_____

_____

_____

_____

Day 12

Stop Photographing the Past with a Lens From the Future

Own it. Own your future. Own your future without referring to what happened to you way back then. Stop looking back. No one ever stepped into their destiny looking back at their past. The dream of having a better childhood may be something you hold dear, but it is time to release it.

You have so much more peace, clarity and healing than you had eleven days ago. Keep your eyes planted on what's ahead. Every day you are becoming stronger. Your future is bright. Take the next step – move forward and vow not to look back. Keep pressing towards the mark.

Write about your future. What do you want your life to be like in the next five years?

Day 12

No one ever stepped into
their destiny looking back at
their past.

Day 13

Take Your Life Back

Unless you view forgiveness as a gift that you give yourself, this part of the journey will seem like a painful burden. Forgiveness is a shining light that allows you to see exactly what has been holding you back for so long. It's a choice. You choose to forgive. Choosing forgiveness does not mean that everything will be perfect, but it will give you the peace you've longed for.

Through the Redemption journey, you learned that you have been forgiven through Jesus Christ. Jesus has afforded this same forgiveness to your father. It's now your turn. Forgive your father and take your life back.

Today, you will need to choose. Remember, the journey cannot continue until you conquer this step. If you choose to forgive, reflect by going back to Day 9 and write the word "Forgiven" next to each wrong your father has done. Take note of this date during today's reflection.

If you choose not to forgive today, that's okay. Perfection is not a component of this journey. You have come so far. Have patience with the process and start the forgiveness journey over, beginning with Day 8.

Day 13

Choosing forgiveness does not mean that everything will be perfect, but it will give you the peace you've longed for.

_____
_____
_____
_____
_____
_____
_____
_____
_____
_____
_____
_____
_____
_____
_____
_____
_____
_____
_____
_____
_____
_____
_____
_____
_____
_____
_____

Day 14

Receiving Beauty for Ashes

You're doing a great job! Let's keep up the momentum.

When you exchange something with someone, you rarely receive something better in return. Well, God does not work that way. He will always beat your giving, because His love runs deeper than the ocean. He blesses His children.

God would love to give you beauty, but in return, He wants everything that is dead in your life. In order to receive beauty, you must first trust God and release your ashes. Are you ready? Every dead relationship, every dead thought, every dead dream. It must all go.

Today, tell God that you want to make an exchange. You are giving up the ashes and expecting something beautiful in return.

Write and reflect over today's lesson.

Day 14

In order to receive beauty, you must first trust God and release your ashes.

_____
_____
_____
_____
_____
_____
_____
_____
_____
_____
_____
_____
_____
_____
_____
_____
_____
_____
_____
_____
_____
_____
_____
_____

Day 15

Who You Are

You made it! We're officially on Restoration Highway.

I am so excited for you! You have finished two of the journeys, and only one remains. Today, we will focus on who you are. During this in-depth process of healing, we strip away all of the hurt, pain, depression and anger, and all you are left with is the real you. Who are you? What have you become? What would you like to become? How have you changed? What more would you like to change?

Write the answers to all of these questions in your journal. Also, capture some actions you will take to change.

Day 15

We are officially on Restoration Highway! Let's journal your thoughts so far.

_____
_____
_____
_____
_____
_____
_____
_____
_____
_____
_____
_____
_____
_____
_____
_____
_____
_____
_____
_____
_____
_____
_____
_____
_____

Day 16

Restoration from the Inside, Out

Restoration may not be visible with the naked eye, but it can be noticed in every situation. From your attitude changing towards your father, to the way you treat others, restoration is one of the strong pillars of championing your life in order to change it. How do you obtain restoration? You let God lead the way. He is the restorer of all things. When you submit and believe in Him, *anything* is possible.

Meditate on this verse:

"He restores my soul; He leads me in the paths of righteousness for His name's sake."
Psalms 23:3 New King James Version

Read chapter seven today. Write down what restoration means to you.

Day 16

Restoration may not be visible with the naked eye, but it can be noticed in every situation.

_____

_____

_____

_____

_____

_____

_____

_____

_____

_____

_____

_____

_____

_____

_____

_____

_____

_____

_____

_____

_____

_____

_____

_____

_____

_____

_____

Day 17

Walking Hand in Hand

Commit to walking hand in hand with God every day. Have a conversation with Him. It's easy. Just tell Him how you feel and He'll take it from there. His guidance will lead you on this continuous journey of restoration. He won't restore you back to what you were before; you'll be so much greater!

Write down your fears, your weaknesses, and anything you may need help with. He will always be there for you, *always*!

Day 17

He won't restore you back to
what you were before; you'll
be so much greater!

Day 18

Conquering the Mountain

This lesson will take every bit of strength that you have.

Reuniting with your father can give you great relief. You can walk through life knowing you've done all you could. Although he shouldn't have walked out of your life, that doesn't inhibit you from walking back into his. Have peace in the fact that you have made it over the mountain and that you are pursuing patience.

Step 1: Write a letter to your father. Include everything you've ever wanted to say to him. You will be emotional, but that's okay. Cry. Let it all out.

Step 2: Read it to him. Even if your father cannot be reached, read the letter out loud and take solace in the fact that it is finished!

Day 18

Have peace in the fact that
you have made it over the
mountain and that you are
pursuing patience.

_____
_____
_____
_____
_____
_____
_____
_____
_____
_____
_____
_____
_____
_____
_____
_____
_____
_____
_____
_____
_____
_____
_____
_____

Day 19

Starting Fresh

After twenty years of separation, my father came back into my life. My expectations were much higher than reality. I really wanted to go back and have the life I longed for back then. I was clearly disappointed, but I had to remember the lessons I learned along the journey.

Although you cannot get back your dream of a relationship, you can definitely start a new one. It does not need to be perfect, in fact, there is perfection in imperfection. If you want to start a relationship, do not have any expectations. Just take it one day at a time.

Write and reflect on today's lesson.

Day 19

It does not need to be perfect, in fact, there is perfection in imperfection.

Day 20

Only Joy Remains

You have reached a pivotal point on your journey. Reading a heartfelt letter to your father released all the emotions you've kept inside for so long. Peace has overcome you and transformation is ahead of you.

You still have one more exchange to make with God – the oil of joy for mourning. You have mourned the dead relationship of your father for too long now. Make the last exchange. Give the mourning to Him. He will give you joy instead.

Write and reflect on today's lesson.

Day 20

You still have one more exchange to make with God— the oil of joy for mourning.

_____
_____
_____
_____
_____
_____
_____
_____
_____
_____
_____
_____
_____
_____
_____
_____
_____
_____
_____
_____
_____
_____
_____
_____
_____

Day 21

Continue Healing

Congratulations! You did it. You finished the 21-day kick off to healing. Be proud of yourself for all the work you've accomplished. This is no easy task, and although you may have struggled at times, you made it. You may not be completely healed yet, but you are definitely on your way.

Don't stop now! Revisit your journal every day to reflect and remember what you have accomplished and the lessons you have learned. You will continue to heal every day that you walk with God, hand in hand.

Day 21

You will continue to heal
every day that you walk with
God, hand in hand.

_____
_____
_____
_____
_____
_____
_____
_____
_____
_____
_____
_____
_____
_____
_____
_____
_____
_____
_____
_____
_____
_____
_____
_____
_____
_____
_____

Living in Your Testimony (Bonus)

You are worth every step it takes to take your life back. Every day is a new day filled with possibilities to transform your life into what it should be. Always keep your goal in mind. Your beautiful ending is filled with freedom, forgiveness and faith!

Go ahead and start living in your testimony. There's no need to wait. While you're still going through your healing process, you'll inspire others to start theirs!

Below, you can write every person's name that you've shared your testimony with.

1.	11.
2.	12.
3.	13.
4.	14.
5.	15.
6.	16.
7.	17.
8.	18.
9.	19.
10.	20.

Thank You

This isn't the end, but rather the beginning. My story is your story, so as fatherless daughters, God is continuously working on our journey.

I'd love to help you with your healing process. You can sign up for a complementary 30-minute session with me where we'll discuss how you can let go and be free to live again. To schedule, use my contact information below. I can't promise you that your journey of healing will be easy, but I will promise you changing your life will be worth the journey.

Are you already living in your testimony? I'd like to hear your story. Send me your testimony and any feedback you'd like to share about Invisible Dad. I can't wait to read it!

I'm also available to speak to your group about Invisible Dad and my journey of healing. Let's discuss your group having me as a speaker at your next event.

Whether you're just starting your journey or you're living in your testimony, I'll see you on Restoration Highway!

To schedule, visit www.CandiceCrear.com.

About the Author

Candice Crear's mission is to serve fatherless daughters around the world. Ready to challenge the new 'normal', she provides people the tools they need to come face-to-face with their true story of power and strength, despite the overwhelming feelings of their past. As a woman full of determination, she continues to make great strides in her life. She's a Life Coach,  entrepreneur, empowerment speaker, and volunteer.

Candice holds a Bachelor of Science degree from Winston-Salem State University and a Master of Business Administration degree from Xavier University. She enjoys traveling and meeting new people and currently resides in Cincinnati, Ohio.

You can reach Candice at www.CandiceCrear.com.

9 780998 930626

I continued to watch, wondering if this person had pulled over for me.

A man left the driver's seat and stepped into the pouring rain, just a silhouette at first, a tall man with thick arms that were visible because he didn't wear a jacket. When he came closer to my car, he was displayed in my headlights.

And wow…he was *fiiiiinnne.*

Dark hair and eyes, a hard jawline, a very distinct and unmistakable *"I don't give a fuck about a damn thing"* attitude. When he came to my window, he tapped his big knuckles against the glass, standing in the rain like it was a warm shower.

I hesitated before I rolled down the window, taking a second to snap out of the reverie. The second the window was down, the sound of the rain became amplified, a cacophony we had to yell over to hear each other.

He put one hand on the roof of the car and leaned down to speak to me, already soaked to the skin. There was a shadow on his jawline, popping tendons up his neck, veins down his muscular arms. "You alright?" A deep and masculine voice released into the night air, authoritative without aggression.

There were no words on my tongue because I was paralyzed by the sight of him.

"I saw your tire blow out when you ran over that scrap metal."

"Oh, I didn't see it." I felt dwarfed by his confidence, felt hideous even though I'd looked my best for the art gala I'd just attended.

"You shouldn't be driving in these weather conditions."

"I-I had work." I had a tough time just stringing a couple words together. All of my confidence was gone, and I didn't like it.

"Pop the trunk. I'll change it for you."

"What?" I asked in disbelief.

He reached inside my car, and that was when I saw the ring on one of his fingers, a large diamond carved into the shape of a skull. He hit the button, and the mechanism clicked in the trunk to provide access to the spare tire.

"You don't have to do that. If I could just borrow your phone—"

"It'll only take me five minutes."

"It's pouring down rain—"

"Trust me, sweetheart. You don't want to be on this street in the next fifteen minutes." He walked to the back of the car, and the vehicle shifted as he pulled out what he needed to get to work. The car tilted sideways as he used the jack to lift it and the tire iron to loosen the lug nuts.

I felt guilty as hell, sitting in there warm and dry while some stranger worked on my car.

Some *hot* stranger…

I pulled on my jacket, put the hood up, and went over to his side.

He was kneeling down, his muscular back visible in the soaked fabric of his shirt. He loosened the tire, pulled it off, and carried it back to the trunk. When he walked back toward me, that was the first real view I got of him. Six-foot-something, the lines of his hard chest and abs visible because his shirt stuck to him like a papier-mâché. "Get your ass back in the car."

"Get my ass back in the car?" Did he just say that to me? "You need help—"

"No." He returned to the side of the car and slid the spare tire onto the axle. Then he grabbed the tire iron and manually tightened each lug nut around the wheel, securing it in place. He released the jack, and the car returned to its flat position.

He really did do it in five minutes. Probably less. "Are you a mechanic?"

A smirk moved over his face as he carried the jack to the trunk then shut the lid. "You're good to go."

"Can I give you some money—"

"No." He came back toward me. "Just get off the street."

That was the second time he'd said something like that. "Why?"

"Don't drive in these conditions. And if you do it anyway—*pay attention.*"

He was a gentleman for pulling over to help me in a downpour, but he was also a dick at the same time. I would normally snap back at an insult like that, but because he was literally soaked to the bone from changing my tire, I kept my mouth shut. "Thank you. I wish there was something I could do for you—"

"You can get in the car and drive away." He turned his back on me and walked back to his black Range Rover.

He opened the driver's door and hopped inside, and the taillights lit up once again, but he didn't drive away, waiting for me to get back in the car.

I got behind the wheel and dropped the hood of my jacket before I started the engine. My dashboard alert had cleared because he'd successfully fixed the wheel.

His Range Rover stayed put, waiting for me to leave first.

I pulled out onto the road and waved at him as I passed, but his window was completely tinted black. The light was green, so I drove through the intersection and then headed home.

2

THEO

I entered the double doors and stepped into the lobby, my boots squeaking because they were full of water. Both of the guards stared at my appearance but didn't say a word. I stepped into the grand room, an old room with old paintings of people dead and gone on the walls.

Derek spoke on the phone, his pistol visible as it stuck out from the back of his jeans. The room was filled with more of my men, all armed to the teeth. "Alright, alright. Got it." He hung up then turned to look at me. "Where the fuck have you been?" Then his eyes narrowed as he studied me up and down before he gave me a quizzical look.

"Something came up."

He looked like he wanted to say more, but the expression on my face dissuaded him from making the greatest mistake of his life. "Anyone got a change of clothes?" He looked around at the other guys.

"It's fine."

"We can't meet Bolton with you looking like that—"

"I said it's fine."

Derek's eyes shifted back and forth between mine, but he didn't press his argument. He grabbed his phone again and made another call.

Whether I was soaking wet or buck naked made no difference. I could make a grown man shit his pants, regardless.

Derek finished his call then came back to me. "They're close."

"Alright. Let's do this, gentlemen."

I sat behind the wooden table in the center of the enormous room, the cold fireplace behind me, the hearth so large it was bigger than the average person's living room. It was a historic building that was sometimes used for tours—and a good friend had let me borrow it for the night.

Guards were posted in every corner and on the surrounding rooftops, some with sniper rifles and some with assault rifles. I was certain Bolton had his men expertly placed as well, finding holes in my defenses because that was his specialty.

We came together under the veil of a temporary truce, but we both knew that veil was so thin, the tip of a paper clip could pierce it.

Derek approached me. "They've entered the building." Then he stepped away, leaving his pistol in the back of his jeans.

A few minutes later, Bolton entered through the open double doors, flanked by the armed men he brought with him. His eyes focused on me, his mouth stretched in a subtle smile. He did a quick scan as he came closer and looked at the chair across from me.

One of his men pulled it out for him—like he was a fucking girl.

He got comfortable and looked me over. "Did you walk here?" He cocked his head slightly, an arrogant shine to his eyes.

"I like the rain."

He gave a slight nod. "Spoken like a sensitive pussy."

It was hard to stay in that chair and do nothing—not because of what he said, but because of who he was. If I could strangle him with my bare hands, I would. I would watch the life seep from his eyes and squeeze harder. Make sure he disappeared in an old oil drum and sank to the bottom of the ocean for all eternity. "You know what I want, Bolton. Make your demand."

"And you know my demands because I've already made them, Theo." He turned serious, switching into negotiation mode.

"I'm not giving you a cut of my empire—"

"Then I'm not giving you his bones."

Grief was a strange sensation. There were days when I felt nothing. And there were days when I felt it all at once. Guilt. Rage. Loss. But I had to wear a mask so sharp it could slice through brick.

"And I'm not giving you a name."

"You have the north. You don't need the south."

"Well, I'd love to have another yacht…so I disagree." He smirked.

"You came all the way here to negotiate, but you don't seem interested in doing that."

"I could say the same for you, Theo." He sank into the chair and crossed his arms over his chest. "The Brotherhood never shares the source of its contracts. Once I give you the name of who ordered the hit, my reputation will take a blow. So you need to pay me for that."

"And I've offered to pay you handsomely—"

"I don't want a lump sum. I want another source of income. Five percent of your business would suffice."

"If I do it for you, I'd have to do it for others—"

"We can keep it between us, Theo."

"The answer is no, Bolton. Your request is unreasonable, and we both know it. You think my emotions will cloud my reasoning, but they won't." It might kill me inside, but I would never show them, not to anyone, not even to Axel. "Take my offer, because it's the best one you're going to get."

A flicker of rage moved across his gaze, but once he blinked, it was gone. "I thought your brother would have meant more to you."

"He meant more to me when he was alive, Bolton. But he's dead—*because of you.*"

"You know it wasn't personal."

"It is personal because I could have outbid your contractor."

"You know that's not how it works, Theo."

"Then let me tell you how it's going to work." I controlled my voice as best I could, but it rose slightly. "You're going to take my deal and give me his body. We go our separate ways. You keep the north, and I keep the south. Refuse, and I will take both territories and do worse to you than what you did to my brother. The Brotherhood will be under my regime—and I will deploy it for my own gain."

Bolton listened to my words with a hardened gaze.

I waited for him to yield, to realize greed wasn't worth poking the bear. A big, pissed-off bear.

"Reputation is everything, Theo. And I'm not going to compromise it without substantial gain."

Wrong answer. "Whether you tell me outright or I cut the answers from your throat, the outcome will be the same. But let's do it your way because it'll definitely be more fun."

ASTRID

When I got home, the house was quiet and abandoned, like no one had been there for days. I flicked on the lights and hung my wet coat on the coatrack before I kicked off my heels. The kitchen island still had the bottle of wine I'd left there and the wineglass I hadn't finished. My phone finally had enough power to turn on, so I turned it on, expecting text messages, but there was nothing.

I set my dress to the side for the dry cleaners and washed away my makeup. It was late and I was tired, but I wanted to stay up and wait for my husband to come home. The husband I hardly saw these days...

The man who'd changed my tire was still on my mind, battling the storm like he was a mighty oak that didn't bend in the wind. He'd told me to get off the street, and those words still bothered me.

That was probably why I couldn't sleep, because I was worried.

I sat on the couch with my favorite bottle of wine from Barsetti Vineyards. It was from the 2016 harvest, my favorite year. I sat there alone, looking out the windows and seeing the rain hit the panes. I was on the ground floor of our three-story villa, so I couldn't hear the rain hit the roof.

I stared until I grew sleepy and pulled a blanket over me. I didn't remember falling asleep, but at some point, I did. And I woke up when I heard someone else in the house. My eyes opened, and I sat up, looking at the man who stood in the kitchen through my squinted eyes. He had dirty-blond hair and blue eyes, and the sleeves of his long-sleeved shirt were pushed to his elbows. He opened the cabinet and pulled out a decanter of booze before he drank straight from the bottle.

He didn't seem to notice I was there. "Hey."

He finished his drink then released a quiet sigh. "Didn't think you'd be awake."

"I was worried."

"Why?" He left the kitchen and joined me in the sitting room, taking the seat beside me. "It's just rain, Astrid."

"I know, but…I know you said you had something to do tonight."

"I always have something to do." I'd met him at a bar years ago, and we'd hit it off right away. We'd dated for a while, and then once we were serious, he laid a bombshell on me. He wasn't an accountant—but a hit man. I'd broken it off because I was disturbed by what I'd learned, but he wouldn't let me go, and then we got married shortly afterward. He never shared the details of his work explicitly, and when he left the house for days at a time, he didn't give me an explanation. I met other men he worked with and understood it was a network rather than an independent job. But I didn't know details because I didn't want to know details.

It was better this way.

I didn't want to know who he killed or why he killed them, but he told me they were always bad men who'd made enemies with their wrongdoing, that he wasn't killing innocent people who were in the wrong place at the wrong time.

I hoped that was the truth.

So, whenever he was gone, I always worried. He told me not to text or call, to wait for him to text or call me in case it put him in a compromised position. Those stretches of time when I didn't hear from him were always the worst.

"How was the art thing?" he asked.

"It was fine." I should tell him about the flat tire and that man who'd helped me, but for some reason, I didn't.

"I'm going to shower then go to bed." He left the couch and my side and walked off.

He used to grab me all the time, yank me into him and kiss me, but lately, he seemed disinterested in physical intimacy. He was always stressed or tired or distracted. "Is something wrong?"

He halted then slowly turned back to me. "It's four in the morning, Astrid. It's not okay for me to be tired?"

"That's not what I said—"

"Why would something be wrong?" he demanded, his voice rising.

"There's no reason—"

"You asked me for a reason. Did you not?" He didn't raise his voice further, but it felt like he was screaming.

"You've just been gone a lot."

"And you think right now, at four in the morning, is the time to discuss it?"

He managed to turn everything around on me, making me look like the bad guy. "It's never a good time. You're always busy."

"You're being clingy, Astrid. Really fucking clingy."

"I'm being clingy?" I asked incredulously. "Because I want to see my husband more than a couple days a week? Because I'm tired of him disappearing for days without telling me if he's okay? Because I want to discuss when we're going to have a family, but you shut me out every time? I would much rather be clingy than what you are—neglectful."

His arms remained by his sides, but he stared me down with a threatening gaze, like I wasn't his wife, but one of the men he was hired to kill. "I'm sorry I haven't been around much lately. Work has been busy—"

"I don't care what your reason is. It's unacceptable."

21

"You asked me to talk about it, and then when I speak, you interrupt me?" His voice rose a little louder. "You think that's wise?"

"I'm just angry right now."

"Well, I'm fucking angry too. I give you a life that women dream of. Diamonds, cars, yachts, villas in every beautiful region in this world—"

"I married you because I wanted *you*, not the shit you can buy me. And instead of finding that clingy, I would hope you'd find that romantic. Because you can get any woman you want who wants your money, but I actually want you for you."

He stared me down, his breathing elevated.

"You're gone so much, sometimes I'm afraid…I'm afraid I'm not the only one."

"Only one what?" he barked.

"The only woman in your bed."

"I fuck you when I come home, do I not? I fuck you like a goddamn sailor on leave."

"You didn't address what I said—"

"Because it's fucking ridiculous. And insulting." He turned away again. "I'm going to bed, Astrid. We can pick up this pointless conversation in the morning if you really want." He moved to the stairs, walked to the next floor, and disappeared.

I stayed on the couch and felt my eyes water with tears I refused to release.

The next morning, we barely talked about what had happened the night before. He apologized, but it was obvious he only did it to make the conversation go away. Nothing had been fixed, exactly as he wanted. He spent the day with me, but the air between us was tense and not the least bit enjoyable.

I went to work the following day at the gallery where I worked. Once I'd finished school, I'd taken a few art classes because I wanted to be an artist. But that dream had never panned out, so I sold art rather than made my own.

My husband was a very rich man so I could stay home all day or go shopping, but since he wasn't around often, I got lonely sitting in that big villa by myself. Florence was one of the most romantic cities on earth, but it didn't feel romantic walking the streets alone or eating lunch in a café with no one to talk to.

It was nice to be around art, to have clients who appreciated the work of the artists we represented. Some of our paintings could be ten thousand euros— or a hundred thousand euros. We also had a lot of clients who didn't give a shit about art but needed it on their walls to look rich or pretentious.

When I was home, I worked on my own art but never deemed it good enough to show anyone. My husband never asked about my work, so I didn't have to hide my canvases. They stayed in my art room, a room he never entered.

My boss told me we had a new client who needed his drawing room to be touched up with artwork, so it was my job to visit the house, take all the measurements, and absorb the ambiance of the room and what would complement it. I was an art dealer, but I was also a bit of a decorator too, a job with many responsibilities.

I drove to the address, a building that was distinct and separate from the others in the heart of the city. Iron gates blocked the entrance, and Gothic statues guarded the outside, which seemed odd, considering this city had flourished during the Renaissance. After I parked my car, I tried to enter through the gate, but it was locked. I noticed the speaker and the keypad there, so I pressed the button and spoke into the intercom. "Um, hi. This is Astrid. I'm from Hemlington Art Gallery."

A buzzer beeped, and the gate was unlocked.

I let myself inside and approached the enormous double doors, black like obsidian against the stone wall.

The doors opened before I could knock, and I was greeted by a man in a collared shirt. "Hello, Astrid. I'm George."

I remembered him from the email. "Yes, it's nice to meet you."

He shook my hand then escorted me inside. The foyer of the house was beautiful, two staircases in the back, dark and masculine tones everywhere. It was very clear that a bachelor lived here all by himself.

"Let me show you the space." George escorted me to one side of the villa, and we entered a grand study with a large fireplace, a mahogany desk, and a sitting area positioned on top of a rug. It was well decorated, but the walls were bare. "The owner of the house has been here for years but never got around to selecting his artwork. He's a very busy man."

I'd already sized up the room, realizing the potential of the space. "It's a lovely room."

"Yes, I agree."

I took a look around, examined the open walls and took measurements, trying to decide how the layout should be. I sat down on the couch and took notes.

George continued to stand there, as if I might steal something if he left me alone.

"I have some ideas," I said. "Do you have any idea what kind of artwork the owner likes or...?"

"He's not picky. Just something to fit the space."

"I would hate to put in all this work without having *some* idea of what he likes." Some of my clients like paintings of naked women exclusively, some preferred floral arrangements and landscapes, and others wanted specific types of art, either religious or evocative. "Does he like images of historical significance? Does he like landscapes? Does he like portraits of people? If we could just narrow it down, that would be helpful. If this is his study, then it's his domain, and he needs to enjoy the art in his space."

George stood there with his hands behind his back, drawing a slow and deep breath as he deliberated with himself. He had to decide whether he wanted to bother his employer with a matter as insignificant as this.

"I've taken all the measurements and have a feel for the room. Maybe he could meet me at the gallery whenever he's free. We could walk through it together, and he could give me his input. Our collection is enormous. We have everything you can think of."

"I'll speak with him," George said. "Expect an email from me."

My husband and I went to dinner that night. It wasn't a romantic night on the town for the two of us, but a work event for him. I wasn't sure if he had a client or some other connection because my husband wore a lot of different hats.

When we arrived, he pulled out my chair for me like he always did, and then we sat across from a man in his late fifties with a woman who looked like she could be his daughter. Beautiful in a scandalous dress, she had only one purpose, and that was to look stunning on his arm.

I was used to this sort of thing because I'd been in this world for so long, but it still surprised me that people lived this way, lived lives very different from the average person.

The wine was ordered, along with an appetizer, and then the men got down to business.

"Tyrone has been a cockblock to my business for a long time," the man said. "We formed a partnership when we were in our early twenties, but he's gone off the deep end in the last few years. Because of the contracts we signed, there's nothing I can do to stop him. But at the rate he's going, he's going to sink the ship."

My husband listened intently, ignoring the sound of the loud restaurant around us, his focus absolute. "Is the ship already sinking?"

The other man cocked his head slightly. "It's starting to creak…"

"And you've spoken to him?"

"We've had our shouting matches. He's an arrogant son-of-a-bitch."

"If he suddenly dies, you'll be the first suspect."

He gave a shrug. "I don't care at this point."

"You don't care about revenge?"

"He has a wife and a couple kids. I'm not afraid of them. They'll still get their cut. But I need to take the wheel and avoid the iceberg we're about to hit. He won't listen to reason, so I see no other option."

I sat there and listened to all of this, partially desensitized to these conversations. They talked about killing people like it was a simple contract with no consequences. My husband said it was real life and fairy tales didn't exist…only nightmares.

I wasn't sure why he brought me to these, because this wasn't the quality time that I craved. I wasn't the bombshell on his arm like the woman across from me, who seemed completely zoned out of the conversation. She either didn't care that her date wanted to kill someone, or she was used to it.

"For a contract like this, it's going to be at least thirty."

"Thirty?" he asked in slight surprise.

"Keep in mind, that's a cheap contract. I have clients who pay in the hundreds. It all depends on the potential fallout we have to face. I took a contract for the Skull King's brother, and it's created quite the headache."

I immediately thought of the ring on the man's hand the other night, the diamonds set into a skull shape. I'd forgotten about it right after I saw it, but it sprang back to my mind in that moment.

"The Skull King?" the man asked. "You thought that was a wise contract to take?"

"This was before he was the Skull King. Game has changed a lot since then."

He gave a slight nod. "I accept your fee."

"Then it looks like we have a deal."

We arrived at our villa, and my husband left his coat on the rack before he walked inside, his muscular arms covered in thick tendons. He was tall and muscular, so his physique was well suited to his line of work. He was a handsome man, and that was the first thing I'd noticed when I'd met him. If he weren't so handsome, I probably would have been smart and left the relationship when I'd had the chance.

But now, I was stuck.

Sometimes I liked being stuck, but I hadn't liked it in a long time.

He poured himself a drink right away and didn't offer me one.

I didn't know what to say. Now, when we were alone together, it was tense and not tense with sexual tension and desire, but with awkwardness. I sat on the couch and slipped off one of my heels.

He moved to the armchair and set his glass on the coffee table. His arms were on his knees, and his hands came together. His eyes found something else to stare at for several seconds before he looked at me. "If you're ready to start a family, I'm ready."

I slipped off my remaining heel then stilled when I let the words sink in.

"I know your window is closing, so let's do it."

It took me a moment to find the words, because we'd been fighting and ignoring each other for the last few days, and then he said this. "This came out of nowhere."

"You've been wanting to discuss it for a while."

"I know, but this is the moment you choose to pursue it?"

"What's wrong with this moment?"

"I—I don't know. We haven't been happy lately."

He looked away for a moment. "That's how marriage is. It has its highs and its lows. It'll come back."

I kept myself busy with work, but I'd rather keep myself busy with my children, growing a family and building a legacy. But once it was placed on a pedestal before me, I didn't want it. "I-I don't know."

His eyes found mine, a hint of surprise there. "What don't you know?"

"Are you going to leave the business?"

He answered without hesitation. "No."

"Well, I don't see how that will work."

"I disagree."

"You could be killed—"

"I've been doing this a long time, Astrid. No one is a match for me."

"What if someone comes after us—"

"We've been together for three years. Has anyone come after you?"

I blinked several times. "No."

"Because no one is dumb enough to fuck with me." Now, his voice deepened, growing angry at my provocation. "I would never let anything happen to you or our children. You can leave the gallery and raise them."

"And where are you in all of this?"

"I'll be around…when I'm around."

"Do you actually want to have a family, or do you just want me to raise your children?"

He stared at me without blinking, without taking a breath. "I want to have a family. But let's be honest here. I provide—and you nurture. I want to spend time with my children, but you're going to be the primary caregiver. I won't insult you by promising to be there all the time when I know I won't be."

It angered me, but I couldn't feel angry when he was honest with me. As far as I could tell, he'd never lied to me. And even though he was harsh sometimes, I treasured that honesty. "I always imagined we would do this after you retired."

"I'm too young to retire. And I don't want to be an old dad."

"I don't know if I could bring a child into our lives in good conscience, knowing what you do."

"How would you feel if I said I didn't want to have a child with you because you're a whore or a stripper?" he snapped. "No one should be ashamed of how they earn a living—and I won't be."

"Being a hit man and an erotic dancer are not comparable."

"I'm not going to change my stance on this. If you want to have children, this is how we're having them." He grabbed the glass and finished it off before he stood up. "I need to do a few things in my office before bed." He walked up the stairs, and then his steps disappeared when he reached the next landing.

I sat there alone…like I always did.

I sat down at my desk and opened my emails.

I read the message from George. *Mr. Bianchi will be there at three this afternoon. This will be a private viewing, so make sure your gallery is vacant for his arrival. Take care, George.*

It was a bit presumptuous and arrogant, but I was used to these types of clients. But to assume I would clear my schedule for a man I'd never met—that was over-the-top. He was probably an old, insufferable man who had turned into a jackass in old age because he had no one to keep him in check anymore. His wife had left him, taking half his money when she couldn't stand him anymore.

Thankfully, all my appointments were in the morning and my schedule was clear in the afternoon, so it was easy to accommodate the diva-like request. I made sure there was champagne and a plate of appetizers so I could greet him like the queen that he was.

I sat behind my desk and realized it was fifteen minutes after three and the guy hadn't shown up yet.

Typical.

My eyes were on the floor-to-ceiling windows at the front of our gallery, and that was when I saw a man in a gray t-shirt that fit snugly around his thick arms step into my view. He wore black jeans and boots, and he spoke on the phone, stopping in front of me to finish the conversation.

My eyes moved to his tight ass in those jeans.

The sex with my husband used to be good, but it'd become irregular and obligatory in the last six months. It never scratched the itch that I had. It seemed like he didn't care whether I came or not, like his mind was so preoccupied that he just wanted to get the deed done so he could go to sleep or finish up something in his office.

So it was hard not to notice this hunk of a man in front of the window.

He finished his phone call and shoved the device into his pocket—and that was when I noticed it.

The skull ring on his left hand.

My heart gave an enormous lurch, and my back muscles spasmed like I was about to fall over in my chair.

He turned the corner and approached the double glass doors before he walked inside, the same man I'd seen in the rain, six-foot-something of pure masculinity and raw sexiness. He had the shadow on his jawline, the dark eyes straight from the underworld, the muscles that had as much horsepower as a race car.

His shirt didn't stick to his hard chest like it had in the rain, but I remembered the visual quite well. My eyes quickly roamed over his body and appreciated every inch because he was god's gift to women...and men.

A slightly annoyed look was in his eyes, like he didn't want to spend his time picking out art. But then his eyes found mine, and a slow look of recognition appeared there. His dark eyes hardened at the realization, but he didn't say a word.

I left the desk and walked up to him, my heels wobbling left and right because I forgot how to walk in them. Even with the four extra inches of height they provided, the man still towered over me like the Eiffel Tower over the old buildings in Paris. I stood directly before him now, but I still hadn't found the words to greet him. Everything in me died at the sight of him, like I'd completely forgotten how to be human.

He didn't say anything either, taking in my appearance as if trying to memorize it.

My mouth was dry, and my palms were slick with sweat. "Small world, huh?"

He didn't speak, and his silence countered my icebreaker. His eyes had been almost black the last time I saw him, but now that it was daylight, they were brown like a hot cup of coffee. There was so much confidence in his stare, like he thrived on others' discomfort. "I hope you've become a better driver since."

I gave a slow nod. "It's not my fault there was a pile of shrapnel in the road—"

"It's your fault you didn't see it," he said. "We can't control what happens to us, but we can control what we happen to." He stepped away to the gallery opening as if the matter had been settled.

I watched him pass, seeing the way the muscles of his incredible physique shifted and moved underneath his clothing.

"Let's get this over with."

I grabbed my pen and notebook and followed him into

the other room, seeing him walk through the gallery and barely glance at the Tuscan landscapes.

"So you're nice enough to pull over and change a lady's tire in the rain, but then you're an insufferable asshole the rest of the time?"

He slowly turned his head to look at me, a slight look of surprise on his face.

"I'm not going to put up with your attitude just because you're a client. Helping someone choose their artwork for their space is a very intimate task, and if you're going to be a dick to me, then this isn't going to work."

His hard expression didn't change, but he absorbed my gaze like I was one of the paintings on the wall.

I held his stare and didn't back down, waiting for him to blow up and scream at me.

But the corner of his mouth rose in a subtle smile. "Fair enough."

He was so hot when he looked angry, but that smile made him even hotter. It took me a second to snap out of it. "I get the impression you don't care for the landscapes—"

"I didn't change your tire to be nice." He cut me off like I hadn't spoken. "I don't do nice. I did it to get your ass off the street, as I already said." He stepped away and moved down the wall of paintings, snapping back into his foul mood just like that.

I followed him. "Why did you want me off the street?"

He walked past more landscapes and barely looked at them.

I suspected I wouldn't receive an answer. "What are you interested in? I have historical pieces. I have nude pieces. Religious stuff. I also have some collector's pieces created during the Renaissance."

"Nude pieces?" he asked.

"Portraits of naked men and women. They tend to be a favorite of most of my clients."

"I'm in my study to work, not be distracted."

"Alright, then let's look at the historical pieces." Our galleries were separated into sections, the lighting different to match the moods of the artwork. I showed him the displays of the Greek ships as they sailed on Troy, Alexander the Great in the battle of Persia, Mussolini minutes before he was executed.

He stopped and stared at those for a long time, taking in the artwork with a curious eye. His arms crossed over his chest, and he stared at the image of Mussolini with the most interest. "He was my great-grandfather."

"Mussolini?" I asked in surprise.

He nodded without taking his eyes off the painting. "His daughter Edda was my grandmother, although I don't remember her. My family has a bloody history, and it only got worse as the line went on."

Dictatorship had clearly been passed through his bloodline, judging by the way he spoke and treated others. "Do you like the painting?"

"No." He stepped away. "I don't want my ancestor's final moments haunting me in my study." He went past the other artwork, looking at history told by artistic historians. These weren't paintings created during the time the events took place, but modern painters who'd taken a stab at a historical narrative.

I was quiet as I watched him look at all the paintings, taking them in with interest. "Are any of these suitable for you?"

"I respect the work, but no, they aren't suitable."

For a man who wanted artwork on his walls, he didn't seem to care that much for it. "Then let's check out the other exhibits." I took him to the others we had. It was no surprise that he didn't care for the watercolor section full of lilies and ponds. He didn't like the religious section either and even said, "I don't believe in that bullshit."

At some point, we ran out of artwork. "Well, I don't have anything else to show you. I can make us an appointment with our other galleries in the city—"

"What's downstairs?" He noticed the stairs that led to the basement.

"Oh." It was an unusual collection of paintings, a section I didn't bother to show most people because they are so disturbing. "It's hard to describe. They don't really fit into any category. They're sinister, dark, disturbing..." I wasn't even sure why we kept them.

"In case you haven't noticed, I'm all of those things. Lead the way."

I looked into his face, seeing a handsome man with dark hair and eyes, but none of the other things he claimed. His words always had a bite, but he'd still allowed himself to be soaked to the bone so he could help me leave whatever danger he'd enigmatically warned me about.

"Sure." I went down the stairs and flicked on the art lights. We didn't bother to turn them on because so few people were interested in this collection. "Most of these paintings are hundreds of years old. The artists are lesser known. They depict some of the crueler things in society, the plague, demons, torture…things of that nature."

He stepped into the room and looked at the first painting. He didn't just look at it, but he stared without a hint of uncertainty, facing the horror head on. It was a demonic creature in a darkly lit room, its grotesque features impossible to describe. It occupied a cabin in the woods…and appeared to eat the corpse of a faceless human as it hung upside down.

"It's a changeling," I explained. "It's a supernatural being who replaces someone who's been taken by the devil or a demon or a monster. It resembles a human when it's been spotted and shows its true form in solitude."

He continued to stare at it.

I expected him to reject these paintings like he had all

the others, even though he seemed just as interested in their evocativeness.

"I want this one."

I almost did a double take as I looked at the side of his face. It wasn't my place to judge another's opinion about art, but I'd never had anyone ever want these paintings on their wall, never heard of anyone wanting to look at them more than once.

He stepped away and looked at the next one, dark monsters creeping out of the forest and surrounding a lone traveler by a campfire. A sword lay on the ground near the campfire, but the man didn't reach for it, like he knew there was no escape. "And this one."

I wrote it down and kept my judgment to myself.

He looked at a few others and wanted them too. But then he came back to the changeling and continued his stare again, because the first pass hadn't been long enough.

"What do you like about this one?"

His arms were crossed over his chest as he stared, his head cocked slightly. "Do you ever feel that way?"

"What way?" I asked quietly.

"Like you died a long time ago, and now there's this other version of you that lingers…a changeling." His stare lasted a few seconds longer before he turned to look at me directly, gazing at me with the same interest he showed the painting.

I felt an invisible spotlight on my face. Felt like another painting he wanted on his wall. I swallowed, the intensity of his stare like fire from the surface of the sun.

"Tell me your name."

For a brief moment, I forgot what it was. "Astrid."

He continued his stare.

"Yours?" I had his last name, but not his first.

"Theo."

My eyes dropped to his hand, seeing the enormous rock on his finger, a piece of jewelry that was probably worth more than all the paintings in this gallery. It was so striking and potent, there was no way people didn't notice it—and that was the way he wanted it. "That's an interesting ring."

He didn't look down at his left hand. Didn't seem to

care about the comment I made or feel pressured to address the questions I never asked.

"I'll deliver your paintings and arrange for them to be hung on your wall." The energy that emitted from him was just as substantial as the energy from all these paintings, their ability to evoke a range of emotions with just the color of their paints. "I can probably get this done tomorrow—"

"Let's have dinner." He spoke over me like he hadn't been listening to a word I said, just watched my lips move while nothing came out. "I know a good place around the corner."

"Um…" He caught me off guard, and I wasn't sure if that invitation was personal or business. Whether it was business or not, he'd selected his paintings, so there was no reason for us to continue a conversation. But I wanted to say yes…and that made me writhe in both disappointment and gut-wrenching guilt. "I'm married."

His expression didn't change, so he either had a great poker face or he really felt no disappointment at my rejection. "You don't wear a wedding ring."

My fingers automatically felt my left hand where my

naked finger sat. "I was in a hurry this morning and forgot it."

Those dark eyes continued to pierce me with judgment. "If I had a wife, I'd make sure she'd never forget to wear hers." He turned away from me and the painting and headed back to the stairs, his muscular back filling out his shirt in every sexy way.

I watched him go, a sharp pain in my chest, a wave of guilt coupled with inexplicable longing. Marrying my husband had been a foolish decision, but I had been wildly in love. But that love had fallen apart like a house that descended into ruin from a lack of maintenance. First, the pipes had turned to rust, then the walls filled with mold, the roof cracked in a storm...and then it came tumbling down into a pile of rubble that no one wanted to clear away.

I looked at the painting again, and for just a second, I saw myself standing there, eating the corpse of a victim...a changeling.

4

THEO

I sat alone and stared at the girls on the stage, drinking my scotch the way finer people enjoyed their wine. The bass from the music blared and drowned out the sound of nearby conversation. Watching naked girls dance around in a room with other men with hard dicks was strange to me, but I did it for business. Businessman did most of their deals on the golf course, and I did mine in the strip club.

Axel finally arrived, catching up with the bouncer he used to see all the time. After he fist-bumped him, he made his way over to me but got a drink from the waitress along the way. His wedding ring was distinct on his left hand because no other man wore a wedding ring in a place like this.

He dropped into the armchair beside me, his head turned to greet me. Not once did he look at the topless girls as they grinded on the pole, their tits out and their G-strings stuffed with bills. "You look pissed."

"You look tired."

"Fuck, I'm always tired." He chuckled before he took a drink.

"Scarlett doesn't care that you're here?"

"What are you talking about? She loves you."

"I meant the atmosphere." I nodded to the girl in front of me, who seemed to take it as a personal offense that I didn't seem interested.

"Oh, she doesn't care."

"She doesn't care that her husband is visiting strip clubs?"

"My baby knows I've only got eyes for her." He grabbed his drink and took another sip. And just like he said, he never looked, didn't even glance at the naked girl who passed right in front of us. "You're the one who wanted to meet here, by the way."

"You wanted to catch up, and I told you where I was.

Didn't expect you to come down." I grabbed a cigar and lit up. "How are the kids?"

"Emotional terrorists and fucking cockblocks."

I smirked.

"But I love my babies."

"Do you actually mean that, or do you feel obligated to say that?" I wasn't the family man kind of guy. Never had been and never would be. Every parent I knew was miserable until their kids finally left the nest.

"Is it hard?" he asked with a shrug. "Yes, it's the hardest thing I've ever done. Just when you finally get a routine nailed down, they decide to fuck with you and change it. My daughter is latched on to my wife's tits, so I don't get to play with them whenever I want. The last time I had a good night of sleep was before I was a father. I'm grouchy sometimes, and when Scarlett gets drained, she lashes out at me. But I can honestly tell you it's also the best thing. The best fucking thing ever." He said it with complete sincerity as he looked me in the eye. "The parents who say it's magical every second of every day are full of shit. It's not magical. They pull the shit out of their diapers and smear it on the wall. You get vomit on your five-hundred-euro shirts. The lows are low, but let me tell you…the highs are high." He raised his hand in the air as far as he could. "The best way to describe it is like going on a trip. You've got to pack, you've got to sit on a plane, you're sleep-deprived by the time you land, then you gotta get to the hotel, and that's when you realize you forgot to pack something important. But then you look at the ocean or the mountains or whatever the fuck you came to see, and the view makes it all worth it."

I let the smoke fill my mouth as I listened, letting the smoky flavors of chocolate and licorice coat my tongue in a cloudy haze. "You think you're going to have more?"

"No," he said with a quiet chuckle. "Two is enough. Don't want to be outnumbered." He took a drink of his scotch and looked relaxed, not annoyed by the blaring music he had to scream over. "What about you?"

"What about me, what?"

"You think you'll ever change your mind about kids?"

"No."

"Maybe if you meet the right woman, you'll feel differently."

"I already met the right woman—in case you forgot."

He stilled as his eyes quickly darted away in shame. "You know that's not what I meant."

I blew the smoke out of my mouth and let it float in front of my face before it drifted away.

"You're in a bad mood."

"I'm always in a bad mood."

"Not when you see me."

A sarcastic smirk moved on to my lips. "That's what you think."

"That's what I know. So, what's up?" He reached for a cigar from the tray and lit up, continuing to ignore the entertainment directly in front of us. This part of the club was exclusive to members like me, so the hottest women were put in here, while the rest were for the public.

"I figured out who killed Killian."

When Axel heard that, he stiffened in seriousness. He didn't bombard me with questions.

"I warned him I don't know how many fucking times, and he didn't listen."

"Who was it?"

"The Brotherhood."

"Who paid for the contract?"

"That I don't know." I spoke with the cigar tucked in the corner of my mouth. "I tried to make a deal with Bolton, but he wouldn't negotiate. Says his integrity can't be bought, but how much integrity can a killer really have?"

Axel let the cigar rest between his fingertips as he stared at my face.

"He said he would give me the name for a chunk of my business. In his fucking dreams…"

"Where does that leave you?" Axel asked.

"I told him I would come for him, and if he doesn't want to end up like my brother did, he better see reason." Killian had been gone five years now. His death had been shrouded in mystery. He'd gotten involved in the banking sector, not the banking system most people knew, but the corrupt one that no one knew about. Full of fraud, corruption, and scandal. The kind of shit that made major banks fail. I wasn't sure what he'd done to get a hit put on him, but he'd obviously pissed off the wrong person. I didn't have any leads and didn't uncover any once I had the power of the Skull Kings in my grasp, so I'd gone to the Brotherhood directly. Most people wouldn't challenge a group of merciless killers, but I wasn't most people.

"You think he'll come around?"

"No," I said. "But that's fine because I want to kill him anyway."

"You want to kill the leader of the Brotherhood?" he asked with slight skepticism.

I let the smoke coat my tongue once more, felt my mouth grow dry as the smoke absorbed all the moisture. "I want to kill the man who ended my brother's life—and I will."

ASTRID

My husband was gone for a couple days on assignment. He didn't give me the details of his whereabouts because I'd rather not know. Whenever he left, it meant he was about to kill someone and hide the body so well that no one would ever find it.

My husband was a killer.

Even if he only killed bad men, it made me sick sometimes.

He came home just before dinner, wearing the same outfit as when he'd left, his jeans, boots, and his olive-green coat. He hung it up on the coatrack then stepped into the kitchen. "Something smells good." He greeted me with a warm smile and a twinkle in his eyes, like he was happy to see me.

I moved around the kitchen island and greeted him with a hug and a kiss. "It smells good because it's your favorite."

"Thank you, Astrid."

We opened some wine and ate at the table together.

"What'd you do the last couple of days?"

I immediately thought of Theo, that sexy man with dark eyes who was moved by the most disturbing artwork I'd ever seen. The man who'd changed my tire in the rain. The man I never thought I'd see again…but seemed to see everywhere. "I got a new client at the gallery. Needs artwork for his study, so he came by to see what we have to offer."

"Did he buy anything?"

"He bought five paintings—expensive ones."

"That's a nice commission for you."

"Yeah." I hadn't delivered his paintings yet. Been purposely dragging my feet on it. "He didn't like anything in the main galleries, so I took him to the basement to see all the artwork that…that doesn't really belong anywhere. Those were the ones he liked."

"You're talking about the demented ones?" he asked before he took a bite.

"Yeah."

"Sounds like a weird guy."

He didn't seem weird to me. Just…a little lost. I almost mentioned the ring he wore, but I kept it to myself—for a second time. I thought I knew exactly who Theo was, but I didn't want my husband to know that. The criminal underworld was a small place, but I'd somehow crossed paths with a man who was talked about like a myth rather than a person. "How was your trip?"

"It was fine." He didn't tell me where he'd been. Hadn't texted me while he was gone. I didn't know whether he'd left the country or if he'd been right down the street. "I'll be home for a while. My contract list is empty at the moment."

"That's good." It was rare for him to be around for an extended period of time. He would work in his office during the day and meet with other members of the Brotherhood at their headquarters underneath one of the oldest restaurants in the city. He took me there sometimes, but I was always bored sitting there listening to stories with people I didn't know, so he didn't really take me anymore.

He finished his plate then took another drink of his white wine. "There's something I want to talk to you about."

"Alright." His tone didn't sound foreboding, so it didn't seem like bad news. Maybe he wanted to discuss giving the villa a new coat of paint or plan our next vacation.

He stared at me for a while, his elbows on the table. "I want you to keep an open mind to this. Don't react emotionally."

Maybe he didn't want to talk about paint colors or vacation spots. "Okay…"

He took another drink of his wine and finished it off. "I want to suggest an open marriage." He held my gaze as he said it, like he was asking me to take a few weeks off work so we could swim in the Aegean Sea, not asking me to welcome other people into our bed.

"I'm sorry…*what?*"

"I told you not to react emotionally—"

"I'm not reacting emotionally. I just don't understand what you said."

He gave a quiet sigh.

"An open marriage? As in, you want to fuck other people."

"That's not how I would put it."

"Then how would you put it, Bolton?" I snapped. "Because it sounds like my husband wants to fuck someone else besides me."

"That's also not how I would put it."

"Then how would you put it?"

He stilled at my wrath and gave another sigh. "I think monogamy is a bit outdated. I'm on the road a lot, and I'm not home—"

"But that's your choice. We have enough money for you to retire. You're the one choosing to do these things. You could stay home and fuck me every night if that's what you wanted to do—but you clearly don't."

He raised his hand slightly to calm me. "We're just apart a great deal, and I don't see the problem in us seeking a physical connection with someone else during these lonely times."

"Then take me with you."

"Astrid, you know I can't do that."

"We've only been married two years, and you want to sleep with other people?"

He closed his eyes briefly like my reaction was annoying. "Forget I said anything."

"You're just going to fuck someone anyway."

"Astrid, I wouldn't have even brought this up to you if that were my intention. I would just be cheating on you every time I was gone. I haven't done that. I only thought having our own private lives would be beneficial for us both."

"I'm not sure what hurts more." I kept my voice steady, but deep inside, there was a dam of tears ready to explode. "The fact that you want to fuck other people...or the fact that you don't care about another man fucking me."

"It's not that I don't care—"

"If you're encouraging me to do it, then you don't care."

"I'd rather not think about it, to be honest. And I'm sure you don't want to think about it either."

"I admit our sex life isn't what it used to be, but I'm happy to try new things, go to therapy, work on our relationship, do whatever is necessary for the sake of this marriage. I don't think inviting other people into it is the solution. I don't understand where this is coming from because last time we spoke, you said you wanted to start a family. Who says they want to start a family, then a week later asks to fuck other people?"

"Why does it have to be mutually exclusive?" he asked calmly. "Just because I fuck some other woman doesn't mean you aren't the woman I love with my whole heart. Doesn't mean I don't want you to be the mother of my children. Everything I feel for you is still true."

I shook my head because I was appalled by his reasoning. "I'm not going to raise your kids while you're off fucking some woman you met in a bar. If you have that much free time, then you don't need to be gone so long."

He sank into the chair, looking defeated. "Astrid, forget I said anything."

"This is not something I can forget, Bolton. It's not something I can forgive either." I shoved my chair back until it knocked over, and I stormed from the table. I walked to the entryway and slipped on the flats I'd left there. It had started to rain, so I grabbed my coat and prepared to yank the door so hard it flew off its hinges.

Bolton placed his body in front of it. "You need to calm down."

"Get out of my way, or I'll move you."

His blue eyes watched me with a look of hurt. "If you need some space, I'll leave."

"So you can pick up some pretty girl in a bar?" I asked viciously.

He leaned against the door with his weight, so there was no way I'd get past him. "Astrid, forget what I said. It was just a suggestion, and it's fine if you don't like it. The last thing I want is to lose you." He said it with such sincerity, such depth with his blue eyes. "It's the very last thing I want."

I was still angry, so fucking angry, but his words sheathed some of that anger.

He continued to watch me as the air left my balloon of rage, his eyes shifting back and forth.

I turned away from the door, kicked off my flats, and headed upstairs.

He didn't follow me.

Days passed. Even though he was home, we didn't spend time together.

I was too angry.

He gave me my space. We didn't share meals together. We didn't sit on the couch together. I slept in the primary suite, and he took a guest room. Time went by, and slowly, the boiling anger turned to a simmer.

I wasn't sure what to do, but I knew we had to talk about it.

He sat in his study working on his laptop, the hearth warm with a fire that lit up the dark room. For a hit man, he did a lot of paperwork, and I didn't understand what he did on that computer.

I walked inside, and it took him a moment to notice me.

He lifted his gaze and stared at me.

I stared back.

When I didn't yell at him, he slowly closed the lid of his laptop to give me his full attention.

I sat in one of the armchairs.

He continued to stare at me as he waited for me to say something.

I wasn't sure what I wanted to say.

He came around the desk and sat in the other armchair, his chin propped on his closed knuckles, his elbow on the armrest. He stared at the side of my face, his skin illuminated by the flames.

"Let's try it."

His eyebrows slowly rose up his face in surprise. "You made it very clear how opposed you are to this."

"I know." I was still opposed to it. It still hurt. "But I love you." I couldn't look at him as I said it. Our relationship wasn't what I wanted it to be, but I knew I loved him. I'd loved him the moment we met. We fell hard and fast, a whirlwind that didn't stop until we'd tied the knot. I was afraid if I denied his request, he would just cheat on me and that would hurt a lot more. "If this is what you want."

"It's not what I want unless you're okay with it."

I stared at the floor.

"Are you okay with it, Astrid?"

I nodded.

"I'm going to need more than that."

I raised my chin and finally looked at him, and it hurt to see that face, to imagine another woman's lips on that mouth I'd kissed so many times. It was hard to imagine him naked and inside someone else, fucking someone else while I slept alone. It hurt like hell, but I was afraid if I didn't accept it, I would lose him. "I'm okay with it, Bolton."

Despite their unpopularity, the paintings that Theo had selected were expensive. Some of them were hundreds of years old. Pieces of history that only a few people had ever witnessed. They were carefully wrapped and the corners secured with padded edges before they were transferred.

I informed George before my arrival, and the transport team arrived outside the gates and began the process of unloading the paintings from the truck and bringing them into the palace where Theo lived alone.

The second we walked inside, I felt the heat across my flesh, feeling that man's presence even though he was nowhere in the room. His essence was in every inch of the hardwood floor, the luxurious rugs, the portraits that hung on the walls.

The paintings were carried upstairs to the study and leaned against the pieces of furniture so they wouldn't scuff the walls. Unpacking each piece would take time, so I worked on that while the guys left. I still had to take my measurements and then ask Theo where he wanted each one. Knowing him, he probably didn't care, but I would never be that presumptuous.

I unwrapped each painting and made a pile of trash to take back with me, rolls of plastic and tape and padding. His walls were twelve feet high, so the paintings were substantial and grand enough to fill the space appropriately.

I was on my knees, loosening the tape from one corner, and I couldn't explain it, I just knew Theo was there, standing behind me. Raindrops started to hit the window at that very moment, like he brought it with him.

Footsteps sounded, and then he appeared beside me, down on one knee to help me, even though it wasn't his job.

He was shirtless. And barefoot. Just in gray sweatpants like it was a Sunday morning rather than a Tuesday afternoon.

I tried to focus on the painting and not look at him beside me. "You don't have to help me."

He didn't address what I said. Instead, he lifted the painting and turned it on to an alternative set of corners so he could pull the tape off another section.

I was still on my knees when I looked up at him, seeing the muscles of his body segmented by distinct shadows, the cuts of muscle up and down his arms, the tightness of his strong stomach, the defined lines over his narrow hips.

It was a cold winter day, but it felt like summertime in Death Valley.

He finished pulling off the tape and tossed it into the pile I already made.

"Thanks." I forced myself to stare at the painting instead of him.

He turned his head to look at me, his stare on the side of my face.

I avoided his look as long as I could. While I desired his attention, I didn't want him to know that, how tense he made all the muscles inside my body, the way he unnerved me whenever we breathed the same air. But I turned to look at him anyway, to regard him with as much emptiness as I could fake.

His eyes continued to burn in my face. "What is it?"

"What is what?" I asked.

"You're upset."

"I-I didn't say anything." How did he know? How could he possibly know every bone in my body was broken?

His eyes shifted back and forth slightly before he stepped away, turning his muscular back on me. "I can tell." He moved to one of the paintings that leaned against his couch, the fireplace behind it. He regarded it for a while before he looked at the empty space above the fireplace, as if he wondered if that's where he should hang it. "Some men are blessed with great intelligence, others wisdom, and men like me...intuition." He turned back to me. "Don't worry,

I won't pry. I can tell you don't want to talk about it."

My eyes were locked on his face with no desire to move. I was fascinated by his appearance and his presence, and not just because he was drop-dead gorgeous, but for another reason I couldn't describe. I tried to counter the invisible spell he cast with a change of subject. "You look like you just woke up."

"Because I did."

And he looked that sexy when he rolled out of bed? "It's three in the afternoon."

"Long night." He moved past me to examine another painting.

My eyes glanced down at his skull ring.

He caught the look. "You forgot your wedding ring again."

I didn't forget it this time. "Where would you like these to be hung? I'll get to work on that."

"There's no way you can hang these."

Because some of them probably weighed a hundred pounds. "No, but I want to make sure the contractors do everything correctly. Time is money to these guys, so they cut corners and shit. And I don't put up with that. So, which one should go where? I didn't want to be presumptuous."

He looked around at the paintings and crossed his arms over his muscular chest...his very muscular chest. He reminded me of a mighty oak tree, hundreds of years old and rich in wisdom, with thick and powerful roots that reached deep into the soul of the earth. After a few seconds of silence, he made his selections.

I wrote down his directions. "I'll get that taken care of with George."

He moved to one of the armchairs in the study and took a seat, his stomach still flat like a board even when seated. He was that tight, that ripped, that muscular. His elbow propped on the armrest, his fingers resting across his shadowed jawline. His stare was as striking as the paintings he selected. Then he just stared.

It was tense, like he'd asked me a question and I missed it, like we were in the middle of a conversation that had fallen into silence. He had a threatening presence to him, but it wasn't hostility directed at me, just in general.

There was nothing left for me to do but leave, but I continued to stand there.

He didn't look impatient for me to leave. He seemed content letting the seconds tick by on the old clock that sat on his mantel. Like a stone gargoyle that was mounted to stand the test of time and guard a Gothic cathedral, he remained still and solid.

I should say goodbye and leave, but my feet were rooted to the thick rug.

He slowly rose to his feet and turned his back on me as he approached his desk.

I stared at that muscular back, seeing concrete that was bulletproof. The muscles that hugged his spine were so tight as they carried all his weight.

He grabbed a decanter and filled two glasses with scotch before he returned to the armchair and placed them on the coffee table. "Sit." He nodded to the couch near him, his elbow returning to the armrest so his fingers could rest against his hard face.

I took a seat in the corner closest to him, feeling the tension increase tenfold. I stared at the glass sitting there waiting for me, but I didn't take it since it was only three in the afternoon.

He grabbed his, took a drink, and then set it on the table next to his armchair.

"Scotch for breakfast?"

"I prefer it to coffee. Much smoother."

I looked at the glass for a moment before I grabbed it and downed it in one go.

One eyebrow lifted slightly in gentle surprise, but the rest of his face retained its hardness. "You drink scotch."

"Sometimes." I returned the glass to the coffee table.

He didn't interrogate me like he said he would. Just let me feel the pressure of his presence.

There was a tightness in my chest, a mixture of excitement and guilt and sorrow. When Bolton said he wanted an open marriage, I hadn't thought of Theo and grown anxious for that prospect, but now that I was with him…I entertained the idea. "So…how about that dinner?"

When I arrived at the restaurant, he was already there.

He sat at a table by the window, covered in a white tablecloth, a single candle burning low in the center. It was a nicer place, but he wore a long-sleeved black shirt and dark jeans like he didn't care.

I liked that he didn't care.

I stared at him before he noticed me, seeing the way his massive body took up the chair, the way he looked out the window and stared at the people outside, his eyes dark like the night.

I hadn't been nervous like this in a long time. Bolton had left for a mission, so he was out of the house and elsewhere...and I didn't know where he would sleep that night. I had no problem being alone and sleeping in our bed by myself while he was gone, but now it hit different.

I approached the table, and he turned to look at me, his eyes slowly dropping down my body to study the way my curves filled out the dress. He didn't rise to pull out the chair for me like a gentleman.

I liked that too.

I set my clutch on the end of the table and felt my heart try to jump out of my chest.

He stared at me with his hard silence, perfectly comfortable breathing the tense air around us even though it was like a cloud of black smoke.

"I've never tried this place before," I said. "It's good?"

"I hope so." He grabbed the wine list. "Would you like to share a bottle of wine?"

"I'm not really in a wine mood tonight." Wine was calm and relaxing, heightening the experience of the food you consumed. But every muscle in my body was so tense, they were all about to lock up.

"Scotch it is." He got the attention of a waitress the second he looked across the room. When she came over, he immediately ordered two glasses of scotch on the rocks, and she disappeared. A moment later, she returned and placed the drinks in front of us. "Never met a woman who likes scotch."

"I only drink it occasionally." After Bolton and I had a huge fight. On the nights when I felt so alone it seemed like I was the only person in the whole world. Right before bed when I wanted to make sure I wouldn't remember my dreams.

"People drink scotch for a reason," he said. "And I think I know what your reason is."

I deflected the observation by taking a drink and letting the liquor hit my tongue. It was smooth on the way down but then burned when it reached the bottom. It was like liquid fire, but I'd felt that kick enough times not to react to it. "You don't seem like the kind of man interested in art."

"The blood of a dictator pumps in my veins, and my heart was born in the birthplace of the Renaissance. I don't possess an ounce of artistic ability, but that doesn't mean I don't have a deep reverence for it."

Floored by what he said, I repeated his words in my mind just so I could hear it again.

"You must appreciate art if you work in a gallery. You don't need the money."

"What makes you say that?"

"The car you drive."

It was a Porsche SUV, one of the high-end models. The downpour hadn't hidden the details from him.

"The clothes and jewelry you wear," he said. "The way you carry yourself. It's all there."

My fingers rested on the top of my glass, but I didn't take a drink, knowing if I drank it too fast on an empty stomach, I would get smashed and make an idiot out of myself in front of the sexiest man who ever lived.

"Answer the question." He never asked for what he wanted, just demanded it in a gentle manner.

"I appreciate art. And I've always wanted to be an artist myself."

"Then be an artist," he said simply.

"It's more complicated than that."

"I disagree," he said. "It's either something you are or you aren't. So, which is it?"

"I paint sometimes, but…"

He gave me a moment to finish, and when I didn't, he pressed me. "But what?"

"It's just not good enough." My own inadequacy stared me right in the face every time I looked at the canvas. When I set out to create something, it turned into something completely different…and not in a good way.

"Says who?" He grabbed his glass and took a drink. "Art is subjective. Those paintings I bought. How long did they sit in your basement before I came along?"

"I-I don't know." They had all come at different times, sold to us by different dealers, sometimes donated as part of an estate. "A couple years, I guess."

"Every piece of art is meant for a different buyer. You just have to find yours." He took another drink.

I noticed the waitress never came to take our order. She attended the tables around us but didn't disturb us, like she was waiting for him to specifically call her over. "You haven't seen my artwork—"

"Then show me."

The only person I showed my work to was Bolton, and he didn't seem that interested in it. He wasn't the kind of man who cared about art or décor or design. He just cared about money, so I tried not to take his lack of interest personally. "It doesn't look anything like the paintings you bought."

"Then what do they look like?"

"Hard to describe," I said. "I guess they're moments..."

He cocked his head slightly.

"Like when you take a candid photo of someone or see a group of friends talking across the bar or when you see a couple talking intensely at a restaurant, and you wonder what all those moments mean. Are they good moments? Are they bad moments? Or are they the last moment those two will ever share?"

He didn't blink as he listened to me.

"It's hard to explain."

"You explained it perfectly. I'd love to see one of your paintings if you're ever brave enough to show me."

Heat moved down my throat and mimicked the scotch I'd stopped drinking. My eyes moved to the menu even though I didn't have much of an appetite. There were a lot of good things on there, though. "What do you get?"

"Bistecca alla fiorentina. But I doubt that's something you'd order."

"I drink scotch. Maybe I like steak too."

A subtle smile moved over his lips. "Do you?"

"I do, but I'm just not that hungry right now," I said. "Maybe I'll get a salad."

His grin widened before he took a drink.

"What?"

He gave a slight shake of his head. "Nothing."

"What?" I repeated.

"I was right," he said. "That's what." He made a slight gesture, and the waitress immediately came over. He asked for another drink because he'd already finished.

When she was gone, it was just the two of us again, the war of eye contact ensuing.

He kept his word and didn't ask me about the one thing I didn't want to talk about. His eyes tried to pierce my exterior, but he never used different methods to pry.

"Tell me about yourself."

"What do you want to know?"

I didn't want to interrogate him since he was nice enough not to interrogate me. "Whatever you want to share."

He considered my words in silence, relaxed in the chair, his thick arms pulling hard on the fabric of his shirt. "I like cigars. Collect them."

"Collect them?" I asked. "Like wine?"

"Yes. I have a humidor to keep them at the right temperature and humidity."

"How long do they last?"

"About thirty years, if you intend to smoke them. But I have a collection that dates back the last hundred years. I can't smoke them, but I can still smell them... and you taste the history in the smell."

"That's interesting."

The waitress brought his second drink and took away the empty glass. He took a drink before he caught a drop with his thumb. "I have some that belonged to my great-grandfather. That's the only piece of him that I have."

"Do you revere him?"

"No. I just think we're a lot alike."

"You identify as a dictator?"

He stared at me for a long time like he might not say anything, but then he spoke. "Sometimes."

My eyes glanced down to the skull ring that he always wore. It was huge, and I could tell it was heavy just by looking at it. I wanted to ask about it, but I wanted to respect his privacy the way he respected mine.

He reached for his hand and twisted the ring off his thick knuckle. Then he placed it on the table in front of me, the diamond casting a spectrum of colors against the window. It glittered in the light of the candle.

I reached my fingers toward it. "May I?"

He nodded.

I took the ring and stilled when I felt how warm it was. I'd expected it to be cold like a stone sitting in the winter fog, but it was hot like fire, because his skin burned like the sun. I'd never touched him, but now I knew how my palm would feel against his chest, how warm my fingers would feel if I touched his arm. If I were tucked into his bed with him beside me, I would sweat from the heat. I wouldn't need a heater or a fire because he was more than enough. The ring was heavy as I'd assumed, its concentrated mass making it like a paper weight. After I examined it for several seconds, I returned it to the center of the table. "That's an interesting ring…"

He twisted it back onto his knuckle and took a drink. "I have two more."

I'd heard Bolton and others mention Theo by a different name—The Skull King. He was the leader of an underground group of men who moved drugs across the country. They monopolized other illegal sources of income. I didn't know much more than that, other than the fact that he was lethal.

His eyes hardened on my face, reading my expression like words on a page. "You know who I am."

The lights from his eyes hit me like a spotlight, and I had nowhere to run. Once I was under that piercing stare, my armor was knocked to the ground. I'd heard he was dangerous and vicious, but it was hard to be afraid of a man who changed my tire in the rain and appreciated art.

"You aren't scared, sweetheart?" He looked down into his glass before he looked at me again, confidence in his eyes, a hint of arrogance in his stature.

"Should I be scared?" A broken heart made me careless. It made me do things I wouldn't normally do. But I felt like I had nothing to lose.

"No." He swirled his glass before he brought it to his lips for a drink. "I don't hurt women—not unless they ask me to." He casually got the attention of the waitress and ordered our dinner, getting himself a steak and me a salad.

I felt a flush in my cheeks when I heard the echo of his words, when I pictured his big palm leaving a mark on my ass from smacking me so hard. When I pictured his long fingers gripping me by the throat, just to the point where I struggled to breathe. I didn't usually think about fucking other men besides Bolton, but I'd thought about it a lot since I met Theo.

"That means your husband is in the game."

The mention of him made the guilt burn in my stomach. I was free to be here, free to go back to his place and ask him to hurt me, but I still felt a shadow of betrayal move across me like a rain cloud.

"And that also means he'd be irate if he knew you were here with me."

I didn't know how he would feel about it. He probably assumed I would hook up with someone at work or maybe with someone I met in a bar when I went out with my friends. He probably didn't imagine I would bump into the Skull King on the side of the road.

He swirled his glass again, and a slight smirk moved on to his lips. "Good."

We returned to his villa after dinner, and instead of entering his study, we went upstairs to the third floor, the walls covered in textured black wallpaper with dark sculptures and mirrors. He wanted every inch of his place to be marked by his presence, for any visitor to know he lived there alone—and he liked it.

His bedroom was like a fancy suite at an expensive hotel, a room that had its own living room with a large TV on the wall. Double doors led to his four-poster king-sized bed in the next room, sitting on a thick rug, the wood of the furniture dark, the duvet cover storm-gray.

The second we entered, my heart was in my throat, the pulse making the skin of my neck vibrate from the rush of blood. Bolton provided a luxurious life for me that gave me everything I could ever want. But the moment I was in Theo's bedroom, I understood there was an even greater level of wealth.

Even greater level of power.

He made his way to the bar area and poured two glasses before he set them on the coffee table. "Help yourself." He walked into his bedroom, and once he crossed the threshold, he yanked his shirt over his head then stepped out of view.

I caught sight of his skin for just a brief second.

I was so nervous, more nervous than I could remember ever being. The combination of excitement and dread and self-loathing made a cocktail of anxiety. When he asked if I wanted to come over, I said yes, and I felt like shit for that answer. But I wondered where Bolton was sleeping that night, and I didn't want to be alone.

When Theo returned, he was just in his sweatpants, these ones black, and they were dangerously low on those narrow hips. His chest was thick like concrete, and the details of all the different muscles of his core were pronounced as if they'd been made with a paintbrush.

I let myself look, but I didn't let myself stare.

He came close to me then grabbed a glass from the table.

His smell hit me—soap, shaving cream, pine trees.

Bolton had a completely different smell, and I wished I didn't notice.

When he took a drink, his throat shifted to swallow. He licked his lips when he was finished with his drink then sat in the armchair, just as he had in his study downstairs. He didn't rush me with an aggressive kiss on the mouth while his hand snaked into my hair. In fact, he was distant, as if I was a friend rather than a lover who'd come to fuck him. He hadn't even tried to touch me, place his hand on my thigh on the drive, brush a loose strand from my face.

I wanted him to, but I also didn't.

I sat on the couch and left the drink on the table because I'd already had too much. "Thank you for dinner."

He stared at me, his cheek against his closed knuckles, his eyes on me.

It'd been so long since I'd done this. Gone on a date with someone then fucked them afterward. But I was glued to my chair, more unsure of myself than I'd ever been. I couldn't even meet his stare.

"I know we aren't going to fuck, sweetheart. Relax."

My eyes immediately flicked to his.

"When the time is right."

I didn't want to relax in front of him, but I felt an invisible weight lift off my shoulders. I'd asked him to dinner so he probably assumed sex was on the table, but he didn't make me feel pressured or obligated. "My situation is...complicated."

His dark eyes stared at me, his knees spread apart as he lounged in the armchair.

"I'm married, but it's an open marriage." My eyes dropped down to the glass on the table, the one I wouldn't drink.

"But not by choice."

My eyes flicked back to his. "I think you're sexy...like crazy, insane sexy...but I just can't." I didn't even kiss him. Didn't try to initiate or give him an invitation. The chains of matrimony were still locked around my wrists even though I had the key.

He didn't grin at the compliment. Seemed more focused on my despair than the flattery. "I hope your husband is as loyal to you as you are to him."

My eyes flicked away again because I knew the answer to that.

"Tell him what you want, sweetheart."

"I did, but...it's complicated."

"It's not complicated. He wants to fuck other people,

and you don't. If he doesn't accept that, then leave him."

"He'd do it if I asked."

"Then I don't understand the problem."

"I-I want him to want it too." I kept my emotions bottled inside because I refused to let them burst free in front of Theo. I hardly knew him, and I wouldn't treat him like my therapist or priest. "And if he doesn't, then maybe I can learn to get used to it."

He continued to stare at me.

"You're judging me."

"I'm not the judgmental type," he said. "Marriage means different things to different people. To some, it's a business arrangement. To others, it's just about procreation. And to some, it's about love. It doesn't matter which one it is—as long as both parties agree."

Bolton talked about starting a family in the same week he mentioned an open marriage. It was so sudden and abrupt, so polarizing, I couldn't wrap my head around it. But when I thought about what Theo said, it made me realize Bolton wanted to change our marriage into a business relationship. It wasn't about love anymore.

It was about our wealth and our future kin. It was about pursuing other interests.

"I don't judge you for being in an open marriage—if that's what you both want." His eyes remained on me, slightly flicking right and left as he watched me with his observant stare, saw right through me.

I wanted the attention off me, wanted his pity to disappear. "What does marriage mean to you?"

He dropped his closed knuckles from his cheek and rested them on the armrest.

"Is it a business arrangement?" I expected him to say marriage was off the table altogether, that he desired a life of solitude until his past caught up with him in a dark alley and claimed his life.

But to my surprise, he had a different answer. "I'd marry for love."

For a brief moment, my pain disappeared as I looked at him, seeing this hard man in a softer light.

"I already have business arrangements. I don't need another. I'm not the judgmental type, but I'm possessive and jealous and territorial. A man looks at my wife, he's going to lose his eyes. He tries to touch my wife, he's going to lose his hand. If she left the house without her ring, I'd bring it to her—and then I'd make sure she never forgot it again." He said it with a tone of anger, like he didn't realize how romantic he was.

"You've been in love before…"

His eyes remained locked on mine. He didn't confirm or deny the statement.

"Have you been married?"

His hard stare indicated I would never get my answer. "Why do you stay with him?"

I knew I'd hit one of his buttons when he fired back like that. "I-I don't want our marriage to end. And I guess I'm afraid if I don't do this, then it is going to end. But maybe if we do it his way, he'll realize it's not right and come back to me. They say after a man cheats he becomes the most committed husband there ever was because he finally appreciates what he has. I guess I hope that's how it'll be for us."

His stare didn't change.

"They say half of men cheat, and I bet the real number is higher than that. At least he was honest with me."

"An odd thing to be grateful for."

"I thought you said you weren't judgmental?"

"I'm not judgmental of the way people choose to live their lives. This isn't a choice for you, sweetheart. But I won't say any more about it." He reached for his glass and took a drink. The ice cubes slid down and tapped his lips when he finished the contents. He returned the glass to the table. "I have stuff to take care of. My driver will take you home."

Bolton came home the next day.

My stomach was tight and tense—and not in the way when I got butterflies. This was just painful.

I was in the kitchen and had just finished making a roast chicken covered in lemon slices. I didn't care to cook, but when I made big meals like this, they lasted for days and made the effort worth it. Bolton said he liked my cooking, so I mainly did it for him, because when I was home alone cooking for myself, it made me sad.

He came in with his bag over his shoulder. He dropped it in the entryway and shed his coat before he joined me in the dining room. "Nothing better than coming home to your beautiful wife after she's made you dinner." His arm moved around my waist, and he dipped his head to kiss me.

I kissed him back, feeling the same love for him that I always felt.

He stepped away and grabbed a bottle of wine and two glasses.

He was in a good mood. A better mood than he'd been in in a long time. I hoped that meant our separation had made him reconsider what he'd asked, that it had given him second thoughts about changing the parameters of our relationship. "I'm glad you're hungry."

"Baby, I'm always hungry for your cooking." He turned back to me and placed the bottle on the kitchen island before he began the process of uncorking the wine. His left hand bore no ring, like he hadn't taken it with him or had forgotten to put it back on. And then just above the collar of his shirt, I saw a distinct mark … the color of pink lipstick.

He didn't notice my stare as he poured the glasses of wine.

I was sick. Too sick to eat. Too sick to pretend.

He carried the glasses to the dining table and gave me a moment to myself.

I stared down at the chicken I'd made, the dinner I'd made because I knew he liked it. I'd slept alone in our bed last night after Theo's driver had dropped me off at home. I'd decided to tell Bolton that I'd changed my mind about everything and hoped he hadn't already fucked someone.

But he jumped the first chance he got.

"Baby?"

"Hmm?" I looked up when I heard his voice.

"You alright? I said your name a couple times."

No, I wasn't alright. I'd thought I was already broken after our conversation, but now I realized my broken bones had been ground into dust. And the worst part of it? He was happy, the happiest he'd been in a long time. "Just realized I forgot the rice."

"It's fine." He carried the dish to the dining table. "We don't need it."

THEO

I entered the De Luca, one of the restaurants that I owned, a respectable business that washed my money and housed my criminal activities—and none of my customers had a clue. They got their reservations for anniversaries and birthday celebrations, not knowing about the underworld that lay below.

The lights were left on, but the restaurant was dark, the tables covered in fresh tablecloths in preparation for the next day. The floor had been swept and mopped. After the closing crew locked the doors and set the alarm, my crew descended into the depths.

There was a stairway at the back of the kitchen, locked during business hours. One time, my manager had asked what was behind the door, and when I didn't answer, he didn't ask again. I took the circular staircase down to the bottom, far below the restaurant, to the bunker that had been reconstructed into a bar. There were other passageways that led here through the sewer system, but I preferred not to go that way.

When I stepped through the door, loud music greeted me, along with a cloud of smoke. Some of the guys were gambling at their tables. Others were hustling the waitresses who were also prostitutes—at least most of them.

When they realized I was there, the energy changed. It dipped noticeably, like the guys didn't know what kind of mood I was going to be in when I walked in there.

Shit, I didn't even know.

I found Octavio at one of the tables and dropped into the chair across from him. A beer appeared out of nowhere and was placed in front of me by one of my favorite girls. Another brought a tray of cigars, serving me like some kind of king. "Thanks, sweetheart." I immediately lit up and let the smoke float to the ceiling.

If a bullet didn't kill me, it would be lung or liver cancer—guaranteed.

I looked at Octavio, and the conversation in the underground tunnel slowly returned to normal. One of my properties was another meeting place for us. This was a more casual spot to solidify our camaraderie. Nothing brought men closer together than booze, cigars, and women. "So?"

"He's pretty stealthy."

"Yeah? Stealthy isn't the word I would use to describe running away from a fight like some chickenshit." Draven had captured me as a way to draw out Axel, but in the end, we got the upper hand and he ran off like a fucking coward.

"He's more cautious now."

"He can be as cautious as he wants, but I'll still find that motherfucker." Dante had opened up a can of worms when he'd recruited his *friend* from the north. Draven thought he could take my drug business from me like I was giving out candy on Halloween. "He knows this isn't over, so either he'll strike or I'll strike. There's no way one of us isn't dead by the end of this."

Octavio smashed his cigar into the ashtray to put it out. "I'll keep looking."

"I know you will, Octavio. We've got eyes everywhere."

"Just remember, he's got eyes everywhere too."

I was spread in multiple directions every day, but declaring war on the Brotherhood for my brother's death had spread me even thinner. I always had enemies, but now I had big enemies.

Scarlett's eyes lit up at the sight of me. "Haven't seen you around in a while." She moved into me and hugged me the way a little sister would hug her brother. She wasn't as tall as me, so her cheek moved to my chest.

"You know how it gets." I pressed a kiss to her temple before I let her go.

"You could always retire, you know." She pulled away and gave me a little smile before she stepped away.

"Men like me don't retire."

"Axel did."

"That's it."

"How?"

"He found me."

"And you're telling me there's not some piece of ass out there just waiting for you to walk into her life and set it on fire? Oh, I'm sure she's out there…just waiting." She moved toward the kitchen.

Axel was at the table with Dante, the two of them talking while the kids jumped all over them. When Axel realized I was there, he grinned and rose from his chair before he walked toward me. "There he is." He embraced me with a bear hug and a hard thump on the back. "Thanks for coming."

"I won't turn down Scarlett's cooking."

Their son beelined straight for my knee, grabbing on to my leg and looking up at me with a smile. "Uncle Theo!" he exclaimed. At least, that was what I decided he said.

"Hey, little man." I ruffled my fingers through his hair as I smiled down at him, seeing the spitting image of Axel looking back at me, with that same dirty-blond hair and blue eyes. "Been good for your mama?"

He smiled wider and shook his head. "No."

"I figured."

He let go of my leg and ran off to his mother.

Axel's daughter was on Dante's thigh, and judging by the smile Dante wore, he enjoyed being a grandfather. Dante put her on the floor, and she toddled off.

On the way, she bumped into my leg and grinned up at me.

"Hi, sweetheart." I smiled as I watched her go then turned to regard Dante.

My smile immediately disappeared.

Dante stuck out his hand to shake mine. "It's been a while."

I didn't take it. "Not long enough." I still had to clean up his mess, a monster that he'd unleashed from a cage.

"Theo." Axel said my name lightly.

"I'm not fucking his daughter, so I'm not so inclined to forgive and forget." I moved to the bar behind Scarlett and helped myself to the bottle of wine sitting there. I poured myself a glass then came to Scarlett's side. "What's for dinner?"

"Bistecca all Fiorentina with scalloped potatoes and sauteed broccolini."

"My favorite. Sounds fucking amazing."

She gave me a quick nudge in the side before she nodded toward her daughter.

"Sorry." I took a drink.

"I'd appreciate it if you tried to get along with my father, Theo."

"Trust me, I am getting along with him." If I weren't, he'd be bleeding all over the tile.

She gave me a hard look.

"You and Axel are out of the game, but I'm not. There are consequences to his actions—and I'm still dealing with them."

After dinner, Scarlett and Dante took the kids upstairs to get them ready for bed.

Axel and I left the kitchen so the butler could take care of the dishes and clean up. We entered the study and took a seat in the comfortable armchairs. It was the only room in the house where we were allowed to smoke, so that was where we lit up.

"So." Axel crossed one ankle over the opposite knee.

"So." I let the smoke fill my mouth and nostrils before I released it in a cloud.

"How are things in the underworld?"

"You aren't in the game anymore, Axel." I brought the smoke into my mouth again and let it simmer on my tongue.

"But you are, so a part of me always will be."

"You don't need to worry about me."

"If I don't, who will?" He let the cigar rest in his fingertips as his arm lay on the armrest.

I'd been alone a long time, but the loneliness had worn off. Now, I thrived in solitude, preferring to spend my nights alone or with a woman who knew she would never mean anything to me.

"What's your plan with Bolton?"

"Corner him and make him talk. But he's hard to nail down."

"What if you hire him?"

I released the smoke and let the cigar rest between my fingertips.

"Hire him to kill someone. And when he shows up to meet you—kill him."

"Not a bad idea."

"I can do it for you. I never had dealings with the Brotherhood, so they don't know who I am."

"You're out of the game, Axel."

"Doesn't mean I don't want to help you."

He was more loyal to me than my own men. Our blood was different, but it felt like it passed through the same heart. He was the last person in my life I genuinely cared for. Everyone else was a situationship, but he was family. "I appreciate the offer, but that's never going to happen. I would never do that to your wife."

"She would understand. She loves you too, Theo."

I'd liked Scarlett the moment I met her, the way she commanded a room and stated what she wanted without hesitation. She looked me in the eye and told me what she wanted, having the kind of confidence that was uncommon in a woman. Even though she and Axel had been broken up for months at that point, I knew she was still his woman, so I walked out on her. It was the precursor to the relationship we had now. She really did feel like a sister. "You have a beautiful family, Axel. I would never risk what you have."

He smirked. "Yeah, I do."

"So, don't worry about me." I'd get my brother's bones and bury them in the cemetery where they belonged. His tombstone had been engraved when he passed, and the soil was ready to receive whatever was left of him. The plot next to him was reserved—for me.

"Easier said than done, man."

Dante walked into the room a moment later, casting me a wary stare as he moved to the couch.

There was a scar on his temple from where I'd thrown a glass at his head in this very room.

He sat back and crossed his ankle on the opposite knee.

I stared him down and waited for him to leave.

He held my look. "If there's anything I can do to help you with Draven—"

"Do you know where he is?"

"No."

"Then you have nothing to offer me, Dante."

"I can call him."

"How stupid do you think he is?"

Axel's eyes shifted back and forth between us.

Dante didn't reach for the cigars on the table between us. "A few years of silence have passed. I think it's fair to assume he's focused his attention on his own territory and spared yours."

"I assume nothing, Dante," I said coldly. "He had you as an ally before, so he assumed he had his conquest in the bag. But now he knows who he's dealing with, and he's taken his time to plot and think. He almost killed me, and he knows I won't forget that. So if he doesn't kill me, he knows I'll kill him. The fuse has been lit, and at some point, it'll explode."

Dante didn't drop his gaze from my stare, holding it without shame.

"I'll kill him—and then I'll take his territory. I've had my sights set on it anyway."

I showered after my workout. By the time I woke up and was ready for the day, it was noon.

I looked at my phone before I headed downstairs and saw the message from George. *Your artwork is currently being hung in the study.*

Which meant Astrid was here.

The bombshell brunette who was so damn fine. With almond-shaped eyes, green like emeralds and an ass that looked like a summer nectarine in her tight dresses, the woman had a mouth that fired off like a pistol.

Her husband was a fucking idiot.

I hoped she realized that sooner rather than later—and not just because I wanted to fuck her.

I made it to the bottom floor and stepped into the study. Painter's tape was on the walls to mark exactly where the paintings would go, and I assumed that was her doing so the guys knew where to put their nails.

A group of four guys picked up one of the biggest paintings then lifted it to the wall, catching it on the nails that had been hammered in to support it. It hooked correctly, and they stepped back to see where the painting sat.

It was perfectly straight.

Astrid stood there and examined it, wearing a pencil skirt and boots, her black blouse tucked in. She picked up a level and climbed the ladder until she placed the tool on one side of the painting to check that it was perfectly straight.

I looked at her ass—and I wasn't the only one.

"It's good." She climbed back down the steps and turned to the guys. "Alright, on to the next—" She froze when she saw me, the color in her face so pale it was as if she'd seen a ghost. She did her best to recover, but the damage had been done. "Theo, I wasn't expecting you. I was hoping you could see it when we're all done."

I looked at the painting they'd just hung up. "Looks good so far." I was in just my sweatpants because I wasn't going to change my clothes for her or anyone else. It was my home, so I could wear whatever the fuck I wanted. "I need something from my desk."

"Oh, of course."

I moved to the chair behind my desk and unlocked my laptop.

They got back to work, moving on to the next painting, this one over the fireplace.

I pretended to look at my screen, but I looked at her instead, and so did the guys. Her wedding ring was absent once again. As I stared at her, I noticed the melancholy in her eyes, the same sorrow that had been there since the moment we'd met. That meant she and her husband were still having problems…or she didn't have a husband.

I hoped it was the second one.

An hour later, they finished the last painting, and my once-bare walls were now full of the disturbed paintings that no one else valued. When others saw horror, I saw beauty…misunderstood beauty.

The guys filed out first and returned to their truck outside.

Astrid looked around at the paintings one more time before she approached my desk. "So, what do you think?" Her hands came together at her belly button, her shoulders back and her spine straight, a professional with a hint of elegance. It was hard to take her seriously when she was so damn beautiful. I was unsurprised to learn she was married to a rich man, because women like her were always promoted to trophy wife, a position they were happy to take because of all the perks. But in her case, it seemed like she actually loved her husband, which made the whole thing sadder.

The idiot didn't know what he had.

"You did a great job."

She turned around to take another look, admiring the paintings in the dark space, not realizing just how tight her ass looked in that skirt.

My eyes dropped to stare, wishing I could have a painting of that ass on my wall.

"Everything you chose really does fit the space perfectly."

"You mean, fit me perfectly." Dark. Disturbed. Enigmatic.

She turned back to face me, that hint of melancholy in her eyes once again.

I stared back at her, holding her eyes like I was squeezing them in a closed fist. There was a magnetic pull to her, affecting every object in the room with her, like the sun pulled on every planet in our star system.

She could hold my stare without looking away, which was what most women did. Whether it was across the bar or in a crowded room, they looked away the second our eyes connected. Sometimes they spoke to me, and sometimes they accepted my drink—but they couldn't sustain the eye contact.

She could.

I could stare at her all day...like another painting in this room.

She cleared her throat. "I guess this concludes our business."

"It does." I left my desk and walked past her, catching a whiff of her perfume, wet roses in spring. My decanter of scotch was on the table where I'd left it, but I went to sit without pouring a glass. I sat at the side of the couch, one arm on the armrest.

She moved to the armchair, the seat I normally occupied.

I didn't usually ask a woman to dinner, to a place where we could talk over candlelight, because I wasn't much of a talker. Never had been and never would be. I had no desire for a relationship except for the fuck-buddy kind, where you would get that random phone call in the middle of the night to fuck.

But I wanted to ask her out again.

She sat with her ankles crossed, her delicate hands in her lap, looking like a queen without a crown, invisible weight on her shoulders. Her chin was tilted down, and her thick lashes curled away from her cheek.

I wanted to ask her, but I didn't.

I wanted to ask what had happened with her husband, but I didn't.

I wanted to know everything about her, but I had to accept I never would.

She lifted her chin and looked at me again. "Are you free tonight?"

My expression didn't change, but I felt an uptick in my heartbeat, a subtle change in my pulse. "What did you have in mind, sweetheart?"

"Thought I could take you out to dinner."

No woman had ever said that to me, and it was really sexy. "I have to reject the offer, sweetheart."

Her stare remained steady, but I could see a hint of disappointment.

"Because I'm the one taking you to dinner."

She parked her car at my villa, and we went together.

I assumed that meant she intended to stay over, but I would never assume that until her dress was on my bedroom floor. Until her heels dug into my ass because we were in too much of a hurry to take them off.

I drove us in my blacked-out Range Rover, the vehicle I preferred to take because it was a special build, the windows and the body bulletproof. She was beside me, her legs crossed in her little black dress, the material up dangerously high.

I tested out the waters and moved my hand to her thigh, feeling the soft skin of those beautiful legs. My eyes stayed on the road with my hand on the wheel, so I didn't see her reaction if she had one.

She didn't push my hand away. Instead, she hooked her arm around my forearm, her small hand resting partially on top of mine, her skin cold to the touch against the heat of my skin.

We drove the rest of the way in silence, the radio off.

She wasn't a talker like most women. She didn't run her mouth a million miles a minute. Whenever she spoke, it was deliberate and purposeful. Silence was a sign of confidence, so if she could withstand the tension that built between us, that meant her spine was metal rather than jelly.

I parked the Range Rover then placed my hand against her lower back as I guided her to the entrance. Even in her sky-high heels, she was still a foot shorter than me. My hand rested right above the top of her perky ass, and I wanted to slide it down farther.

I pulled out her chair when we made it to our table then sat across from her.

She was a bombshell in that little black dress, thin straps over her shoulders, her tits stretching the fabric the way my arms nearly ripped through my shirt. She'd taped down her nipples instead of wearing a bra, but she was cold, so her nipples were slightly visible as they pebbled.

I'd offer her my jacket if I had one.

But I was glad I didn't.

I ordered two scotches the second the waitress walked up, then we were left alone again.

"I appreciate scotch, but I don't drink it the way you do."

"You'll get there."

A little smile moved on to her full lips. "I'd be hammered all day if I drank that much."

I couldn't remember the last time I had a buzz. Scotch was like water to me now.

The waitress returned with the two glasses.

"She'll also have a water."

The waitress nodded and walked away.

"I'll drink yours if you don't want it."

"And you'll be able to drive out of here?" she asked incredulously.

"I can do more than drive, sweetheart."

Her smile slowly disappeared, and so did her gaze.

I was desperate to know what had happened between her and her husband, but I would never ask. I didn't like to pull information out of people, only receive it freely…unless they were stupid enough to cross me.

The fact that she'd asked me to dinner told me some of the story—that she was either ready to give the open marriage a try or she was ready to move on. Maybe she would tell me by the end of the night.

The waitress returned with the water.

"Thank you," Astrid said quietly, her eyes dark with the shadow she wore. She had catlike eyes, and she'd done something with her makeup to make them appear bigger, smokier and sultrier.

This woman sold art, but she could easily sell herself. I'd been with escorts who charged a million dollars for the evening—and she could charge double. I hadn't fucked her yet, but even if she just lay there while I did all the work, that'd be just fine with me.

I picked up the menu and took a look. "I hope you aren't getting another salad."

She smirked slightly, like she might laugh. "I don't want to look bloated."

"Why?"

She seemed to realize what she'd just admitted and looked down into her water glass before she took a drink. "Just don't."

"A belly isn't going to make my dick less hard, sweetheart."

Her eyes immediately flicked up.

"Get what you want," I said. "I'm getting the lasagna." I set the menu down, confident in my selection.

She continued to stare at me before she looked at the menu again.

When the waitress returned to the table, I ordered first to give her another moment to decide. "I'll take the meat lasagna."

She took one final look at the menu before she handed it over. "I'll have the same."

I smirked before I took a drink. "Attagirl."

"My parents are from Milan," she said. "We moved to Florence when I was about ten."

"They still live in the city?"

"No...they're gone."

I gave a slow nod in understanding, absorbing her sadness. "I'm sorry."

"Yeah, it's been a while now."

"Can I ask what happened?" Unless her parents were older when they had her, they should still be mobile and healthy. It must have been a tragedy, like a car accident.

"Well, my mom got sick. By the time they caught it, there was nothing they could do. She was gone in three weeks. And then my dad..." She stopped and stared at her water glass, taking a moment to combat the pain inside. "He killed himself a month after she was gone. He just couldn't live without her..." She moved her stare from the water glass to her half-eaten plate, keeping her emotion locked behind an invisible dam as best she could.

Sorry was such an empty and ambiguous thing to say, so I avoided saying it at all costs. But I truly felt sorry for her. "I'm sorry." I repeated the words I'd already said, but I wished there were something else I could have said instead.

She grabbed her fork and cut off a small piece of her lasagna, but she let it sit on her plate instead of taking a bite. Her eyes were down for a few more seconds before she had the strength to look at me once more.

"Do you hate him?"

"Hate him?" she whispered. "No, I could never hate him."

To leave behind his only child was a cowardly thing to do—in my opinion. Even if she was an adult who lived on her own, every child needed their parent. Different stages of life presented different needs. You needed a parent to hold you when you were scared at night, and then one day, you needed their friendship and advice.

"How old were you?"

"Nineteen."

"And how old are you now?" It was hard to tell. She didn't look as young as a twenty-one-year-old, but she didn't look thirty either.

"Twenty-eight. So it's been about ten years."

"Time doesn't make things easier. It just puts distance between the past and the present."

Her eyes narrowed slightly on my face, looking at me with a greater depth. "Who did you lose?"

"My brother."

She said the phrase that I despised, but she said it with such sincerity that I didn't mind. "I'm sorry."

"He was my twin."

She gave a slow nod, like she understood how much more painful that made it. "I can't imagine two of you."

"One of me is enough."

"How did he die?"

I hesitated, unsure exactly how he'd met his end, but the tidbits I did know were torture. "Someone wanted him dead. He had a habit of pissing off people everywhere he went."

She didn't smirk. Her eyes remained serious. "Did you kill them?"

"I still haven't figured out who it is. But I will...eventually."

She returned her gaze to her plate.

I said horrible things, but she didn't flinch at the words. She seemed accustomed to this life. Death and torture didn't faze her like they did most women. I didn't talk about work with my women because it always made them uncomfortable. It was a breath of fresh air telling her the truth without seeing the cringe. "How did your father do it?"

She stared at her plate a moment later. "Left the car on in the garage."

"No chance it was an accident?"

"He left a note."

I gave a slight nod in somber understanding.

"Said he was sorry…and he loved me."

But that wasn't enough. The love of a parent for their child should always be enough. "I wouldn't show so much grace."

Her eyes found mine again. "Why?"

"Because he had something to live for." A beautiful daughter, who was as smart as she was pretty.

"My father was in a lot of pain when he lost my mother."

"I'm sure he was. But that's not good enough."

"I thought you weren't the judgmental type?"

"I'm not—"

"That's exactly what you're doing. My parents had been together since high school. Blissfully happy at every age. Grew old together with grace. They tried to have a family for a long time, but it didn't happen... until I finally came along. I was their miracle baby, and they treasured me like a miracle. I won't replace the love in my heart with anger and resentment. I won't forfeit all my good memories because of a tragic decision he made. Don't judge people for feeling such inescapable misery just because you've never felt it yourself. Just be grateful that you don't understand. And if you're lucky enough, you never will."

I got lost in those words, bumps forming on my arms from the wisdom of her words and the depth of her heart. Unlike me, she didn't let the bad tarnish her soul. She continued to shine on, pure and vibrant like the sun that appeared from behind the buildings every morning. "You're right. I apologize." It was the first time I'd said that in a decade—and she had no idea.

She had no idea the power she already had over me. "I feel protective of you. And knowing you were abandoned at such a tender age provoked the worst in me."

"Protective of me?" she whispered. "You barely know me."

"And you barely know me, so you don't know that I never take a woman out to dinner—but I've taken you twice."

Her eyes flicked away for just a second in reaction before she looked at me again. Her confidence faltered, and a moment of vulnerability shone through. My words struck a chord...a couple of chords. "Why?"

"Why what?"

"Why have you taken me out to dinner twice?"

I cocked my head slightly. "I want to fuck you."

She didn't flinch at the audacity of my words.

"And I care for you."

When my hand went to her thigh on the drive home, it slipped underneath her dress, almost to her panties underneath.

I wanted to look and see exactly what color they were, but I kept my eyes on the road.

She took a deep breath when she felt my touch, but she didn't push my hand away. A moment later, her hand moved over mine, and then her fingertips lightly traced my hard knuckles.

I parked on my property behind the iron gate, and then we entered the home that was far too big for a single man. But I needed somewhere to put my money, and I needed something substantial to keep out the vermin. The windows were bulletproof, and the main doors were thicker than the walls of a vault. It was disguised with elegant décor, but it only distracted onlookers from the truth—that it was a fortress.

We walked to my bedroom upstairs, and along the way, I felt her anxiety increase, felt her energy change from calm and confident to erratic. It was a subtle change in her breathing, a drop in her shoulders, just her presence.

I walked inside first and grabbed the bottle of scotch from the bar.

She entered my room slowly, like it was the first time she'd been in there.

"Want a drink, sweetheart?"

"Sure."

I poured two glasses and carried them to the sitting room. I took a seat on the couch so she could sit next to me if that was what she wanted. There were moments when I could tell she clearly wanted me, but then there would be a surge of sabotage, guilt that squeezed her around the throat and cut off her air supply.

She joined me on the couch, but she kept several feet in between us.

We'd been closer together in the Range Rover.

She liked my touch when things couldn't go anywhere, but now that this could go somewhere, she was withdrawn and distant.

I drank from my glass then put it on the table beside me. I was just about to speak, but she beat me to it.

"You're probably wondering what happened between my husband and me." She looked at the coffee table for several seconds before she looked at me again.

"You don't owe me an explanation, sweetheart."

She watched me for a while before she dropped her gaze again. "I've decided to give it a try."

I'd never felt aroused and disappointed at the same time, but it happened now. She deserved better than this asshole, but that was something she needed to figure out on her own. I wanted her, and I would settle for a piece of her if I had to.

"Is-is that okay with you?"

"My opinion doesn't matter."

"I meant…will you sleep with a married woman?"

I'd done it before—and not because they were in an open marriage. "I don't have a problem with that."

She hesitated, as if she expected me to say something more about it. To talk her out of it. To put a stop to it.

"Sweetheart?"

It took her a moment to look at me again.

"There's no rush."

She released a breath like she'd been holding it. "I'm sorry. I just—"

"Don't apologize to me." My words came out harsher than I meant.

Her eyes darted away.

"You owe me nothing. Not an explanation. Not a debt."

She stared at the black TV on the wall, the fireplace underneath it. She sat that way for seconds before she finally turned to look at me once more, more confident than she'd been a minute ago. "I don't want to talk about him when we're together."

"I don't want to talk about him ever."

"I want to do this. It's just… It's hard." She looked away again. "I feel like I'm doing something wrong, even though I'm not… Even though he's already done it."

Her words shouldn't make me angry, but they did. *They made me really angry.*

"But I'll get there."

I wanted to ask why she stayed in the marriage at all, why she didn't just pack her shit and leave. But since she'd just said she didn't want to talk about it, I let it go. Maybe it was because she loved him. Maybe it was because she thought he would get it out of his system and they'd be what they used to be. I didn't know.

But I would enjoy her until that time came. "And I'll be here whenever you're ready, sweetheart."

7

ASTRID

Bolton was home for a couple of days, and like the last time he'd come back, his mood had lifted considerably. Instead of expecting me to cook, he took me out to dinner. He was engaged and thoughtful. We slept together, but I wasn't totally there. I thought about the others.

I thought about Theo.

I didn't usually think about Theo when I was with Bolton, but I thought about him more and more. I wondered what he was doing, if he was sleeping with other people since I was sleeping with Bolton. He hadn't texted me, and I wondered if he was waiting for me to text him first, like he didn't want his message to be seen by the wrong person.

I was on the couch in the living room when my phone lit up with his name.

My eyes immediately shifted to Bolton.

He was on his computer, working in front of the TV like he usually did in the evenings. He used to go into his study, but now he spent that time with me.

I felt a jolt of guilt, but then it quickly faded away, because I was innocent of any wrongdoing.

I grabbed my phone and read his message.

Let's have dinner tomorrow.

He didn't ask women to dinner, but now he'd asked me three times. All he'd done was touch my thigh, but our relationship felt far more intimate. His dark eyes and hard appearance flicked across my mind. Then there was the desire, the image of his naked chest that burned behind my eyes, the excitement that made my hands tremble.

I glanced at Bolton.

He was too absorbed in his computer to notice.

Can I take you out this time?

I heard his deep voice in my head when I read his response. *No.*

Come on…

But I'll let you pick the place, sweetheart.

———

Bolton and I never discussed the terms of our new relationship, but I assumed the open marriage only applied to the times he was gone from the house. That meant my time with Theo was restricted to a couple days a week.

I wondered who Bolton was spending time with, if it was a woman he liked…or if it was a line of nameless women who were only in his bed long enough to crinkle the sheets. I tried not to think about it too much. Otherwise, it would crush me.

I drove to Theo's place like I did last time, an overnight bag in the back seat, the same bag I'd brought last time but didn't use.

I wasn't sure if I would use it this time either.

If Theo was frustrated by the slow pace, he didn't show it. For a man with a ruthless reputation, he was quite the gentleman. Said things to me I'd never heard another man say. Made me feel his touch even when he was across the table. In the short amount of time I'd spent with him, I knew he was a special breed of man.

When I arrived at his place, he was ready for me, wearing a long-sleeved shirt with the sleeves pushed to his elbows, showing off the cords that popped in his forearms, the ink across his beautiful skin. Every time I saw him, he dressed casually like this, not having any desire to impress anyone around him.

But I found that confidence more impressive than anything he could wear.

He could wear a burlap sack and still look like a sculpture made by da Vinci's own hands.

He had to tilt his chin down to look at me, even in the high heels I wore, because he must be six and a half feet tall. A behemoth of height and muscle, a gourmet cut of meat, he was the finest specimen of man.

I held his stare, feeling my skin melt under the heat of his gaze. Whether I wore a little black cocktail dress or a pencil skirt for the office, he looked at me like I was wearing the sluttiest lingerie ever made.

No one had ever looked at me like that, not even my own husband.

"Where are we going?"

I hadn't thought about it once. I'd been thinking about him all day, running my fingers through that dark hair and kissing that hard mouth. "I liked that place close to the gallery."

"You had a salad."

I smirked. "Are you ever going to let that go?"

He didn't smile at the taunt. His eyes remained as hard as ever. "I never let anything go." Without taking his eyes off me, he wrapped his big hand around mine, and he gently pulled me out the door to his Range Rover.

He pulled onto the road, and like last time, his hand went to my thigh, his fingers sliding all the way until he could touch my black thong underneath. His hand was so big it took up my entire thigh, and it made me wonder how big the rest of him was.

With one hand on the wheel and the lights striking his dark eyes, he looked sexy as hell driving us to dinner, commanding the road with confidence and calm, not caring about the traffic or the asshole who'd run the red light.

"I'm surprised you don't have people drive you around." Sometimes Bolton had men pick us up and transfer us elsewhere. Theo had had one of his men drive me home on our first night together, but I'd never seen him be driven anywhere.

"My men don't need to know where I am every minute of the day."

"So, you don't trust them?"

"I don't trust anybody."

I looked down at his hand and saw the tendons pop across his hand and connect to his knuckles. There were little scars in the skin, like he'd been cut with a couple knives and the wounds had healed over long ago. I had one person in my life I trusted...until he asked to break our marriage vows. I could appreciate his honesty—or wonder what would have happened if I hadn't given him my blessing.

Theo parked the Range Rover, and then we entered the restaurant. We were given the same table as last time, and just like last time, no one came over until he motioned for them to.

He ordered a scotch and let me order whatever I wanted.

"I'll take the Bordeaux—Barsetti Vineyards."

The waiter walked away.

He sat with one arm resting on the table, his shirt tight on his muscular arm. It was a cold winter night, so I'd worn my coat, but he was so muscular that he was probably hot, even when the temperature was in the forties.

He looked out the window for a moment, and when he caught my stare, he shifted his gaze to me.

"Why do the waiters wait for you to signal to them?"

"Because this is my restaurant."

"Oh…" Good thing I'd only given compliments. "Do you like to cook?"

"I don't know shit about food. I just bought a couple places to wash my money…among other things."

I wondered what those other things were. "I'm glad we came back so I could try something else."

The waiter returned with the drinks. He poured me a glass of wine and left the bottle behind.

"You like their wine?" He glanced at the bottle between us.

"I love it. Why?"

"Do you know the Barsetti Family?"

"No. Do you?"

"I know Crow. He's the one who started the winery. Bought it to wash his money."

"Whatever the reason he bought it, I love it." I picked up the glass and took a drink.

"I like that about you."

"That I like wine?"

"That you know my world."

"I wouldn't say I know it…" Just seen it indirectly, at dinners and galas, late nights with Bolton's men.

"But you're aware of it—and unafraid of it."

I had no reason to be afraid of it. Bolton's immoral work never affected my life. He hid his trail well, so it never came back to me. He had several different names, so our marriage license was tied to one of those aliases. Our properties had been bought under other names and identities. I wasn't sure how he kept track of all of it. "What do most women think when you tell them?"

"I don't."

"Then how do you meet them?"

"I pay them." He grabbed his scotch and took a drink.

"You sleep with prostitutes?"

"Escorts. There's a big difference."

"There is?"

"An escort is an exceptionally beautiful woman who charges a fortune for her time. Her livelihood is dependent on her health—so they're clean. It's one of the things you're paying for."

I wasn't sure if I should be concerned that he openly paid for sex…or respect his honesty about it.

"That bothers you."

"I wouldn't say that."

"I can tell it does. But I'm not going to lie about it."

"Are those the only kinds of women you sleep with?"

"No. I meet women when I'm out. In a bar. At an event. Wherever."

"And it doesn't bother them that you pay for sex?"

He stared at me across the table, not showing his annoyance even though he must have felt it. "Those are one-night fucks. Not much talking going on. I always wear a condom, so where my dick has been before them is none of their concern."

I continued to stare at him, picturing him throwing a wad of bills at a woman in a hotel room. "So, you don't have relationships?"

His answer was immediate. "No."

"When was the last time you were in one?"

He grabbed his glass and took another drink. "This feels like an interrogation."

"I'm sorry," I said quickly. "I didn't mean for it to sound like that. I just...want to know you more." Neither one of us had expected to spend so much time together, so all the basic and inconsequential information had already been discovered. That left the important stuff, the deep stuff.

"Have long have you been married?"

"I said I didn't want to talk about him."

"And I didn't ask about him."

I knew if I wanted him to answer my question, I had to answer his. He was a master of conversation, controlling the temperature because he was the thermostat. "Two years. We've been together for three."

He didn't react. Didn't voice the thought that was probably in his head—that you shouldn't want an open marriage after just two years of matrimony. Whatever he thought, he kept it to himself. "I was in a relationship ten years ago." He gestured to the waiter who'd been standing on the other side of the room waiting for the signal. Theo clearly wanted to change the subject because he looked at his menu. "Chicken marsala."

I hadn't looked at the menu, but I found something at a quick glance. "I'll do the cheese ravioli with red sauce."

The waiter took the menus and walked away.

I didn't press Theo on the topic. It had red tape all over it. "I can tell you don't want to talk about it, so I won't pry. But if you ever want to talk about it, I'm here to listen."

His fingers rested on his glass, and his eyes shifted to look at me.

I froze in his stare, feeling stuck in place by his rigidness.

"I don't ever want to talk about it."

Over the course of our dates, I'd gotten to know him better, but I still felt like I didn't know him at all. However, I did see the pain in his stare, that whatever happened to him was more than a painful breakup. But I would probably never know more. "That's okay."

The hardness in his eyes softened slightly, seemingly touched by the way I backed off. He hadn't interrogated me about my marriage, didn't persecute me for the choices I'd made—the choices that I'd allowed my husband to make. I wanted to give him the same courtesy. There were things we wanted to know about each other, but we would have to settle for keeping our secrets.

"What do you think?"

I'd finished most of my dish, a couple ravioli left on the plate. "A lot better than that salad."

He gave a slight smirk, and his face was so much more handsome when he did that.

"What about yours?"

"I'm not picky. I'll eat anything."

"Then I should cook for you sometime. It'll be nice not to have any pressure."

He wiped away a speck of sauce from the corner of his mouth before returning the linen to his lap. His plate was nearly empty, with the exception of a few mushrooms that were left behind. He washed it down with a drink from his second scotch. "Can I ask you something?"

"Sure." I braced for whatever he wanted to know, but I was so lost in those dark eyes that it was hard to be scared. I never knew brown eyes could be so damn pretty. They had a darkness to them...but also a warmth.

"What did you do after your father died?"

That wasn't a question I'd expected. Figured it would have something to do with my marriage. "That was a hard time in my life. I stopped my classes, slept around a lot because I felt alone. When I lost my home...I lost myself."

"Why did you lose your home?"

"Couldn't make the mortgage, so it was repossessed by the bank." I took the possessions that mattered most but lost the rest. "Slept on a friend's couch for a while. The years after that were one struggle after another. Tried to make it as an artist, but I was just broke and hungry. My dad had a life insurance policy, but the company didn't honor it because he killed himself. I don't think he'd anticipated that."

He didn't make another negative comment about my father. He seemed to have let that go.

"I got a job at the gallery and finally got my own apartment. Then I met my husband shortly after, got married, and moved in to his place." All the wealth I had came from him. He elevated me from rags to riches. I used to consider myself lucky to marry for love, and the money was just a perk. But the wealth did drastically change my life. I never worried about money or bills or car repairs. All the money I earned at the gallery was just extra spending money that I didn't need. I worked a job because I wanted to, not because I had to, and that was the ultimate sign of privilege.

Theo listened to every word I said. His eyes didn't glaze over like he'd lost interest. He was with me in every moment, in every word I spoke, entranced by the mundane mediocrity of my life. "The death of your father was the most defining moment of your life…"

My eyes locked on his.

"We all have moments like that. If that moment hadn't happened or if it'd been different…what else would have been different?"

I couldn't imagine how different my life would have been. I probably would have lived with my dad for a long time, not because I needed to, but because I wouldn't have wanted to leave him alone until he was ready to be on his own. Or maybe I wouldn't have left at all because I enjoyed spending time with him. There wouldn't be nearly as many notches on my bedpost. Wouldn't be so many scars on my heart. "What's your moment?"

His eyes shifted slightly.

"The moment that changed your life."

He considered the question for a long time, letting the silence hang heavy between us. "I have more than one." His big arms crossed over his chest. "The first was when I lost the family business to a fire…and had nothing left. I needed money, and I didn't care how I earned it. If that hadn't happened, I probably wouldn't be who I am now."

"And the other moment?"

All he did was give a slight shake of his head. "That one…dies with me."

Theo motioned for the tab, and it was brought to him instantly because it'd been sitting in the front pocket of the waiter's apron. Theo opened the folder and dropped a wad of cash inside.

"I want to pay for this one."

He closed the folder and stared at me.

"You're one of those guys who insists on paying for everything?"

"You mean a man?" he asked quietly. "Yes, I am." He left the folder at the edge for the waiter to take.

"Why are you paying if you own the place?"

"Just easier this way. Bookkeeping purposes."

"Well, thank you for dinner…again."

He grabbed his scotch and took a drink.

"Wow, baby. Look who it is."

I turned to the man who approached our table, a six-foot-something fine piece of man with a nice smile. A woman was on his arm in a skintight black dress. She wore a wedding ring on her left hand, and she smiled at me.

Theo released a quiet sigh.

The man moved to Theo and gripped him by the shoulder. "A very nice surprise." He looked at me then reached his hand forward. "Axel—Theo's brother. And this fine piece of ass right here is my wife, Scarlett."

Her cheeks flushed deep red, and she quickly rolled her eyes. "Nice to meet you." She extended her hand to shake mine.

"You too," I said. "I'm Astrid."

Axel turned to the waiter. "Pull up two chairs. We'll be joining them—"

"We were just leaving," Theo said, giving him that don't-fuck-with-me look.

"Then we'll have a drink together." When the waiter brought a chair, Axel positioned it so his wife could sit down first. Then he took the other seat the waiter brought, closest to Theo.

Theo stared at him.

Axel stared back, a full grin on his face. "So…how do you know each other?"

"Axel." Scarlett moved her hand to his thigh. "Give it a rest."

"Listen to your wife," Theo said coldly.

"I only listen to my wife when she tells me how to fuck her." Axel gestured to the waiter to get his attention. "I'll have a scotch. My wife will have a Bordeaux." He looked at me next. "You're a scotch drinker too."

"On occasion," I said. "Not like Theo."

"Sounds like you know Theo pretty well, then." He looked at Theo and gave him a knowing look.

"It's been a long time since I hit you," Theo said. "I'd rather not break that streak."

Axel seemed undeterred because he grinned. "It'll be worth it."

I looked at Theo. "I didn't realize you had another brother."

Axel looked at Theo again, his eyes narrowing like he'd discovered something else.

"Yes," Theo said. "But not for long…"

"You don't look alike." Theo had dark hair and dark eyes, whereas Axel was a dirty-blond with blue eyes. They were both tall and muscular men, men who could have any woman they wanted. I could see why Axel wanted his wife Scarlett because she really was a fine piece of ass, but me…not so much.

"Adopted brothers," Axel said. "Known each other a long time."

"Astrid," Scarlett said. "What do you do for a living?" It seemed like she was trying to get the heat off Theo.

"I work at an art gallery. I acquire pieces from clients who have estate sales, old paintings that come back on the market to find a new home. I work with modern artists as well, local ones in Tuscany. And then I have clients who hire me to fill certain spaces of their home with artwork."

The waiter brought their drinks, and Axel took a drink as he continued to watch me.

"That's fascinating," Scarlett said.

"And she's also an artist herself," Theo said, looking at me.

"Oh really?" Scarlett said. "What kind of art do you make?"

"Theo is being generous," I said quickly, feeling flustered by the attention. "I've always wanted to be an artist, but I haven't made it there yet. I paint my paintings and then never let them see the light of day."

"Why?" Axel asked.

"I don't know," I said with a shrug. "I don't think they're good enough. I stare art in the face all day, every day, and mine don't really match what I see."

"The artwork I chose didn't match anything else in your gallery," Theo said. "And I think they're perfect. Perhaps yours are perfect too, waiting to sit over someone else's mantel for ten years. At some point, you have to grow a spine, sweetheart."

Axel turned to look at Theo again, covering his grin by taking a drink.

"So that's how you know each other?" Scarlett asked. "You visited her gallery?" She asked the question as she looked at Theo.

"I needed something for the study, and George arranged it," Theo said.

"But you physically went down there and looked at art?" Axel asked incredulously. "*You?*"

Theo gave him that cold look again.

Axel smirked then took a drink.

When Theo had said he never took other women to dinner, I hadn't been sure if it was just a line to make me feel special, but judging by the way his brother reacted to our date, it was the complete truth.

"I apologize for my husband," Scarlett said. "He just likes to start shit."

Axel moved his hand to her thigh, way up her dress in the middle of the restaurant, and leaned into her. "Come on, baby. You know you like it." He pressed a kiss to her neck and then another, to the point where she had to push him off.

"We don't get out much," she said. "If you can't tell."

"Why?" I asked.

"We've got two babies at home," Axel said. "They're with the nanny tonight. We'll have dinner, go back to a nice hotel and fuck, and then—"

"Axel," she snapped. "Stop talking."

"Please," Theo said.

Axel smirked and took another drink of his scotch.

Theo rose from his chair. "Let's go, sweetheart. Before we catch the live show."

I rose from the chair and looked at Axel and Scarlett. "It was lovely to meet you both. Enjoy your dinner… and your fuck-a-thon afterward."

Scarlett released a chuckle.

Axel was about to take a drink, but he set down the glass as he released a laugh. "I like her, Theo."

Theo ignored him as his hand moved to my lower back, and he guided me out of the restaurant. He didn't talk about his brother and sister-in-law as we headed back to his Range Rover. The drive was spent in silence, and his hand didn't move to my thigh like it normally did. He seemed annoyed by the unexpected guests at our dinner table, even though they seemed nice enough to me.

We entered his bedroom minutes later, the primary suite the same size as most apartments. It even had its own dining table behind the sitting area, the ceiling ten feet high, curtains drawn closed over all the windows.

He went straight to the bar like always and made two drinks without asking what I wanted. Then he walked into the room that had the four-poster bed, probably to change into his signature sweatpants and nothing else but a bare chest.

I sat on the couch and looked at the glass he'd left for me. I'd been nervous every time I'd come over here, but I was a lot less nervous tonight.

He came out a moment later, black sweatpants on his narrow waist, dark ink visible on his tanned skin. Every time he stepped into the room, he brought a presence so profound it filled the room with smoke—because he was the fire. He sat on the couch, leaving an open space between us because he never crossed the boundary I never had to put up.

"I liked them."

"Really?" he asked. "Because I don't. Well, I like Scarlett. That piece of shit...not so much."

"What did he do?"

He grabbed his glass and shook the ice inside. "Just being a dick."

My eyebrow cocked. "Were we at the same table?"

"Trust me." He took a big drink and set the glass on the coffee table. "I don't want to talk about them anymore." He sat forward with his elbows on his thighs, his flattened palms gently sliding back and forth. His muscular back was like the trunk of a mighty oak. After a stare at his drink, he turned to look at me.

I was paralyzed by that stare, the darkness of his eyes and their shadowed depth. He touched me without crossing the divide between us. He made me hot without drawing close. Made my lips ache without being kissed.

For the first time, I forgot I was married.

I had a connection with this man. It had started off slowly, with the roots puncturing the soil, but every time I saw him, those roots dug deeper, reaching far down, away from the surface.

He hadn't blinked since his gaze locked on mine. "If you aren't ready, then leave. Because if you stay…" He gave a slight shake of his head and never finished the sentence. His stare hardened, hinting at the inferno that was about to erupt from his chest.

Bumps formed on my arms as if a draft had entered the room. A tightness formed in my stomach. The trepidation was still there, but the excitement had built so much over the last few weeks that it triumphed over everything else I felt. It gave me a jolt of confidence that I rarely felt. "Get over here."

His stare immediately hardened as all the impressive muscles of his body flexed in desire. His hand reached to the back of my calf, and then he tugged me, so strong that my hips rolled and the back of my head dropped to the seat of the couch. He moved on top of me, one of his big hands diving underneath my dress to feel my hip and the lace of my panties. This mountain of a man blocked the sun as he rose over me, tugging my dress up my body, forcing it up until my tits were revealed, the nipples taped down.

Instead of kissing my aching lips, he looked down at my body as he slid one of his hands up my stomach to explore me, and he released the sexiest moan at the sight of me, making me feel desirable rather than ordinary, like I was worth the price of the other girls he paid for.

He ripped the tape off one nipple without any gentleness.

I winced when it tugged hard on my skin.

He did the same with the other, ripping just as hard. Then he dipped his mouth to the valley between my tits and kissed me there, breathed in my scent. One of his big hands squeezed my tit as he sucked the nipple as hard as he'd ripped off the tape.

My hand dug into his short hair, and I felt my hips lift to push my body farther into his mouth. His touch brought my body out of its dormancy and set it on fire. When Bolton and I fucked, that was all it was. No foreplay. Just our naked bodies coming together before we raced to the end. But Theo stopped to treasure my body, to appreciate it and memorize it, to lavish it with kisses and touches.

He moved down and played with the lace of my panties, kissing the skin over my hips and running his tongue just above the top of my waistband.

I closed my eyes and dug my nails into his shoulders. God, they were so thick and strong, like pieces of concrete on either side of his neck.

His thumb hooked into the lace of my thong, and he tugged it down, getting it over each hip and then over my ass. He grabbed my ankles and forced my knees to bend, to pin my legs as deep into my body as my flexibility would allow. He pulled the thong up and over my feet before his big hands pushed down on my thighs, and he pressed his face right between my legs.

And then breathed.

I stiffened when I felt his face between my legs, felt the air from his breaths over my folds and my opening. Bumps formed on my arms, and my nipples sharpened like knives. My ankles rested over his shoulders at the back of his neck. I was frozen to the spot, feeling him smelling me like a rose.

Then his mouth kissed me, a hard kiss that would have bruised my mouth. It started off slow and purposeful, and then he added his tongue to the lineup and I was a fucking mess. I lay there and squeezed his head with my thighs, my ankles batting at his shoulders. My breaths came out as pants, and the tension in my stomach made the muscles cramp. It was so damn good, the best kiss my girl had ever experienced.

I already knew he was going to make me come. "Theo..."

He sucked me hard in his mouth, sucked my folds and my nub and gave me a gentle bite before his tongue swirled with the pressure of an iron fist. It was a testament to his experience, because a man didn't eat pussy like this without it. He knew exactly what I would like, what would make me come in just a few minutes.

I expected him to stop, to make sure I wouldn't say no when he tried to fuck me, but he followed through and pushed me over the edge, causing my hips to buck against his face as the tears sprang to my eyes.

My fingers tugged on his hair as I shoved my pussy at him, fucking his face without an ounce of shame. "Jesus...Theo." The wave I rode was long and high, building to a beautiful crescendo before I slowly rolled back down the hill.

He gave me a final kiss before he lifted himself up, his lips shining like he was wearing lip gloss. "You've got a nice pussy, sweetheart." He moved over me, his heavy body making the cushions shift under his weight.

My thighs immediately squeezed his torso, and my ankles locked together at his back as I brought him close, desperate to kiss those lips that made me feel so damn good. My hand cupped his face as I kissed him for the first time, tasting myself on his mouth, my fingers digging into his hair as I felt another burst of sparks.

His kisses started off slow and purposeful like they did before, and he took the moment to enjoy my kiss rather than blow right through it. His hand slowly slid up the back of my neck before he fisted my hair into a ball. He'd barely touched me on our dates, but once permission had been granted, he showed how physical and affectionate he was. He loved to touch me everywhere, loved to feel every piece of me instead of just the main attractions. He was a thorough lover.

He ground his hips into me, to make me feel him.

To feel that big fucking dick.

Jesus Christ.

He wasn't inside me, but my lips quivered like he was stretching me wide apart. It'd been a long time since I'd been turned on like this. I'd been happy with my sex life with Bolton before he'd asked to open our marriage to other people, but I hadn't felt like this…ever.

Theo moved his kiss to the corner of my mouth and then my jawline. He made his way down my neck and smothered me with his kisses as he tugged his sweatpants down to unleash his super dick.

He pulled away to tug them down to his thighs then fished into his pocket to pull out a foil packet.

I propped myself up on my elbows and looked at that monster cock. "Uh, whoa…"

He didn't grin at the compliment and ripped the top of the foil packet.

I suddenly realized what would happen next, and that realization made me go ice-cold. The guilt returned to the surface as I confronted what I was about to do. I'd kissed this man. I'd let this man fuck me with his mouth. But once that monster cock was inside me, it would really seal the deal.

My hand reached for his wrist before he could roll the condom down his length.

His eyes found mine, and instead of disappointment, there was just a ruthless stare.

I sat up and moved to my knees. "My turn." My hand gently pushed him in the chest and forced him back.

He lay back, his head propped up on the edge of the couch, looking like the hunkiest piece of man meat ever.

Just as he did with me, I kissed his body, worshipped his hardness, the way his muscles separated over his hard frame. There was salt on my tongue from his sweat, and I kissed the tattoos that marked his skin.

I moved down, getting closer to the big dick that lay against his stomach, a fat vein up the middle, perfectly groomed balls at the bottom. He was a different beast of man, more animal than human.

I came closer to the tip but avoided it, kissing and licking everywhere but the place he wanted me most.

His breathing picked up slowly, that big chest rising and falling at a gradual speed. His dark eyes hardened with impatience.

I decided to start at the bottom instead of the top. I pressed my soft lips to his balls, and the gentle contact unleashed the sexiest moan from his throat. A deep breath accompanied it, his mountain of a chest filling with the air he pulled in.

I kissed him again and again then let my tongue swipe the soft skin. It started off slow before I soaked his flesh with my tongue, sucking one side entirely into my mouth as I gently rolled it over my tongue.

He seemed to like it.

When I had him breathing hard, I moved up and dragged my tongue up the vein of his rock-hard dick.

That elicited another moan from him, a deeper one than the others, sounding more like a bear than a man.

I made it to the tip then pressed a kiss to the head, getting the precome on my tongue.

That was when his hand dug deep into my hair, and he grabbed himself by the base. His impatience took over, and he guided my mouth down his dick, forcing me down until there was no more throat for his length.

I wanted to gag right away, but I bottled the impulse deep inside.

"Slow." He guided me by the hair the way he liked, still holding his base for me like some kind of gentleman. "Just like that, sweetheart."

I flattened my tongue and kept going, feeling like a horse that was guided by the reins, feeling his cock push inside over and over, blocking my airway and forcing me to abstain from oxygen.

He'd been anxious to fuck me just a minute ago, but he seemed to want to stretch this out and make it last as long as possible, to put me to work and get the most out of me like a laborer on the clock.

My jaw ached because of how far open my mouth had to remain, and the back of my neck was already sore from lifting my head over such a great obstacle.

His eyes watched me the entire time, hard like his dick, dark like the night outside the windows.

When I went down, he forced me down farther, wanting me to take more than I could. Even when I struggled, he forced me to do it, like he got off on the struggle. Tears sprang into my eyes because it was hard to breathe and hard not to choke, but he didn't give a damn.

He breathed harder as he watched me work, the cords of his veins tight from the way he flexed his whole body. Then he guided my head down faster, increasing the pace slowly until he had me going at breakneck speed.

My eyes watered until tears formed. I gasped between breaths, sucking in whatever air I could while it was available.

"Does my dick make you cry, sweetheart?" He started to thrust from below, slamming his dick into the back of my throat. Air supply became more limited and the need to gag increased, but my tongue remained flat to take that big cock like he demanded. My body wanted the strain to end, but I'd never been more aroused giving head before. My knees could be on cold concrete and I could sweat in the heat of a furnace, but I would still enjoy every second of making this man come in my mouth.

His face flushed red with desire. The skin over his chest became blotted with different spots of red. All the cords in his hands and neck popped like they were about to burst. His jaw clenched as his breathing turned ragged.

Then he released a loud moan as he finished, his fingers tightening in my hair and keeping me in place, his dick fully in my mouth so I wouldn't miss a drop. The heat and the substance came a second later, dumping into my throat and making it impossible to breathe.

"Attagirl," he said as he filled me.

When the moment passed, his fingers loosened on my hair so I could finally be free.

I sat up and straightened, but I didn't get far before he grabbed me by the neck. His thumb swiped up over the bottom of my lip as he stared at me. "Show me."

I hesitated before I stuck out my tongue, showing that I'd already swallowed it.

He released me when he got what he wanted. He left the couch, buck naked because his sweatpants were left on the floor, and walked into the bathroom to clean himself up.

I sat there, naked on his couch with my dress still bunched up above my tits. I pulled it down over my body, my hard nipples visible through the thin material now that the tape was missing. My black thong was on the floor where Theo had left it. I stared at it for a moment before I pulled it back on over my heels…because I'd never taken them off.

I was dead tired and could fall asleep right on this couch, but I needed to get home. I left the couch and grabbed my purse.

Theo came back into the room in a pair of black boxers, six and a half feet of pure man. His dark eyes took me in as he drew closer. "Next time you come over here, you're going to get fucked." He almost looked angry, like the nice blow job that had made me cry wasn't good enough. "You've been warned."

8

THEO

I sat behind my desk and looked at the painting directly across the room, the image of the changeling that had been stored in the basement of the art gallery with other portraits and sculptures that no one seemed to care about.

Except me.

My laptop was ignored on my desk as I stared past it, seeing something new every time I looked at it. But there was one thing I always saw when I stared... Astrid. I saw her standing beside me as we looked at the painting. I saw her in my study, measuring the walls in her tight pencil skirt. I saw a broken woman so fascinating she belonged in her own painting.

George knocked on the open door before he entered. "You have a visitor, sir."

My eyes shifted to him, already knowing who it was.

"Should I bring Axel in here?"

Motherfucker. "Sure."

George left.

I gave a heavy sigh before I left my desk and moved to the sitting area, the chairs outlined in gold, the coffee table with beautiful ornate legs. The man who'd owned this place previously was French, so it looked more Parisian than Tuscan.

I sat in the armchair and waited for him.

He walked in a moment later in jeans and a gray shirt. "Didn't expect George to let me in."

"I knew you would come back, like a fucking cockroach."

Axel grinned like that was a compliment. He took a seat and helped himself to a cigar, lounging on the cushions like this place belonged to him as much as it belonged to me. "So...how was dinner?"

"Fuck off, Axel."

"The only person who should be mad here is me, asshole."

"Really?" I asked coldly.

"You've been seeing someone and didn't tell me? I told you everything about Scarlett. Except the intimate details that are reserved for me."

"You were serious with Scarlett. It's not serious with Astrid."

"You took her out to *dinner*." He made it sound like I already married her. "*You*. Theo Bianchi. Skull King."

Imagine his reaction if I told him how many times I'd taken her out to dinner. "I said it's not serious."

"It's not casual either. Otherwise, you would skip dinner and head straight for dessert. And if it really were casual, you would have mentioned it to me."

"I wouldn't."

"You mention your other rendezvous pretty often."

"Not as often as you think." I kept a lot of stuff from him because I wasn't the type to fuck and tell.

"Theo." He turned serious, letting the smoke leave the tip of his cigar and rise to the ceiling.

"How many times do I have to say it?" I barked. "It's not serious."

He cocked his head. "The last woman you took to dinner was—"

"Shut your fucking mouth, Axel." I could tolerate the jokes and the grins, but there was one thing I couldn't tolerate and that was her fucking name. She haunted me every day, had haunted me for a decade. Time may have passed, but her memory had never faded.

That was the only line Axel didn't cross—and he didn't cross it again.

We sat like that for a long time, the silence slowly suffocating us both.

Axel finally sucked on his cigar and let the smoke escape his mouth. "Scarlett wants me to quit."

"Are you going to?"

"I don't smoke at home or around the kids, just when I'm out."

"Didn't answer my question."

"I want to honor her requests, but fuck, there's nothing like a cigar in your mouth after a shit day."

Every day felt like a shit day lately—except when I was with her.

Axel stared at my cold fireplace before he looked at me again. "You like her, right?"

"We aren't in sixth grade, Axel."

"You want more than sex, Theo."

I hadn't gotten sex. "Like I said many times, it's not serious."

"Why not—"

"Because she's married."

He was about to bring the cigar to his lips again when he stopped. His eyes hardened on my face. "Why are you taking a married woman out to dinner? Shouldn't affairs take place in beautiful hotels room and shit like that?"

"It's complicated."

"Doesn't sound complicated to me. Sounds like you want to get caught." He sucked on his cigar and let another puff of smoke leave his mouth.

"It's an open marriage."

"An open marriage?" he repeated with disdain. "Then why be married at all?"

"I don't know." It didn't make sense to me either. "We don't talk about it much, so I don't understand it."

"If you don't talk about it, then what do you talk about?"

"That's my business."

He straightened in his chair as he stared me down. "Why are you being so defensive right now?"

"I'm not being defensive—"

"I'm your brother. I'm not coming to you to gossip or talk shit. I haven't seen you with a woman in years. Unless it's a girl on your lap at the strip club or some shit like that. We tell each other everything, but now you've shut me out and I don't know why."

"I'm not being defensive," I said calmly. "I told you it's not serious how many fucking times, but you don't believe me. So, yes, I'm getting a bit annoyed with the redundancy."

"Well, you're lying."

"Fuck you. I'm not lying," I snapped.

Axel stared me down. "Then why are you taking her to dinner?"

I grew frustrated at the line of questioning and almost reached for a cigar to dissolve the annoyance. "I asked her out, and she said she was married. But then her husband said he wanted an open marriage, so she asked me out. But she's needed some time to get used to the idea of fucking someone besides her husband, so we've gone to dinner a few times. That's it, Axel. That's the whole fucking story." I propped my cheek on my knuckles and waited for him to finally lose interest in this story.

But he looked just as confused as when I started. "Why are you wasting time with her, then? Instead of taking her to dinner, you could be fucking someone. You've taken her out multiple times, so it sounds like you like her. Have you fucked her?"

I continued my stare.

"You like her."

"I think we have a lot in common."

"Such as?"

Misery. "That's between us."

Axel put the cigar back in his mouth and let it sit there.

I continued to watch him. "Her husband is in the game."

His eyes found mine again.

"I don't know who he is or what he does. But she knew I was the Skull King when she looked at my ring. It's a nice change, being with a woman who's unafraid of who I am and my world."

"That means you could be in deep shit if you get caught."

"It's an open marriage—that he asked for."

"But I doubt he expected her to fuck you, of all people."

I gave a shrug. "I don't care."

"Because she's worth it?"

"Don't put words in my mouth, asshole."

"That's why it was a question and not a statement. Asshole."

I finally grabbed one of the cigars and lit up because it

seemed like this conversation was nowhere near finished.

"It's okay to like someone, Theo." His voice was suddenly gentle. "You know that, right?"

I turned to look at him, the cigar hanging between my fingertips.

"I want you to have what I have."

Memories flashed across my mind, the kind I wished I could erase from my memory. They said it was better to have loved and lost than not to love at all, but those people didn't know shit about loss. Or pain. Or grief. Or anything. If I could do it all over again…I wouldn't. "I did have what you have, Axel—and it haunts me every fucking day."

ASTRID

I held the flute of champagne in my hand and eyed the hors d'oeuvres spread on the table, little pieces of bruschetta and filet mignon wrapped in crispy bacon. I'd already had enough to make my dress tighten over my stomach so I should exercise some self-control, but I was also bored.

Bolton was across the room, sitting in one of the armchairs, talking to his older brother with a glass of red wine in his hand. His light-colored hair was combed back away from his face, showing off the handsome features that made me fall for him the moment I saw him. He wore a serious expression, but his eyes had a light that never faded.

I still loved him despite the suggestion that broke my heart, but it was changing, slowly drowning with resentment and anger...and self-loathing. The worst part of this was knowing I wasn't enough for him. That his desires had to be supplemented with women I didn't have the courage to ask about.

"You alright?" Denise, my sister-in-law, walked over.

"Yeah." I covered my consternation with a false smile. "Just trying not to eat all your appetizers like a fat-ass."

She smirked. "You're not a fat-ass, Astrid."

But I wasn't a fine piece of ass either, the kind that Bolton wanted to keep all to himself.

She continued to watch me. "You sure you're alright?"

"Just had too much champagne. It's always been my weakness."

Denise accepted my explanation. "Michael tells me you guys are thinking about starting a family."

Bolton told him? Did he also tell him the other thing we'd started? "Yep, it's on the table."

"That's exciting. I was so nervous when our first one came, but once he was here, it all just came together. We knew what to do."

"And I'm sure a nanny helped with that," I teased.

"Oh, definitely," she said with a chuckle. "I'm a grouch without sleep, and Michael is even worse."

I used to see Bolton's family as my family, the family I'd never had, but now everything felt different. The connection that bonded us had been severed by his desires. I hated to admit it, but I even felt differently toward my niece and nephew. I didn't have a family of my own, and I really believed in-laws would be enough, but I realized nothing would ever come close to a blood relative. All Bolton had to do was fuck someone else, and everything came unraveled.

"I'm sorry. I know I've asked twice already, but you just have this look in your eye…"

My eyes found hers again.

"Like you go somewhere else, somewhere sad."

I forced that smile to come back. "The gallery has been really hectic lately. Just got a lot on my mind."

"Well, you don't *have* to work."

"I know. But I want to." I needed something that was just mine. I'd thought Bolton was mine, but he only wanted to be mine part time. "Need something to do while Bolton is away." Something other than the dark hunk who brought me to life with his electric touch.

———

Bolton talked about Michael on the way home. "Said we should all take a trip to Paris this summer. The kids are old enough now."

"Yeah, that would be fun."

He drove with one hand on the wheel, but his other hand didn't reach for my thigh. "What did you and Denise talk about?"

"Work...kids." I liked Denise, but I had been in the mood to sit alone and eat in a corner.

"I told Michael we were thinking about trying."

"Yeah, she mentioned it."

He approached a stoplight and brought the car to a slow stop. "Well?"

"Well, what?"

"You wanna start trying?"

My heart dropped into my stomach with dread. It was the same feeling of terror I felt when things heated up with Theo, the heavy realization that I was about to cross a line I could never uncross. But this was a different level, an anxiety that went from zero to sixty in a nanosecond. "Um…" I'd been on birth control a long time and continued to take it. Once I stopped taking it, I didn't know what would happen. Would I get pregnant right away, or would it take a year?

The light turned green, and he continued down the road. "That sounds like a no." Disappointment was heavy in his voice as he grabbed the wheel with both hands.

I didn't know what to say, so I focused my gaze out the window and ignored him in my peripheral. My pulse raced, and despite the cold, I felt sweat on my palms.

Bolton let the conversation die, but the tension was very much alive.

We parked in the underground garage then entered our villa, the light low because only a few lamps were lit. I hung my jacket on the coatrack and slipped off my heels by the door.

Bolton didn't have a jacket, so he immediately took a seat in the living room.

I moved to the stairs so I could go to our bedroom and get ready for bed.

"Astrid."

I froze on the first step.

His back was to me. "Sit with me." He didn't raise his voice, but there was a hint of a threat there.

I took a breath before I walked into the living room, moving behind the back of one of the couches before I came around and took a seat. I was on a different couch from him, our bodies perpendicular to each other. I crossed my ankles and sat with bumps on my arms.

His stare burned into the side of my face.

I didn't want to look at him.

"Astrid."

I obeyed his command and met his gaze. He was a handsome man who could get any woman he wanted. But he was lean and toned, an athletic build like a soccer player, and Theo was...like a bull. Muscle on top of muscle, with dark ink over the burning hot skin, with that dark hair like midnight. The men couldn't be more different, and now I couldn't stop comparing them. Theo was taller, quieter, and even his…package was bigger. The difference in size was substantial enough that I noticed it every time Bolton and I were together, even though I hadn't actually slept with Theo. Having him in my mouth was enough.

His eyes burned into mine, treating me like an enemy he was about to interrogate. "You were the one pressuring me to have a family. Now you've changed your mind?"

"I haven't changed my mind—"

"So, you want to do this."

"I-I just need some time—"

"So, you don't want to do this?" he pressed.

"Just because I don't want to do it right this second doesn't mean I don't want to do it at all."

He hadn't blinked once since the interrogation started. "Then what changed?"

"Having a kid is a big responsibility."

"You've been hounding me for six months about this."

"I'm just not sure if having a baby when you're still in your line of work is a good idea."

His eyes flicked back and forth between mine. "We talked about this. I'm not leaving my job, Astrid."

"Okay, then I need more time to think about it."

"Nothing will happen to either of you, I promise."

"You can't make that kind of promise."

"I've got a lot of enemies, but no one has ever knocked on your front door, baby." His voice rose slightly. "I've seen the way your eyes glaze over when I speak. I feel the distance in your touch. You spent more time with the hors d'oeuvres than you did with us. Something is wrong, and you must think me a fool not to notice."

My eyes flicked away as I felt the weight on my shoulders. The air was suddenly too thick to breathe, like it was humid and mixed with smoke. He had me cornered, and there was no escape with this man.

"You said you were fine with it, Astrid."

I still wouldn't look at him.

"Those are your words."

"I'm aware of what I said."

"But you clearly aren't," he said. "I can see that."

A part of me wanted to burst and tell him it killed me inside, that I'd been broken ever since the moment he'd admitted his desire for other women. It was a hit to my confidence, an axe to my heart. I could make it all stop right now if I asked for it to stop, but if I did… that meant I would never see Theo again. That meant his dark eyes would never pierce my flesh. He would never kiss me like I was the sexiest thing he'd ever seen. Those big hands would never squeeze my hips again, never squeeze my tits. Now, everything was complicated because I was invested in a man who wasn't my husband. To get what I wanted from Bolton, I would have to let Theo go…and I just couldn't do that.

It made me feel like shit, but then I remembered none of this was my fault.

It was his fault. "It's been hard to adjust to the change, I admit that. But I'm okay with it." I looked at him as I said it because I needed my sincerity to come through. Weeks ago, I'd just wanted my marriage back. I was ready to walk away from Theo…until Bolton walked in with lipstick on his neck. That was the catalyst for all the events that led to this moment, made me desire a man more than I'd ever desired anyone, including the man beside me. "But I do think it's strange to try for a family when we've just started this arrangement."

Bolton peered into my face, his blue eyes like the lens of a microscope, analyzing everything. "If it works for us, it's not strange."

"Do you even want a family?"

"Of course I do."

"But do you actually want it, or are you just doing it because your brother has kids, because that's the next stage in life? You're gone a lot, and you won't see them much. You don't want to change that?"

"My job is to provide for my family. To put our kids in private school. To give them the best lives they could possibly have. Maybe they'll be disappointed when they're young, but when they're older, they'll understand and be grateful."

I'd rather have my father around than attend an expensive school with snobby kids. That was just my opinion.

"Baby."

My eyes had drifted away and came back to him.

"If you ever want this to end, all you have to do is tell me. You understand that, right?" His eyes bored into mine again. "Because I love you with my whole heart. These women mean nothing to me—but you mean everything."

Women. *Plural.* There'd been different lovers in his bed—and I hadn't even slept with Theo. Guilt and obligation had restrained me. I couldn't just jump into bed with someone else so quickly, not the way he could. But I meant everything to him?

He searched my face, wanting my answer.

"Yes," I said with forced calm. "I understand."

———

The second Bolton was out of the house, I fired off a text. *Can I come over?*

The three dots were instant. *I meant what I said, sweetheart.* His deep voice sounded in my head as I read the words, the subtle threat that he somehow made gentle.

I didn't feel the anxiety anymore. Didn't feel the moral injury. I felt nothing at all, no guilt or shame. The tight handcuffs on my wrists had sprung free. *Why do you think I want to come over?*

Then get your ass over here.

I packed my bag and drove to his place fifteen minutes away, south of the Duomo. The gates automatically opened when my car pulled up, and I left my car down below in his underground garage.

He had an elevator that rose to the ground floor, so I stepped into his beautiful villa and was immediately smothered by his distinct presence. The hardwood floors were made of walnut, so they almost looked black. The décor that someone else had picked out was all in shades that matched his exterior, dark and complex.

George didn't come out to greet me, so I headed to the stairs to begin my journey to the top floor, but when I heard his deep voice, I stilled.

It came from the study, the one where his artwork hung. I hesitated before I turned back and approached the double doors that were partially open.

"Tell him a deal's a deal." Theo's voice was calm but deep with anger. "If he doesn't want to honor it like a man, then I won't honor my end of the deal either."

I stopped when I realized I'd just stepped into the underworld, the world that Bolton barely mentioned to me. The only evidence I witnessed was the interactions he had with people at parties or at dinners. It didn't feel so threatening when I wasn't part of it, and I thought that was intentional on Bolton's part.

Theo seemed to fire off a list to someone who listened. "Talk to Fender. I know he's out of the game, but that man still knows shit. He still knows all the big players because he'll always be the biggest player there ever was. And if the Colombians are still giving us pushback, tell them I'll personally pay them a visit." There was a pause before he spoke again. "Sweetheart, get in here."

I was blocked from view by one of the doors, but he somehow knew I was there. I rounded the corner and entered the room, Theo sitting in his usual armchair with a lit cigar resting between his fingertips. In just his gray sweatpants, he commanded the room with that skull ring on his left hand. There were two other guys, both smoking as they sat on each of the couches. Neither one of them looked at me. I stepped inside, my bag over my shoulder, feeling completely out of place.

"Octavio." He nodded to one guy. Then he nodded to the other. "Nico."

Both of them looked at me in acknowledgment.

"Guys, this is Astrid."

"Hey." I didn't know what else to say. It was obvious I'd come over there to get fucked by this man, and the bag over my shoulder showed that I intended to stay until morning. It was his house, so there was no reason to be embarrassed, but nonetheless, I was.

"We're done here, gentlemen." Theo looked at me as he spoke.

The guys put out their cigars before they filed out of the room. They didn't look at me as they passed me on the way out.

The room was like an ashtray, smoke visible all the way to the top of the high ceiling.

I entered the room and glanced at the artwork that was still hanging. "I didn't realize you were busy."

"I'm always busy." He brought the cigar to his lips and pulled the smoke into his mouth before he smashed the cigar into the ashtray. "I just ignore everything when you walk into the room." The smoke left his mouth with his next breath, clouds of gray drifting above his head.

I knew he smoked because I could taste it on his tongue when I kissed him, but it was different from cigarette smoke. It had flavors of licorice and chocolate and a hint of coffee.

When he rose from the armchair, I was reminded of how tall he was, that my highest heels were still no match for this behemoth. He stepped toward me and circled his arm around the small of my back, pulling me into him for a soft kiss on the mouth.

My eyes shut when I felt his kiss, and I was suddenly taken to a sandy beach at sunset, the air warm around me, my skin kissed by heat. My hand moved to his bicep and felt the hunk of muscle there as I rose on my tiptoes, hooking my other arm around his neck for support.

When he felt my enthusiasm, his big hand moved to my ass and squeezed it hard. He kissed me hard too, his fingers digging into my flesh through my jeans. His mouth parted my lips, and he gave me a swipe of his tongue, turning a simple kiss into a passionate one, his other hand diving into my hair to fist the strands.

Fuck, he was a good kisser. He took his time, made every embrace purposeful, squeezed my body so hard it nearly left a bruise. He made me feel desired without saying a word, showed his desperation for me with so little, but also so much.

When he pulled away, his eyes were on my lips, like he might kiss me again. His fingers were still deep in my hair, and he cradled my head the way he wanted, my chin up so I could meet his gaze. He handled me like a rag doll that he could twist and turn and leave on the floor, but at the same time, he handled me like a delicate rose.

He reached for the bag stuffed with clothes and makeup and put it over his shoulder before he took my hand. He guided me up the stairs and into his suite, but instead of stopping in the living room where we usually sat together, he took my bag into his bedroom and set it on an armchair near the window.

I slowly entered his bedroom, eyeing his four-poster bed and the mahogany nightstands on either side. A large rug covered the hardwood floor and complemented the other colors in his room, the gray and the maroon.

My heart raced, not in fear, but with excitement.

He came back to me, thick arms at his sides, his eyes like hooks that sank into my flesh. He stopped before me, his head angled down to meet my gaze because our height difference was even more apparent in my flats. He was almost a foot and a half taller than me and at least two times my size, maybe even three.

His hand went to my neck, and his thumb traced my bottom lip until it rested in the corner. His hold was firm and threatening, like there was no way I could escape his grasp unless he allowed it. "Last chance, sweetheart." He gave me a harder squeeze, like he expected me to try to leave.

My face turned into his hand, and I kissed his thumb.

His eyes narrowed in a subtle look of desire.

I turned more and kissed the inside of his palm, the callused skin over his fingers. He smelled like a fresh shower with a hint of pine. I gave him my kiss, gave him my body, handed it all over for him to take.

His fingers relaxed as I kissed him, but then they hardened around my neck again as he brought me into him for a deeper kiss. His hand supported the back of my head as he dipped down to kiss me, the Eiffel Tower bending down to kiss the Seine. The disparity in our height made it difficult for us to embrace without my heels, so he scooped me up in his powerful arms and gently lifted me into him, our chests together.

His kiss deepened further, his powerful mouth taking the reins of the embrace. His big hands squeezed my ass as he held me to him, turning his head to kiss me at a different angle, swiping his tongue in my mouth before he breathed his life into me.

I melted like butter in a hot pan, aroused by that momentous kiss, the way he held me so effortlessly because he lifted weights heavier than me every day. My arms hooked around his neck, and I kissed this man with a rush of unbridled passion, the kind of desperation that made my lips quiver, made my knees go weak. He swept me off my feet, literally, and brought me into a clandestine heaven.

Instead of rushing me to the bed, he kissed me like that for a long time, his desire not thwarted by the burden of my weight. He tugged me into him so I could feel the outline of his dick in his sweatpants, the monster cock that was about to pound inside me…if it would fit.

He carried me to the bed then gently laid me down as he rolled on top of me, continuing the kiss because the transition was so smooth. The mattress sank underneath me with his weight, making it dip below me. My legs were still hooked around his hips, and I was anxious for my jeans to come off so I could squeeze the hot skin of his core.

My hands planted on his chest, and I felt stone covered in skin, felt a brick wall that lived and breathed. My mouth continued to cherish his as his hand dug into my hair and fisted it, tightening his hold like there was a chance I would slip away.

My hands reached for his hips and tried to push down his sweatpants, but he was so long, it was hard for me to reach when my crossed ankles sat at the top of his lower back.

He grabbed my shirt and yanked it up to expose my bra. He dipped his head and kissed my sternum as he continued to lift the fabric and draw it up my arms. Then he smothered my tits with kisses as he pulled down the straps of my bra to make them come free.

I tried to reach for his sweatpants again, but they were just out of reach.

He pulled away and rested on the balls of his feet as he unbuttoned my jeans and yanked down the zipper. He tugged them hard, dragging my body along with the jeans before the denim left my hips and ass. He got them to my ankles, and I kicked off my flats, letting them thud against the rug.

He moved for my pink thong and hooked his thumbs in the band before he tugged it free, pulling it down my legs and to my ankles. He left it there before he moved between my legs, his shoulders making themselves at home between my knees as he pressed a gentle kiss to my aching lips.

My back immediately arched when I felt that hot kiss. "God…"

He kissed me the way he kissed my mouth, separating my folds with his tongue and swiping at the anxious nub tucked away. He sucked it hard into his mouth and gave a gentle bite before he moved over me again, reaching behind my back and unclasping the bra so it was finally free.

I was completely naked underneath him, and he pressed a trail of kisses up my body until he made it back to my lips.

I growled into his mouth.

He pulled away slightly and looked into my eyes. "What is it, sweetheart?"

I sat up slightly and forced him back, grabbing his sweatpants and tugging them down.

He smirked, and the twinkle in his eye was brighter than a shooting star—and passed just as quickly. He helped me remove them the rest of the way before his monster cock sprang free, the kind that would stretch the condom until it nearly burst. When he was naked, he moved on top of me again, squeezing between my thighs and pressing his fat dick right against my clit.

I sucked in a deep breath because it felt as good as his kiss.

He ground against me, his face just inches from mine, watching me breathe hard every time he rubbed his hard dick against me, giving me the kind of friction that was better than my hand.

My hands went to his bulging biceps, and I dug my fingers into the skin as he dipped his head and kissed me. His tongue was immediately in my mouth as he ground against me, his length starting to pick up the slickness from my opening and smear it over my clit. Over and over, he did that, pushing the perfect pressure into my nub and making me tighten from the pleasure.

My thighs squeezed his waist, and my locked ankles rested at the top of his ass. I rocked with him, starting to pant into his mouth because it felt so damn good—and he wasn't even inside me yet. This man hadn't even fucked me, but he'd managed to make me come twice.

My nails dug deeper into his skin, and my lips paused our kiss, unable to keep up the movements because all I could think about was the burning pleasure that thudded between my legs.

He stopped and pulled away, taking his hot, throbbing dick away from my clit.

He opened his drawer and rolled a large condom down his length.

It looked even bigger when it was wrapped in latex.

He came back, the mountain of a man casting a shadow over my body as he returned to his position on top of me. He grabbed my legs and tilted my hips, putting me in the position that he wanted me before he guided his dick to my entrance. He pushed right away, applying enormous pressure to my opening, trying to fit a square peg into a circle.

My nails dug into his arms again, and I sucked in a breath when I felt him move forward again, pushing past my opening and forcing himself deeper. He was the biggest I'd ever taken, and it was like experiencing my first time again, the anticipation of the pleasure but also the pain.

He gave another thrust and then finally started to sink, driving his tree trunk deep inside my earth, his midnight-sky eyes watching my reaction to him.

I released a cry when I felt him fully, his enormous girth stretching me as far as I could go. "Fuck…"

He tilted my hips farther, both of his arms pinned behind my knees to keep me open. His eyes were unapologetic even when he caused me pain, his desire written in the hard features of his face. He started to rock into me, moving slowly and giving my body a chance to accept his big dick. "You'll get used to it."

My nails were cutting like knives into his skin, and I breathed deep with every thrust, turned on by the pain because his size was so sexy. The fact that he didn't care that it hurt was sexy too, like he knew I could handle it.

He started to thrust harder, keeping me pinned underneath him, the friction disappearing because I was soaked, a river of arousal dripping down my crack to the duvet below me.

I moaned and panted in his face, feeling the same heat deep in my belly that I felt when his dick was sliding over me. The orgasm approached like a sunrise over the horizon, and it was almost at my front door. "Theo…" Tears burned in my eyes, and I wasn't sure if they were caused by the pain or the pleasure that was about to explode.

He moved faster, a subtle red tint marking his skin, but his breaths didn't increase and the intensity in his eyes didn't wane. "Almost there, sweetheart." He leaned over me farther, our mouths almost close enough to kiss, but he did it to deepen the angle and give me a little more when he thought I could handle it.

I felt the orgasm creep up my body before it wrapped around all my bones like tendrils. The grip tightened, and then it pulled, tugged me into him, into the depths of the blissful abyss. The tears pooled an instant before, and then I came with a whimper and a cry, my nails dragging over his skin and his ink, feeling his dick pound into me harder, ruthlessly, pressing me deeper into the mattress.

It hurt, but fuck, it was the best.

He fucked me hard as I finished, as I rode the waves of pleasure until I hit the shore, a burst of ecstasy that I hadn't felt in a long time. I wasn't sure if it was the size of his dick or the size of the man.

When I finished, the tears dripped from the corners of my eyes and made their way to the duvet underneath.

He gave the sexiest moan before he released, filling the condom inside me, shoving himself as far as he could go and making me wince in the process. He folded my legs a little more, showing me just how flexible I could be for the right man. A flush of red moved across his chest and over his neck. He released a breath before he pulled out of me, his dick as hard as it had been when he'd entered me. He left me on the bed and stepped into the bathroom.

I lay there and felt my body crumple with exhaustion, even though I hadn't done anything except lie there.

Theo walked back into the room a moment later and opened his nightstand. His dick was still rock hard as if nothing had happened, and he rolled another condom over his length. His knees hit the bed again, and the mattress shifted. He must have noticed the surprise in my eyes because he said, "I'm not done with you, sweetheart."

I lay in his big bed tucked under the sheets and listened to the shower run in his bathroom. The room was dark, with the exception of the lamp on his bedside table. The soreness made me ache, but the rush of pleasure that dumped into my blood made my entire body relax like I'd just gotten a spa treatment.

Theo left the bathroom and turned off the light before he approached the bed. He pulled on a pair of black boxers, the material snug on his thick thighs and tight ass. The bulge in the front was substantial, even when his soldier was at rest.

He got into the sheets beside me before his big hand snaked over my belly. The smell of pine came over me, and the heat from his body was like having hot coals in the bed. My arm moved over his, and I felt lighter than air.

"You make it hard to leave." Hard to leave this warm bed and this sexy man.

"Then don't." He lay on his side as he looked at me, his shoulder jutting to the sky like the cliff face of a mountain.

"If you don't take a girl out to dinner, then you probably don't have her sleep over."

He stared at me for a while, his hand still on my stomach. "I'd tell you if I wanted you gone."

Bolton was the only man I'd slept with in years. It should feel weird to sleep beside Theo, but it didn't. His bed felt far more comfortable than mine. Sleeping in that villa all alone felt suffocating. That house felt less like home with every passing day. "I'll leave first thing in the morning."

"You have somewhere to be?"

"I have work at eleven."

"Then that means you have time for breakfast."

"You don't look like you eat breakfast."

He smirked slightly. "I eat two breakfasts, sweetheart." He came closer to me and dragged my body into his, turning me on my side so he spooned me from behind. It was like a heater right up against my back. His arm was tight over my waist like a safety belt from a car.

His face was at the back of my neck, his breaths touching my hair.

It only took a few seconds to feel my mind start to slip. "Goodnight."

"Goodnight, sweetheart."

When I woke up, Theo wasn't there.

The bedroom was vacant but still full of his heavy absence.

I went into his bathroom and got ready for the day, taking out the toiletries from my packed bag, brushing my teeth, and doing my makeup. I'd brought a change of clothes so I could go straight to work after this. I hadn't really planned on a sleepover, but I was prepared for it if it happened.

When I was done, Theo entered the bathroom in just a pair of workout shorts, covered in sweat, his skin tinted red the way it was during sex. His muscles were thicker than normal, plumped with blood and tension from the workout he'd just completed. Without saying a word, he came to me and gave me a quick kiss on the lips. Then he turned on the shower and stripped down to nothing at all before he got in.

I hadn't stopped staring since the moment he'd stepped foot into the room.

Water cascaded down his body as he washed his face and ran the bar of soap over his muscles and chest.

I'd never been jealous of a bar of soap before.

I tried to focus on myself, but I definitely lingered unnecessarily so I could sneak peeks of him. When he used the bar on his junk, my eyes glanced back to watch, to see him clean his monster dick.

He turned off the water and reached for the towel.

I packed up my things and walked out before I made it too obvious that I was a creep.

He came out moments later in his black sweatpants. "Let's go."

I assumed we weren't going out to breakfast because of the way he was dressed, so we must be eating in his dining room. I grabbed my bag so I wouldn't have to double back for it. When I looked at my phone, I had no missed texts or calls.

In the hallway, he took the bag off my shoulder and carried it for me.

His dining room was a big space with high ceilings and open windows. It was beautiful, a long table that could accommodate twenty guests even though he seemed like someone who rarely had company.

He sat at the head of the table.

I set my bag in the seat beside me and sat down.

George already had a pot of coffee on the table along with cream and sugar, so we each had a cup. Theo took it black like his eyes, and I drenched mine in cream. Then George brought out breakfast, an egg-white omelet and strips of bacon for Theo, while I had a plate of pancakes and a savory crêpe topped with ratatouille.

We ate in silence.

"So, when do you have a second breakfast?"

"This is second breakfast." He ate with his arms on the table. "I have a shake while I work out."

"That's not breakfast." I took a bite of my buttery pancakes and wished I could eat like this every day. We could afford help if we wanted to, but it was something neither of us cared for. But now that I'd had it, I had a different opinion about it.

"It has calories. And I have to eat four thousand calories a day."

"What?" I almost dropped my fork.

He continued to eat like that number wasn't crazy. "That's what I need to maintain my size."

"I wish I could eat four thousand calories a day."

"It sounds better than it is. I have to eat two breakfasts and two lunches."

"Oh, poor you."

He smirked before he took a bite.

I loved his seriousness, but those little smiles were something else. "These pancakes are fire."

"My chef is from Paris."

"Must be nice to have someone cook for you."

"I don't have the time," he said. "Do you cook?"

"Yes, most of the time."

"What do you make?"

Talking about the dinners I made for Bolton should make me feel like shit, but I felt nothing. "I made braised chicken and artichokes the other day. Mostly casseroles and one-pot dishes so I have less to clean."

"Between work and cooking, when do you find time to paint?"

I gave a shrug. "I haven't painted in a while."

"That's what you should be focusing on."

I looked down at my pancakes. "My paintings aren't very good."

"How will they get better if you don't keep painting?"

"Theo, you're sweet—"

"I'm not being sweet. If you want to be a painter, then paint. It's that simple."

"Making art is more complicated."

"Nothing is complicated if you have discipline."

I set my fork down and looked at him. "I think you're being a little pushy."

"You need a push, sweetheart. You said it's your passion in life. So, either do it...or accept that it's not your passion." His elbows were on the table, and he looked at me as he held his fork in his grasp. "Except the second option isn't really an option."

I looked down at my plate again, my crêpe half-eaten. I didn't usually eat breakfast, and I forgot how scrumptious it could be.

He let it go. "Are you free tonight?"

My gaze returned to his. "I haven't even left, and you want to see me again?" I didn't know where this relationship with Theo would lead, but I did wonder if he would drop me after we fucked. After he got what he wanted, he might lose interest and turn his attention elsewhere.

He took a drink of his coffee. "Is that a yes?"

Bolton wouldn't be home until tomorrow afternoon. "Yes, I'm free."

"Then come by after work."

I'd expected to spend my night alone, but I had another night with this man, another evening with his warmth and affection. That filled me with a jolt of excitement that I didn't anticipate feeling. He fucked me good and left me satisfied, but it only made me want more. "Alright."

I usually enjoyed being at work, but now, it felt like a drag. One of my regular clients came in to see the new shipment of artwork we received, and normally, I was excited for these kinds of days, but all I could think about was the man who had asked me to sleep over another night. Nothing else seemed to matter.

The hours dragged by, and finally, five o'clock arrived.

I texted him when I got to the car. *You still want me to come over?*

His attitude was in full force. *Did I say otherwise?*

Okay. I'm on my way.

Good.

I drove to his villa then parked in the parking garage, in the same spot I'd left that morning. I took the elevator and entered his dark and brooding villa, the place that was always quiet, like a beast lurked on the top floor and never left.

I didn't see George, so I made my way upstairs, assuming that was where Theo was. I entered his primary suite and found that it'd been tidied while I was out for the day. All the surfaces were shiny, like they'd been dusted. His bed was made, and the pillows were fluffed.

But there was no Theo.

I entered the room with his bed and stopped when I spotted the new addition to the furniture. An easel with a blank canvas was sitting there. Paints and brushes were placed on a table beside the stool. It was on top of a black rug, something to capture the spilled paint and protect the hardwood floor underneath. The curtains were open, showing the fading light as the winter sun set.

On the table was a note written in a man's handwriting. *Sit your ass down and get to it. I'll see you at dinner.* I read the note multiple times, absorbing his handwriting and the words he'd written by hand, hearing his powerful voice in my head.

I set the note aside and stared at the blank canvas, releasing a slow breath when I felt the daunting task in front of me. It'd been a while since I'd felt creative in any capacity. After Bolton asked for an open marriage, everything in me felt stunted. I took a seat and noticed the apron sitting there, crisp and white, ready to be destroyed by paint. I decided to take off my clothes so I wouldn't ruin them, leaving only my thong on, and then got to work.

I didn't hear Theo when he walked in. I felt him when he drew close enough.

In just his sweatpants, he came close, examining the canvas that was now splashed with color. His arms crossed over his chest as he looked at it.

"It's nowhere near done." It didn't look like much right now because I layered the background with color, trying to capture the dining room with the window in the background, the chandelier hanging from the ceiling. "I start on the outside and work my way in."

He didn't compliment my work and give me false praise. "How long does it take to make a painting?"

"It's different every time, but at least a week for me."

He gave a slight nod. "Are you hungry?"

"Always. Since I don't eat four thousand calories."

His eyes shifted to me with a hint of amusement.

"Where were you?"

"In the study."

"Working?"

"Always." He stepped away and opened one of his drawers to pull a black shirt over his head. "Where do you want to go?"

"Do we have to go anywhere?" I untied the apron and set it on the table. There were a couple spots of paint on my skin, a spot of champagne gold that I'd used on the chandelier. When I sat across from him at dinner, all I could think about was digging my fingers into his dark hair and feeling him thrust inside me. He seemed to be a beautiful and complex person on the inside, but he was so damn pretty on the outside too.

He turned back to me and subtly looked me up and down. "I'll tell George."

I walked away from the easel and made my way toward him, stepping off the rug and feeling the hardwood floor underneath me.

His eyes were down on my tits, watching the way my body moved as I drew close. Like a lion that studied the movement of his prey, he looked like he would strike at any moment, get me tight in his jaws and never let go.

My hands planted on his hard stomach when I was close enough, feeling the hard muscles under the searing-hot skin. I felt his abs, all eight of them, my eyes tracing the lines that separated each one. "That was thoughtful of you."

He continued to stare at me, his muscular arms at his sides.

"Why do you care whether I paint or not?"

That intense stare continued, seeming to be so lost in my face that he hadn't heard what I said. "I'm not a plotter or a thinker. I just do shit. Wanted to help you do the same."

"If you aren't strategic, doesn't that get you killed in your line of work?"

"Am I dead?" he asked seriously, like he really wanted an answer.

My eyes moved to my fingertips at the top of his sternum.

"I do things when I want to do them—and there's no way for my enemy to anticipate that." His arm curled around my waist and rested on the small of my back before he moved to my ass. Effortlessly, he lifted me to him, bringing our faces level so neither one of us had to crane our necks.

His dark eyes took mine in, always looking at me like it really was the first time he saw me.

"I wish I were a little taller." I was five-three, a valley compared to his mountain.

"I think you're perfect."

"You have to pick me up every time we stand together."

"You weigh nothing, sweetheart." He started to move me to the bed, just as he did last night, showing no signs of strain from holding the weight from my belly and ass. Instead of rolling me onto the bed, he placed me on the edge before he dropped his bottoms, showing that fat dick.

I immediately stared at it, still sore from the night before but too anxious to stop it.

He rolled the latex down his length then tugged me to the edge, gripping me by the backs of my thighs. He licked two of his fingers before he slid them inside me, invading me in a slick motion like he was already innately familiar with my body. Then his thumb started to work my clit at the same time, pulsing and rubbing, making me draw breath between my clenched teeth.

He stared at my face as he continued to finger me, his fingers getting soaked in the arousal that started to flow to my entrance. He smeared it onto his thumb then used that as lube over my clit.

The size of his dick became less of a concern as I ached for him.

He finally pulled his fingers away then guided himself inside me, having to push and wait like last time before slowly sinking inside. He was too big to go balls deep, but he put himself as deep as my body would allow. His big hands pushed back my thighs, and he thrust into me hard the second my body was ready, rather than giving me time to acclimate. This time, he just took me.

Took me hard.

George delivered dinner to the dining table in Theo's bedroom. There was a bottle of wine and two glasses, along with a little vase of pink roses to place in the center. Once he finished setting it up, he silently dismissed himself and left Theo's room.

Instead of taking the head of the table, Theo sat across from me and removed the silver cover of his dish, revealing a roast chicken cooked in a white sauce along with a side of roasted vegetables.

My dinner was different, a plate of pasta with shaved truffles along with a sliced baguette. Both meals looked great, and I was happy to eat either one. "Why do I get pasta and bread, and you get meat and vegetables?"

"Because I need the protein, and you don't." He dropped the linen and sliced into his meat. "I can split this with you or have George bring you the same thing."

"Oh no," I said quickly. "I'm very happy with this. Was just curious."

He ate with his elbows on the table, sometimes having good table manners and sometimes eating like a caveman. Whenever we were out at dinner, he was more refined, but in his own home, he seemed to disregard dinner table etiquette.

We ate in silence, the bedroom quiet because we were above the street and the windows were probably double-paned. It was just the sound of utensils tapping against the white plates. It was very different from eating at a restaurant, where the sound of nearby conversation filled the room like a quiet hum.

My life had changed so drastically in the last few weeks. A month ago, I couldn't imagine ever being with anyone else but Bolton, but now I sat across from a drop-dead gorgeous man who wasn't my husband—and it didn't bother me.

He chewed his bite as he stared at me. When he was finished, he spoke. "You're different."

My eyes hardened on his face. "I'm different?"

He nodded and took another bite.

"How?"

"You're a lot more relaxed." He grabbed his glass and drank the white wine that George had paired with the meal. "You've finally let me see you, all of you."

Because my mind wasn't riddled with guilt, anger, and self-loathing. Now, I lived in the moment without hesitation.

"Did something change?"

I didn't want to talk about Bolton when I was with Theo. But he was a constant presence in our lives. It was like we were having an affair, only we weren't. When I was with Theo, my husband was with someone else. "My husband has embraced the arrangement, so I decided to do the same."

He took a break from his dinner and watched me instead, trying to read all the layers of emotion in my gaze.

"He's noticed I've been distant. Closed off. Cold. Said we could stop the arrangement and go back to what we used to be, but…" I looked at the gorgeous man across from me, the man who seemed to fill the void that my husband had left in my heart. "That meant I'd have to give you up, and I didn't want to." Bolton's infidelity suddenly stung less because Theo numbed it with kisses. The depth of the loss had shallowed because Theo had filled it with his presence.

He smirked slightly.

"What?"

"He's a fucking idiot."

The defensive side of me came to the surface to defend Bolton's honor, but I never voiced it because it felt stupid to do so.

He grabbed his glass and took another drink. "But I'm glad he's an idiot."

10

THEO

The waitress took us to a table, the restaurant dark due to its aesthetic, the chandeliers glowing as they hung from the vaulted ceilings.

We sat down, and the waitress placed the menus in front of us before she walked away.

Axel immediately grabbed the menu. "I wonder what the specials are."

"You don't know?"

He shook his head. "All I know is whatever I pick, it's gonna be *goooood*." He turned the menu over to check the back, but it was blank.

"Can't she just cook for you at home?"

He chuckled. "With two demons running around? I wish."

"Is Dante watching them tonight?"

"Yep. Good ol' Grandpa."

"He doesn't seem like the babysitting type."

"Well, he knows he's our full-time babysitter for all the shit he pulled." He looked at the menu again. "I might get one of those smoked old fashioneds. You know, where they take off the glass, and then all the smoke comes out...pretty cool."

"I'll get one too."

The waitress returned, and we ordered our drinks.

"What are the specials?" Axel asked.

The waitress listed the three, one with fish, a short rib ravioli, and then a vegetarian couscous dish.

"Hmm." Axel looked at the menu. "Fuck, what am I gonna do?"

"It's a big decision," I said sarcastically. "Take your time."

"What are you getting, asshole?"

"Probably the chicken. I like the sauce she makes."

Axel continued to look at the menu. "This is hard."

The waitress returned with our drinks, and when she removed the glass covering, the smoke rose.

"That's sick." Axel brought the glass to his lips and took a drink.

Ever since Axel had settled down and left the game, he'd become more childlike, caring about things that he would have found insignificant beforehand. We had less in common now, but our bond was still tight like a taut rubber band.

"How are your parents?" I asked.

He shrugged. "Things are good, but it'll always be a little...strained. You know? They feel guilty, but there are times when I get pissed off about the whole thing. And then I need space. I don't think it'll ever be what it used to be. It's been too long, and too much shit has happened. But I'm happy that we've buried the hatchet, so I don't have to feel guilty when they're gone."

"Yeah."

"I'm not the type to hold a grudge, but this one is hard to let go."

"That's fair."

He looked at the menu again. "Fuck, I gotta figure this out."

"Why don't you take something to go?"

He looked up at me and gave me a slow nod. "You're a smart man, Theo. Very smart."

"I know."

He chuckled slightly and looked at the menu again.

"Why is she working tonight anyway? She's the owner. Shouldn't someone else be slaving away back there?"

"She likes to come down a couple nights a month. It's the best way to see how the restaurant's doing. She likes cooking and being a part of the team. And I think the biggest reason is she gets tired of being a full-time mom. I think she likes to have some space and do her own thing."

I nodded in agreement.

"I love my babies more than life itself, but they really changed everything. Though, the idea of them needing me less as they get older fills me with a sadness that hurts more than a bullet in the arm."

Once upon a time, I wanted a family. The quiet life that he had. But now, I couldn't imagine it ever. I was exactly where I belonged. This was the path I was destined to take. What happened in the past…was just a lapse in judgment.

When the waitress came back, Axel ordered two things, one to take home.

"I'll take the chicken." I handed over the menu.

Now that the stressful part of the evening had passed, Axel sipped his drink and relaxed. "How are things with Astrid?"

"It's not a relationship, Axel."

"Did I say it was?"

"It's implied."

"Fine," he said. "How's your little affair going?"

"It's not an affair if her husband knows about it."

He cocked his head. "But does he know about it?"

I had no idea what she told him. It was none of my business.

"I think if he knew, you would know," he said. "You aren't the least bit curious who he is?"

"No." I had no respect for him for hurting his wife the way he did. She was one hell of a catch, and he was an idiot to squander her. She deserved better, and it was a shame she didn't believe that herself.

"You guys never talk about him?"

"She said she doesn't want to talk about him. And when I'm fucking a woman, I don't like to think about other men—or other men she may be fucking."

"If you didn't care about her, you wouldn't care if she's fucking someone else."

"I never said I cared that she is," I snapped. "I just don't want to think about it while it's happening." I grabbed my glass and took a drink, finding the smoke taste tame compared to the heaviness of a cigar.

"How long do you think this is going to go on?"

I shrugged.

"You aren't really a one-woman kind of guy, so this is interesting."

"Who said I'm a one-woman kind of guy now?"

"So you're sleeping with other people?" he asked incredulously.

No. "Yes." I looked him right in the eye and lied to his face, something I'd never done before. "Her husband is only gone a couple days a week, so the rest of that time, we don't speak."

He gave a slight nod in understanding. "You want my advice?"

"Not even a little bit, Axel."

He acted like I hadn't spoken and continued. "At some point, this guy is gonna figure out who's fucking his wife. I don't care if he asked for an open marriage. When he realizes his woman is fucking none other than the infamous Skull King, it's gonna dent his ego quite a bit. It's gonna open a can of gunfire and grenades. You've got enough on your plate, Theo. You don't need this added to the top. So, if this woman really means nothing to you, then ditch her before it's too late."

"You think I'm afraid of anyone, Axel?"

"No," he said. "But I know you don't like bullshit, and this sounds like it could be *a lot* of bullshit."

"I'm not worried about it."

"Because you like her—"

"*Axel.*" I gave him a glare across the table. "I don't do back-to-backs because I'm not interested in having any kind of a relationship with a woman. And even though they say they're fine with that, they're *never* fine with that. They sleep over once and then try to leave their shit there so they have a reason to come back. But this is a unique situation because she's married, and I like that she's married because it makes my life a lot simpler. I can have a relationship with her without having to deal with all the bullshit that comes with an actual relationship, like commitment, the future, all that nonsense. Maybe I'll have to deal with her husband at some point, but that's a much simpler problem than dealing with a woman asking me to be something more than a fuck buddy."

Axel listened to all of that with a straight face then gave a nod. "So, you do want a relationship."

"Did you not listen to what I just said—"

"*I can have a relationship with her without having to deal with all the bullshit of an actual relationship. That's what you just said.*"

My eyes narrowed.

"I just don't want you to get hurt, man. You've been hurt once…and you've never gotten over it."

I grabbed my glass and took another drink, washing down the annoyance and the anger.

"Think about what I said. Let this go on too long, and it's gonna be more trouble than it's worth." He was probably going to say more, but then the waitress arrived with our plates. She set them down in front of each of us before she walked away.

Axel looked down at his steaming hot food. "Damn, this looks good." He grabbed his fork and dug in. "I still would have married her even if her pussy weren't so damn pretty, because that hot piece of ass knows her way around a kitchen."

When we were finished and Axel had his to-go container with his other meal, Scarlett emerged from the back, her hair pulled back in a bun so it could be tucked underneath her chef's hat. She didn't wear her apron, but she had splashes of food on her shirt and jeans like a mess was unavoidable during the dinnertime rush.

I saw her first and smirked as she approached.

"You like your food, boys?"

"Yes," I said. "Axel said he still would have married you even if your pussy weren't so pretty because you can cook so well."

Scarlett crossed her arms and gave Axel a hard stare.

"Baby, come on," Axel said. "Guys talk."

"About *that*?" she asked, shocked.

"I've only said good things," he said. "*Very* good things."

Her angry look was already waning.

He rose from his chair and pulled her close for a kiss, not the least bit dissuaded by the daggers in her eyes or how hot and sweaty she looked. His hand snaked down to her ass, and he gripped it in view of all the tables like she wore a black cocktail dress instead of jeans. "Some guys brag about money, some brag about their cars, and I like to brag about you."

She planted her hand on his chest and gently pushed him back. "I should get back."

"Come on, baby," Axel said. "Have a drink."

"I can't," she said. "They need me in the kitchen."

"You own the place. You can do whatever you want."

"I'll see you at home, okay?" She gave him a quick kiss before she walked off.

Axel watched her go, staring at her ass until she was officially out of sight. "Thanks for throwing me under the bus."

"You needed to be taught a lesson."

"What lesson?"

"Not to talk about your woman's bits to other men."

"You aren't other men. You're my brother."

I'd once gone on a date with her, and she could have shown me those bits at the end of the night if I'd let it happen. But I was too loyal to Axel to hurt him like that. He seemed to have forgotten all of that over the years because he didn't appear to see me as a threat anymore. For at least a year, he'd been visibly uncomfortable whenever we were in the same room together, when I just hugged her.

"You want to hit up a bar?" Axel asked.

"Don't you have to get home to the kids?"

"Nope. *Grandpa's* on the clock until I'm good and ready."

I never texted Astrid whenever she'd said she wouldn't be available for a while. It was an open marriage, but a marriage all the same, and I respected the boundaries that she'd never laid out. During those breaks, she belonged to him—and I accepted that.

I dropped my responsibilities when she was free, so when she was unavailable, I threw myself back into work. A lot of shit required my attention that I'd blown off to give my full attention to her. I had two motherfuckers to kill, and it was time to get my hands bloody.

"One of our snitches in the Brotherhood says Bolton usually wines and dines his clients at a few favorite spots across Europe," Octavio said. "And I guess he's got a big contract with Claude Vanderbilt. He wants a lot of people dead."

Claude was in the trafficking game. He had a worldwide organization that operated in several countries. He was always changing his tactics and channels because the authorities were always hot on his tail. He'd managed to shake them for decades, always one step ahead. "You really have to be a scumbag to take a contract from that asshole." I smoked my cigar as I sat across from him at the table. "Who does he want dead?"

"I'm not sure, but he's got a list," Octavio said. "Our informant says they're supposed to meet for dinner next week to finalize the details."

"Out in the open?"

"I guess Bolton considers public dining a flex."

"What did Fender say?"

Octavio sat on the couch with a cigar between his fingertips. "He would ask some old contacts what they know—but only as a favor to you. He said he's made it very clear he's walked away."

"That's bullshit," I said. "He knows you're never really out once you're in."

"He said he'll call you when he knows something."

"Good." I took another puff of the cigar and let the smoke rise to the ceiling. It'd been almost a week since I'd spoken to Astrid, and the withdrawals had started to kick in. I didn't have a replacement in my bed, so when she was gone, I was alone. She probably fucked her husband when we were apart, so she didn't feel the same drought.

Octavio left, and I remained in the armchair, looking at the painting across from me, the painting of the changeling. I'd stared at it so many times but continued to see new details. It was a creature clearly out of place, so distinct it couldn't blend into the world it was supposed to invade, and that was exactly how I felt every day of my fucking life.

I used to be someone else, but I'd changed.

I'd changed a long time ago, ten years, a fucking decade...but I still remembered.

I also saw *her* when I looked at the painting, someone who was forced to change against her will. But then she embraced that change—and made it her own.

At that moment, my phone lit up with a message. It wasn't from one of my guys or Axel.

It was her.

What are you doing?

I hated open-ended questions like that, but it didn't

feel like a nuisance coming from her. *Staring at your paintings.*

Would you like to stare at something else?

My cock instantly came alive in my sweatpants, picturing her bent over the couch with her beautiful ass on display, looking back at me with a sexy taunt. *Get over here.* It'd been the longest stretch of silence we'd had. So long, I'd started to wonder if she and her husband had decided to be monogamous again. Would she let me know? Or was I unworthy of a notice of eviction?

Should I pack a bag?

You don't need clothes in my house—if that answers your question.

Her messages went silent, and her dots disappeared.

My attention turned back to the painting once more... and I waited.

It seemed like she'd gone through a dry spell as well because she was all over me the second she walked inside. She rose on her tallest tiptoes and reached her arms around my neck as far as the distance would allow. Her lips were anxious on mine, kissing me like a lover she hadn't seen in months rather than days.

I hated to bend my neck down so far or strain hers in the opposite direction, so I scooped her into my arms and elevated her to my height, holding her like she weighed nothing, my hands gripping that summer-peach of an ass.

She hooked her arms fully around my neck, and she kissed me slowly but passionately, giving me her tongue before I could give her mine. Her fingers dug into my hair, and she pressed her tits against my bare chest. "I missed you." She spoke against my lips, barely breaking our embrace to whisper those words to me, like the last thing she wanted was a response.

I sat in the middle of the couch and felt her weight on my lap, my hard dick like a log of firewood between us. If she dragged her pussy down fast enough, she would light the match and burn us with the flames.

I yanked her jacket off her arms then tugged her shirt over her head, revealing the black bra that pushed her tits together and made a noticeable line of cleavage in the center. For a woman so small, she had an impressive rack. My dick complemented my size, but she was the opposite.

I unclasped the bra and let her tits come free, the little nipples in the centers hard like diamonds. I palmed one in my hand before I leaned in and sprinkled her neck with my hard kisses, smelling the scent that clung to my sheets after she left.

Her arms hooked around my neck, and she brought us close together, her nipples dragging against my bare chest, warm and soft like rose petals. Her mouth came down on mine, and she kissed me with a moan, drunk on the wine of our passion.

My dick was so fucking hard.

I paid women a lot of money to give me head like it was their damn honor, but she was more enthused than all of them combined. Whenever I was in the mood to fuck a woman in the ass, I paid for that, because no woman wanted my big dick at their back entrance unless they were being paid a fortune to tolerate it.

But based on the way she wanted me, she might do it for free.

I tugged my sweatpants and boxers down so my dick was free then helped her get her jeans and panties off. Piece by piece, everything came off, and then it was just us together, skin to skin, heat against heat.

She lifted herself and pointed me at her entrance.

I grabbed her hips and steadied her when I felt the warmth of her soft folds directly against my skin. "Slow down, sweetheart." As much as I wanted to fuck her without a condom, that simply wasn't possible for us. I hadn't gone bareback with a woman in ten years. I'd forgotten how good it was...until the head of my dick grazed her entrance.

I pulled a wrapper from the pocket of my sweatpants then rolled the condom down to my base, leaving plenty of room at the tip because she always made me come hard. I guided her back onto me and pulled her down, sealing my head in the tight entrance before I tugged her down, forcing my way into her tightness the way Alexander the Great forced his way into Persia. My hands gripped her ass, and I brought her farther down, stopping when I felt the limit. I couldn't fit fully inside her, but I couldn't recall a time I could fit fully inside any woman. Being well-endowed made it easy to bring a woman to a climax, but I wished I could pound into a woman until I was balls deep.

Her breathing picked up, and she planted her palms against my chest to balance herself. There was a wince in her expression and a crack in her voice when she slid as far as she could go, feeling the pain of my intrusion but not asking me to stop. Her nails clawed into me slightly, like a cat about to take a deadly swipe in a fight.

Against the back of the couch, I looked at the petite woman on my lap, the sexy little thing who knew how to fuck. Why her husband wanted to fuck other women besides her was beyond me. My hands squeezed the perfect ass I wanted to take a bite out of, and I slowly lifted her up, bringing her back to my head before lowering her down again. One of my arms was almost the size of her head, and I lifted tractor tires as part of my workout, so Astrid was like a five-pound dumbbell in comparison. I lifted her up again, my fingers sprawled out across her ass cheeks, sliding in and out of her tightness.

Her hands were planted against my chest for support as she rose up and down, rolling her hips at the end to catch my length nice and deep. Confidence and desire burned in her eyes like my fireplace in the midst of winter, her voice crackling as she consumed the log between her legs. Her breaths grew deeper as she continued to move, more enthused but also tired from lifting herself up so high and never letting herself rest on her way down—otherwise, my dick would hurt too much.

I started to do more of the work and lifted her with my arms, not that I minded. Having her little body on top of my mine, squeezing my fat dick into her little channel, was damn sexy. Soon, we were both flushed red with arousal, her breaths shaky, my nostrils flared, the pleasure so good it made us both tighten.

I knew she was almost there. I'd fucked her enough times to notice all her tells. The way she bit her bottom lip more and more. The way her nipples hardened even though the temperature of the room rose to a sweltering heat. We moved harder and faster together, and my cock was anxious to fill the tip of the condom, but damn, what I wouldn't give to fill her little pussy with everything I had, to make myself at home in another man's palace.

Just when the fire spiked in my veins, her nails started to drag across my chest, and she squeezed me with the strength of a boa constrictor, gripping my dick harder than a man's handshake. There were tears and whimpers, marks on my skin from her scratches, echoes of her pleasure bouncing off all of my walls.

I couldn't take it anymore. Her natural sultriness, the deep curve in her back, the way she loved it when my dick hurt. She'd been all over me the moment she'd walked in the door—and now her cream was all over me too. I could feel it building up on my balls. I tugged her up and down harder, my breaths elevated in a heated frenzy.

"Fuck, your dick is even bigger."

I didn't need another reason to come, but she gave me a reason to come harder. I gripped her and forced her down onto my length, ignoring the hiss of pain from between her clenched teeth. My cock twitched and throbbed as it filled the condom that caught my seed, but I pretended it wasn't there, that it was just me and her.

Our dirty plates from dinner were in the other room behind the closed door. I'd sent off a text to George a while ago to let him know he could come fetch it. Like a mouse, he moved in and out without making a sound.

The curtains were still open, and rain splattered the window, the little drops like music in the quiet room. I lay in bed with Astrid, her beautiful body naked beside mine under the sheets. Her bag was on the armchair in the corner.

Her eye makeup was smeared from the various rendezvous that had taken place from the study to the bedroom, and even though she would probably be mortified if she knew how she looked, there was something about it that I liked. Maybe because I was the reason the black color bled down her face... because of the tears.

I liked her without makeup too, first thing in the morning after she woke up. Her eyes looked different when they were well-rested. They had a different kind of shine to them, like the morning light on a summer day.

All those thoughts swirled through my head as I stared at her.

Her eyes gently flicked back and forth between mine as she absorbed my stare the way a cat absorbed the sun. "Can I ask you something?"

"Yes." My eyes were still focused on her face, her high cheekbones, her full lips. She was a painter, but she could easily be the subject of any masterpiece. I could picture her in a painting, her naked body wrapped up in cream-colored sheets, looking out the window as the sun poked through the rain clouds.

"Has...your size been an issue before?"

"My size?" My thoughts were elsewhere, imagining that painting on my wall in my study, her beauty replacing the haunting imaging of the changeling.

"You know..." She glanced down to the sheets at my waist.

It took me a moment to understand. "It's not for everyone."

"So, it's affected your relationships?"

"I would say it's affected my fees." I'd only been in one relationship my whole life, and she'd handled it like a pro.

"Your fees?"

"What escorts charge me."

She gave a slow nod. "Aren't those women professionals?"

"Yes. But depending on what I want, they need to be fairly compensated." I had more money than I could spend, so I didn't care about the price. Perhaps that was why I was a popular client. I'd heard through the grapevine that some of the escorts fought over who got to service me if one of my preferred escorts was unavailable.

"Like what?"

"Well, I like to fuck a woman in the ass. That's a big ask in my circumstance."

The discomfort was in her eyes, so my choice of partners still bothered her. She did her best to hide it, but I knew her tells too well now. "I see." Her eyes traveled slightly down, looking at my chest instead of my eyes, her thoughts drifting elsewhere.

"I'd love to fuck you in the ass."

Her eyes immediately shot back to mine.

"If you're into that."

"I-I don't think I am."

"It sounds like you've never done it."

The hesitation remained in her eyes. "No. It's never come up."

"Good to know."

Her eyes were on mine, like she wanted to say something, but she chose to keep it to herself.

"Does my size bother you?"

"No," she said immediately. "I just wish… Never mind."

"Tell me."

"It doesn't matter—"

"Tell me."

Her eyes turned away again. "I just wish we didn't have to wear anything. It's been a long time since I've done the condom thing, and it would be nice to really feel you."

Heat flushed through my body because just the thought enticed my flesh. I couldn't remember how good it felt because it'd been so long. Even with escorts who insisted they were clean, I still wore protection because you couldn't always trust a sex worker.

"To feel you come inside me…"

I released a slow breath as my chest tightened, the taunt hitting me deep in my bones. It was practically dirty talk. But if her husband was sleeping around and coming home to her, it was too risky. "That would be nice."

"Maybe...we could do that?" She looked at me with an air of hopefulness.

My eyes watched hers. "No."

"My husband has always been a clean freak. I'm not worried about him—"

"No."

Her eyes shifted away. "Because you're sleeping with other people..."

I let her make that assumption because it was better for her to believe that lie than to know the truth. "As much as I wish things were different, they aren't." My hand slid into her hair, and I cradled her face close to mine, her neck so small I could snap it in two with just my grip. "But it's enough."

My alarm didn't wake her up the next morning.

My sleep schedule was all over the place because sometimes I was up at the crack of dawn, and sometimes I was out all night. Instead of embracing sleep as a necessity, I regarded it as a luxury, one of the few luxuries I couldn't afford.

The sound didn't wake her up, and I hit the gym down the hall. Instead of taking the time to travel to the gym every morning, George had had a private gym built into my home, so my commute was a short walk. I never had to wait to use a machine or weight set. It was all for me, and that made it easier to maintain the standards I set for myself. It was a lot easier to scare the shit out of grown men when you were nearly two hundred and fifty pounds of muscle.

When I came back to the bedroom, she was still in bed, right in the center like it was her place instead of mine. The sheets were pulled over her shoulders, and she was on my pillow, like she reached for me absent-mindedly while she slept.

I got into the shower and prepared for the day. I shaved at the sink and dried off before I walked into the bedroom.

She was awake, sitting at the stool in front of her partially completed artwork, wearing nothing but her underwear and the stained apron George had provided for her. Her hair was pulled back in a light bun to keep it out of her face, the sunlight coming through the windows because she'd opened the curtains. She didn't notice me right away, not until I opened the drawer of my dresser and pulled out a pair of boxers. "Morning."

"Morning." I walked over to her and looked at the painting, seeing the vague details of a woman sitting in a café alone, rain splattered all over the windows beside her. It was hazy, and the table was floating without legs. There wasn't a lot of context to the moment—but there was a moment.

"I'm still working on it." She cleaned her brush in the water.

"I like what I see."

She forced a smile. "You're sweet."

"I'm not the kind of man who says what you want to hear, sweetheart."

She set down the brush and looked up at me.

"Just remember that." I leaned down and pressed a soft kiss to her lips.

Her eyes closed slowly and stayed that way when I pulled away. It took her a second to overcome the heat in our kiss, despite how short and simple it was. The intensity I felt, she felt it too. She looked away, cleared her throat, and then rose to remove her apron. Her bag was on the chair, so she opened it and looked through the clothes inside.

"Work at eleven?"

"No. I'm off today, actually." She pulled out a pair of jeans and a bra.

"Then where are you going?"

She stilled at my question before she turned to look at me. "I don't assume I'm going to stay here every time I come over—"

"You should." I opened a drawer and pulled a shirt over my head. "Hungry?"

Color moved into her cheeks, her blush pink like the roses hanging from windows in Paris. "I mean...I'm always hungry."

"Good."

She set her clothes down and walked up to me, naked except for the little black thong she wore. Her hand slid up my chest and my neck until she cupped my face. Then she rose on her tiptoes to kiss me, holding my face in a passionate embrace. "But for my first breakfast...I want you."

11

ASTRID

Theo let the valet take the Range Rover, and we stepped into the restaurant, the place covered in black wallpaper, with chandeliers hanging from the ceiling. The lobby had waiters presenting hors d'oeuvres and flutes of champagne like it was an event rather than a restaurant.

Theo walked up to the host stand. "Table for two, please."

"Do you have a reservation?" the hostess asked.

"No." Theo looked at her like that didn't matter.

"I'm sorry, sir," she said. "We're fully committed."

"Trust me, it's fine."

Did he own this place too?

"*Sir*," she repeated with more attitude. "I said we're fully committed."

"Anna, it's fine." The woman I'd met at the restaurant a couple weeks ago came to the front, dressed in all black with heels, looking like a supermodel once again. "Hey, Theo." She smirked as she looked at him. "No reservation, huh?"

He smirked back. "Thought my sister could help me out."

She did a quick scan in the computer. "Are you fine with a small table?"

"You know I'm not picky."

She spoke to the hostess. "I'll have the guys grab a table and chairs from the back. Seat them in section twelve."

"Sure thing," the hostess said without a hint of attitude now.

"It'll be just a few minutes," Scarlett said before she stepped aside at the counter and opened a binder. She snuck a look at me, and when I caught her stare, she smiled. "Nice to see you again."

"You too." I smiled back.

Theo put his hand on the small of my back and guided me away from the congestion of the entry. A few moments later, our table was ready, and Theo took the lead and pulled out my chair when we arrived.

The table was small and tucked into a corner, but it was definitely quieter.

Theo glanced at his menu for two seconds, as if that was all it took to find what he wanted.

"You like this place?"

"I love it."

"This is the first restaurant you've taken me to that you don't own."

"Guess it's time I stop being cheap." He gave a slight smirk before it disappeared.

The waitress came over, and he ordered an old fashioned.

I ordered a glass of wine.

Then it was just the two of us again. "You know what you're getting?"

"The chicken. I had it a couple nights ago and haven't stopped thinking about it."

I immediately pictured him at dinner with some other woman he'd taken out to eat. She wore a skintight black dress like Scarlett and drank scotch like a man. But then I remembered he said he didn't take women out to dinner, and I realized my jealousy had reared its ugly head out of nowhere. "I'll have to try it."

"Get something else, and we'll share."

"What do you recommend?"

"Axel almost ordered everything on the menu, so I'd say you're safe with anything."

"Is that who you came here with?"

He nodded. "Scarlett was the head chef for the night, so he wanted to eat here."

"Doesn't she cook at home?"

"I asked the same thing, but I guess she doesn't cook a lot these days with two kids running around. Best time to get some of her cooking is when she's at the restaurant. He got one entrée to eat in the restaurant and one to go."

I smiled. "That's cute."

"He's definitely her biggest fan."

"I love that."

The waitress returned with our drinks then asked for our orders. Theo stuck to his decision with the chicken, so I opted for a pasta. Then we were left alone again, the two of us in the back corner, the sound of chitchat coming from behind me.

When he removed the glass cover from his drink, a billow of smoke rose toward the ceiling. He breathed in the smoke like it was air then took a drink. "It's a drink and a cigar in one."

"Two bullets, one heart."

He cocked his head slightly.

"Something my husband says." I wished I'd just lied and said I'd heard it somewhere else, but I wasn't the kind of person who could just bullshit off the cuff. "Two birds, one stone. Basically the same thing."

He grabbed his glass and took another drink, letting my words settle into the silence.

I waited for the awkwardness to dissipate like the cloud of smoke had. It took a long time for it to move, but eventually, it did. "You like this place, then?"

"Scarlett is a talented chef."

"Did she train anywhere?"

"No. She's a natural. Just how you're a natural painter."

A flush of heat entered my neck and cheeks. "You've barely seen my work."

"But I can see what you're trying to capture."

"What am I trying to capture?" I asked.

He stared at me across the table for a long time, his fingers around the cool glass. "Grief."

A pain shot through my chest and both arms, like I'd been caught with one hand in the candy jar. My face remained as stoic as ever, but I felt a sudden panic deep inside me. Like my lies had been spilled. My truth had been told. "Why do you think that?"

"Because I can see it." He hadn't blinked since the start of this conversation. "You said you paint moments. I think I know what moment you painted."

After Bolton had asked for an open marriage, I'd ended up at a coffee shop on my lunch break. For some reason, it hit me there, sitting by myself, that I would probably die alone...even if I were still married. My world had been shattered by Bolton's request, and even though I loved him with all my heart, I knew it would never be the same.

Theo continued to see right through me with a discerning gaze, seeing my flesh and bone and the blood in between. He should be just a good lay, a warm body next to mine in a cold bed, a distraction from my loneliness, a form of revenge against the man who crushed me, but he somehow felt like more than that. "I'm sorry."

My eyes flicked down to my drink.

"But I'm not sorry that you're here with me."

When we finished dinner, our plates were totally clean.

"Damn, that was good."

He smiled slightly. "Don't tell George."

"She really knows her way around a kitchen."

"And the bedroom, according to Axel."

I chuckled. "He tells you stuff like that?"

"Not the details, but the incidents."

"Have you...told him about me?" When we ran into them at the restaurant, there was definite tension in the air. Axel seemed particularly interested that I was there.

It took a while for him to answer. "The incidents. But not the details."

"You really are a gentleman."

"I'm not a gentleman," he said quickly. "Just not an asshole. To women, at least."

"So he knows that I have an open marriage?"

"Yes."

"Does he have an opinion on that?" I'm sure most people would burn me at the stake.

"Like me, he's not the judgmental type. He's a one-woman kind of guy, so he doesn't understand how a man could ever let his wife be fucked by somebody else. But that's just his personal opinion."

I didn't understand how Bolton could stand it either. Whenever I thought about him with someone else—let alone multiple people—it made me sick. It *still* made me sick. The longer I spent with Theo, the more I disassociated from Bolton and our marriage. I wasn't sure where we would end up, but happily ever after seemed less realistic with every passing week.

Theo continued to watch me. "And even if he were the judgmental type, you wouldn't be the one he'd judge." He grabbed his glass and drank what remained of the contents. It was his second drink of the night, and despite the fact that it was hard alcohol, he seemed in complete control of his faculties.

Heels sounded from behind me, and then Scarlett appeared, tall and lean in her sky-high heels, the big diamond on her left hand. "How was dinner?"

"Amazing," Theo said. "As always."

"It's the first time he's taken me somewhere he doesn't own, so I knew it would be good," I said.

"Sounds like he takes you out a lot." She glanced back at him.

I realized I'd shoved my foot into my mouth. "Not a lot, just here and there."

"Well, I'm glad you liked the food," Scarlett said. "We opened the restaurant a couple years ago, but it still feels like my baby. The restaurant business is hard, and the last thing I want is to lose something I care so much about."

"You'll never lose this place," Theo said. "You can't get in unless you make a reservation a month in advance."

"Unless the owner tried to sleep with you once upon a time," she teased.

My eyes immediately darted to Theo.

He smirked like it was an inside joke only the two of them knew about.

"Enjoy the rest of your evening." Her hand squeezed his shoulder before she walked away.

His eyes immediately moved back to me instead of staring at her ass. The waitress never brought the tab, so it seemed like it wasn't coming. And Theo didn't wait for it because he rose from his seat. "Ready?"

"Yeah, sure."

When we returned to his bedroom, I reached for my bag.

He grabbed my hand and steadied it. "Stay."

I inhaled his scent when he stood this close to me. It smelled like a cold forest, the mist a cleanse on the soil. But when I turned to look at him, I saw a blazing fireplace that heated the entire room. My eyes took in his dark midnight gaze as he stared down at me.

"Can you stay?"

Bolton would be back tomorrow evening, so I did have some time. Now, my life was divided between two homes, between two men. My identity was in limbo. "Yes."

With his iron grip, Theo forced me to turn toward him, and then like a bullet coming out of the barrel at the speed of sound, his mouth was on mine, his hand deep in my hair, his other hand making itself at home on my ass.

He kissed me with the passion he always showed when we were behind closed doors. At restaurants and in the car, his affection was restrained and discreet, but once it was just the two of us, he was at me like a hungry wolf. He lifted me into his arms and carried me toward the bed, holding me with my thighs around his waist.

He kissed me there for a while, until he suddenly threw me onto the bed.

My back hit the mattress, and I bounced, my hair flying from the motion.

Then he was on me like a bear crawling over its prey. His shirt was already off because he'd yanked it off while my hair covered my face like a mask. His hands pulled up my dress to expose my bottom as he crushed his mouth to mine, swallowing my moans with his demanding lips.

Just when I thought this man couldn't be sexier.

"Theo..." I was lost in the passion, and he wasn't even inside me yet. My nails clawed at his muscles and his hot skin, and my knees squeezed his hips.

He unbuttoned the top of his jeans and yanked down the front so his cock could come free. My dress was left on, pushed up so the bottoms of my tits were exposed. He pulled a condom out of his pocket, probably having those foil packets in all of his jeans and jackets so he was always prepared for the women who wanted to whisper his name the way I did.

He had to stop everything to roll on the condom, his big dick requiring the use of two hands. Our world came to a grinding halt, and while it built up the anticipation, I'd prefer no pause at all, just the two of us together.

When he was secured, he moved over me again, his tip sinking into my entrance with little resistance because I'd been wet since dinner, wet since the moment I'd seen him. All he had to do was sit there and look at me, and I melted like butter over a warm baguette. His dark hair, his dark eyes, the way he seemed not to give a shit about anything.

He sank fully inside me, the plunge slow and easy so my body could accept his gift. A low growl left his lips when he plunged inside me, like it was the first time he'd had me, even though he'd already had all of me more than once. He took me in the same position almost every time, his heavy mass on top of me, his mountain a shadow over my river. But he seemed to like it this way, to have our eyes locked together like lovers in another night of passion. He did all the work most of the time, but he seemed not to mind it, like he was grateful just to have me, like whatever he could have was taken with gratitude.

When I was the one who should be grateful.

Bolton had ripped the foundation from underneath me, and I'd been in free fall ever since. The only moments I ever stopped were the instances when Theo caught me with his big hands and paused time for a night or days in a row. The chaos and turmoil quieted, the world stopped spinning, and all I could see was this gorgeous man who looked at me like I was his equal…and sometimes his superior.

I lay in his big bed under the soft sheets while he showered. The water ran in the bathroom, audible through the crack he'd left in the door. It almost sounded like rain, soft enough that it acted like a lullaby. My eyes grew heavy and started to close more than once, but I stayed awake, waiting for him to join me.

Minutes later, he came to bed in a new pair of boxers, his skin smelling like soap, some of his hair still slightly damp. He pulled back the sheets and brought heat to the bed the way a fire warmed a room. He didn't hesitate to cuddle with me, to hook his big arm around me and pull me close, to bring me right up against his flames without catching me on fire.

I stared at his hard face, his jaw covered in a distinct shadow from his thick hair. He hadn't combed his hair, so it was a little messy, and some of the ends were still damp because he'd rushed it with a quick towel dry.

His eyes closed for a while, but they opened again, like he felt my stare.

I met his look, seeing those brown eyes turn still like the earth, quiet and confident. He asked a question without moving his lips.

"I swear I'm not trying to be nosy—"

"I didn't sleep with her."

"But she tried to sleep with you…?"

"It's more complicated than that."

"Is it?" I asked, eyebrow raised. "Someone either tries to sleep with you, or they don't."

"Why does it matter?"

"It doesn't matter." He wasn't mine, so I couldn't be jealous of anyone for any reason. I had no idea what he did when we were apart, if another woman occupied this bed in my absence. "But I guess I'm curious. You said Axel was your brother."

"He is."

"Then did you know Scarlett before he did?"

He gave a quiet sigh like he just wanted to go to sleep. "No. You want the full story or just the headlines?"

"Whole story, always."

"Alright." His eyes shifted away as he collected his thoughts. "Scarlett is the daughter of a drug kingpin. A psychotic one who's thrown a fat wrench in my plans. He forbade Scarlett from seeing Axel, so naturally, Axel did whatever he could to have her. He fell hard right off the bat, but then her father tore them apart. Threatened to kill Axel's parents if he came near his daughter again. They broke up for six months."

"Jesus, this guy sounds like a jackass."

"Jackass is too generous," he said coldly. "He tried to make a deal with me and cut Axel out of the business. But he's a fucking idiot who doesn't know how his shit, so he was unaware of my relationship with Axel. We don't exactly broadcast it, but if you have a business partner, you should know where he eats, sleeps, and fucks. But that worked in Axel's favor, so we crossed him when he thought he was crossing Axel."

"As interesting as this is, I don't understand what it has to do with you and Scarlett."

"You said you wanted the whole story, right?"

I nodded.

"Dante—that's his name—asked me to marry his daughter."

Both of my eyebrows jumped up my face. "What?"

"He thought it would be a good business move."

"For him. But what about her? Had she even met you yet?"

"No, she hadn't. So, I asked her out like he wanted me to, and we went on a couple dates."

"She didn't know you and Axel were brothers?"

"No." He shook his head. "She was depressed and bitter. Not interested in intimacy, only sex. She made several moves to get me into bed, but I stayed on my best behavior for Axel. Even if they weren't together anymore, he would have been devastated. Our relationship wouldn't have been the same. Some would argue she was fair game, but I knew he loved her. So she wasn't fair game to me."

I listened to the story and felt an ugly burst of jealousy. "So…that means you wanted to?"

He didn't avoid my gaze or look uncomfortable at the question. "When a woman wants to fuck, I don't say no."

"I mean, you wanted to, even though she used to be with Axel?"

"It'd been six months, and they'd both been with other people. Besides, she laid it on really thick."

"You think she would have done that if she knew who you were?"

"After what Axel did to her, she probably would have tried harder."

"What did he do to her?" I asked.

"Dante made him pretend to cheat. It was the only way Axel could get Scarlett to walk away."

"So he basically had to break her heart irreparably?"

"Yes."

The jealousy disappeared, and pity replaced it. "That's horrible."

"It all worked out in the end." His warm arm hooked around my waist, his skin warm like a pan left on the stove. His fingers gently caressed me as he held me under the sheets, his heavy mass making the mattress dip farther in his direction.

"Does Axel know all of this?"

"She told him."

"You didn't?"

"I'm not cruel. I'm not going to tell my brother that his woman cooked for me and tried to fuck me afterward."

I'd liked Scarlett the moment I met her, and even if I had the right to feel jealous, I shouldn't. Every woman who set her eyes on this man fell under his spell. She wanted him—and not just for a night, but for as many nights as she could get.

My fingers traced the lines of his arm, feeling the mountains of muscle and the valleys in between.

His eyes didn't close to go to sleep. He continued his stare.

I felt the heat of his intrusion, felt the question he failed to voice.

"Does he know about me?"

Bolton had never asked me about how I spent my nights when he was away. It became an unspoken agreement between us, to pretend we were faithful to each other even though we were sleeping in other places with other people. "No."

His eyes narrowed slightly. "This has been going on a while now."

"Honestly, he's never asked. Nor have I."

His eyes continued to absorb my stare. "He said something that pushed you into my arms. What was it?"

"I-I said I didn't want to talk about him."

"I'm not asking about him. I'm asking how he made you feel."

Whenever I thought about Bolton, it was always with a cloud of gloom over my head. Whenever he came home, it took days to get back into normalcy. Every touch and kiss felt foreign until they finally felt familiar again. But even then, it was with a note of bitterness, the sweetness sucked out of the fruit, dried and desiccated while it was ravaged by fruit flies.

"What did he say, sweetheart?"

I'd pried into his personal life and pursued a comment I probably shouldn't have heard in the first place, so I felt obligated to reciprocate. "He'd already been with multiple women...and I hadn't even been with one man."

His dark eyes took me in with a note of sympathy.

"It was hard for me, but it didn't seem hard for him."

A heavy silence passed, his hard stare burning into my face. "This is one of those moments…"

"One of the moments, what?"

"Where you have to decide whether the truth is worth cruelty."

I was in his soft bed that felt like a cloud, and whenever I was in the presence of this man, I was cocooned in safety. But now, I was in free fall once again. "What truth do you speak of?" My voice had been strong a moment ago, but now it wavered…like I didn't want him to hear me.

His eyes shifted back and forth between mine, but he didn't answer.

I didn't ask the question again because I didn't have the spine. A small part of me wanted the truth, but a bigger part of me wanted the lies if they were preferable. I was already broken…and another hit or bruise might make me irreparable.

He seemed to read the fear in my eyes because he didn't pursue it. Instead, he pulled me close, my face planted into the top of his chest, and released a breath as he prepared to fall asleep.

Despite the weight in my heart, I drifted away into sleep, lighter than air.

———

After I finished work, I headed home to our villa in the city. I grabbed some groceries along the way then turned my key in the door and headed inside to the kitchen island. The two paper bags were set on the granite countertop, and I placed my purse beside them. I hadn't been home in almost three days, and I couldn't even remember what we had to eat around here.

"What did you get?"

"Jesus." I nearly jumped out of my skin because I jolted so hard. I'd assumed the house was empty because Bolton didn't usually come home until the evening. My hand immediately flew to my heart as if that was about to jump out of my skin too. "I-I didn't expect you to be home so early."

He came to my side. "I'll give you a hand." He pulled

the items out of the bags and put them in the refrigerator and the cabinets.

It gave me a moment to compose myself, to accept the fact that I was in Bolton's presence...and not Theo's. I swore I could still smell Theo on me since my clothes had been at his place for almost three days. His scent was in my hair, on my skin. I wondered if Bolton could smell it too.

"How was the gallery?"

"Fine. How was..." *How was killing someone?* "How was work?"

"Fine." He shut the fridge and looked at me head on for the first time. It was a long stare, not the intense one of longing he used to give me. This one felt perverse, like there was a secret behind my eyes that he wanted to dig for with a shovel. "What's for dinner?"

"Citrus chicken and risotto," I said automatically.

He nodded slowly but seemed disappointed, like he'd asked a different question that I hadn't answered.

I waited for that hug, that embrace, but it never came. "Is something wrong?"

His stare continued with its sharp edges, plowing deep into my earth to prepare the soil for a new season.

I wasn't sure why I asked the question because everything was wrong. Everything had been wrong for a while now. Ever since that horrible night when he'd punched the air right out of my lungs.

"No." He leaned in and gave me a quick kiss on the lips.

All I could think about was the last woman he'd kissed…if it was someone new…another name to add to the list.

And Theo…the man I'd kissed goodbye before I went to work. He'd asked me to stay again, but I told him I couldn't. He never showed his disappointment, but it was heavy in the air around him, the way an oven raised the temperature of the whole house by a few degrees.

"I need to finish some things in the study." Bolton left the kitchen, left me to make dinner alone like the good little wife I was, and disappeared.

When he was gone, I stared at the fridge, thinking about all the things I did to make him happy. I went for a run every day to stay fit, I cooked all his favorite things, I wore the sluttiest lingerie to surprise him in the bedroom—but he still desired other women.

What could I have done differently? What could I have done better?

Nothing.

Fucking nothing.

He came down when dinner was ready, probably smelling the food once I pulled it out of the oven. I set the table with the dishes and flatware, along with an arrangement of flowers I'd put together myself. I didn't expect a man to care about those things, but I hoped he would appreciate it.

It was becoming clear to me that Bolton didn't appreciate anything.

Bolton took a few bites of his food. "Excellent, as always."

"Thanks." I pushed my food around more often than I actually ate it, thinking about my dinner with Theo one second and then thinking about this moment with Bolton the next. I lived two very different lives, and now the separation between them had become thinner than a sheet of paper.

Bolton lifted his chin and looked at me.

I concentrated on my food and waited for him to look away, but as the seconds passed and the heat of his stare felt like a laser on my face, I knew that look was here to stay. I scooped my fork into the risotto and took a bite before I met his stare.

The second he had my attention, he spoke. "The security system said no one came or went for two and a half days." He spoke in a normal tone, but there was more to his statement, a veiled threat that was inaudible but ever-present.

My fork returned to the food, and I did my best to act normal even though I felt like a deer in the headlights. My heart raced like I should be running from a predator, except I shouldn't feel threatened by the person who'd broken our marital vows first. I'd done nothing wrong, but I felt like a liar and a cheat.

He continued to stare like he'd asked a question.

I held my fork and focused on my food.

"Were you sick?" he asked.

I could just say yes and make this go away, but I didn't like to lie. It came easily to others, but it was the most unnatural thing to me. "No. I went to work."

"Then why did the system say the doors never opened?" He left his fork on his plate and leaned back against the chair, arms crossed over his chest, his head slightly cocked like he was a detective about to complete an interrogation.

I stared at my food again, feeling the race of my anxious heart but also the fury in my soul. I'd never wanted any of this. None of it. "Because I wasn't here the last two and a half days—and you already know that." My strength came from my rage, the rage that had been boiling consistently for a month now, bubbling and spilling over the edge onto the stove. "You're the one who asked for this, so don't put me on the stand for a crime you asked me to commit."

The tendons in his neck tightened as the indignation made his face go taut. His eyes dropped momentarily, the flash of anger like lightning across the clouds in his gaze. His arms crossed and he gripped his elbows as he sank into the chair, his jaw clenched harder than it'd been a moment ago. "I don't disappear for two and a half days—"

"You're gone for three days at a time, Bolton. Sometimes more."

"And ninety percent of the time is spent working—not with someone else. If you're spending two and a half days with the same guy, that sounds more like a relationship than a quick fuck."

I stared down at the dinner I'd made, the dinner that would grow cold. If Theo were here, he would have eaten his whole plate then gone for seconds. He would have complimented my cooking and not to be polite, because he wasn't the type of guy to say things just to be polite. "You never stated the parameters of the arrangement. You just asked to fuck other people, and that was it."

"So, you are fucking someone?" Now, his voice hardened like he was about to burst.

"What did you think was going to happen?" I snapped. "That you were going to fuck a line of beautiful women and I was just going to sit on my ass at home? Maybe you've forgotten that I'm a hot piece of ass that men are happy to throw down on the bed like a fucking rag doll, but that's your damn fault, not mine." I pushed my chair out from the table and threw my napkin right on my plate. "I didn't want this. I never looked at another man from the moment you were mine. So don't turn this around on me like I'm the one who crossed the line, when you crossed every line there is to cross."

He got to his feet. "Baby—"

"It's done, Bolton. You failed to outline the terms of this arrangement when you signed on the dotted line of a contract you shoved in front of me. There's no going back now. So, you do whatever the fuck you want, and I'll do whatever the fuck I want, and we'll come home and act like nothing fucking happened." I pointed at him across the table, and my finger was as sharp as a knifepoint. "Because that's what you wanted."

12

THEO

I sat in my armchair at the strip club and breathed in the smoke like it was fresh air off a mountain. The music blared and thudded off the walls, and the girls danced to pay their mortgages and put their kids in private school.

Octavio dropped into the chair next to me. "The dinner with Claude is tomorrow night. Chez Patrice—right on the corner, surrounded by windows. It's like he wants to get shot."

"He's just that arrogant."

"So." He looked at me. "We doing this?"

"Yes." I'd take out his men along the perimeter then walk right in and drag him out by the collar. The guys would tase him and cuff him, and then we'd be on our way to headquarters for the real fun.

"I look forward to it." He turned his attention to the woman who danced on the pole for our benefit. Probably for my benefit because I always dropped a wad of bills whenever I left. These women worked their asses off for that cash, and I'd rather give it to them than most other people.

I smoked my cigar then looked at my phone light up. It was Axel.

So...how was dinner?

I locked the screen.

Another message popped up. *Don't ignore me, asshole.*

I'm working, asshole.

You're watching a stripper slide down a pole with her ass cheeks.

I looked up and expected to see him somewhere, but coming to the strip club just for the hell of it wasn't his style. He'd cleaned up a lot of bad habits after he'd settled down with Scarlett. He didn't smoke as much as he used to, he cut back on the drinks, and he didn't lounge around in strip clubs. *Where are you?*

I'm at home. But that's how well I know you.

I almost made a smartass comment but chose not to. *Octavio and I just made a plan for Bolton. It's happening tomorrow.*

Need a hand?

Not from you.

Come on, you know I've always got your back.

You're retired, Axel.

Brotherhood never retires.

I said, I don't need help.

Well, if this plan is going down tomorrow, then you're free to come by now.

I'm at the strip club, so I'm not going anywhere.

You've never fucked a stripper, so I know you aren't into that.

If I fucked a stripper, you think I'd tell you? I rarely mentioned who I fucked. If he hadn't spotted me with Astrid, I wouldn't have mentioned her either. I only took her to Scarlett's restaurant because my secret was already exposed, so I didn't have anything to hide. But I guessed that was a mistake because Axel was hot on my tail again.

Just come by. Scarlett made cheese souffles, and they are so good, they even taste better than her...you-know-what.

If you're going to imply it, you may as well just say it.

Fine. They're so good, they even taste better than her pussy. Now get over here.

I'm gonna tell her you said that.

I don't care. She's so sexy when she gets fired up.

Alright, I'll be there in thirty minutes.

Yaaaassssss.

The kids had been asleep for hours when I came by.

Scarlett greeted me with a tight squeeze before she smiled at me, a smile that reminded me of the warmth of a mother. The moment I saw her, I'd thought she was sexy as fuck, but now I saw her as a sister, and any attraction that burned long ago had gone cold and dormant. "I heard you're here for the cheese soufflés."

"Axel mentioned they were good." My eyes shifted to him, threatening to out him.

"He says that about everything I make. Who knows if he means it."

"Oh, I mean it," Axel said from behind her.

She smiled as she pulled away. "I'll let you boys do what you do best…eat and smoke." She turned to Axel and gave him a quick kiss. "Goodnight."

"Goodnight, baby." He spanked her ass as she walked by.

She didn't flinch at the contact of his palm, like this was a regular occurrence between them.

She walked away and headed to the stairs, and Axel craned his head as hard as he could to stare at her ass as she left.

I smirked as I watched him.

Only when she was out of sight did he turn back to me. "They don't make them like that anymore, do they?"

I immediately thought of Astrid and disagreed. "Guess not."

He nodded in the direction of his study.

We walked inside, and on the table, a silver dish covered the soufflés underneath. There were also cigars sitting there, along with the decanter of scotch.

I sat in the armchair and looked at the warm fireplace, which had been lit ablaze to chase away the cold winter. Then I reached for the cigar and lit up before I got comfortable against the chair. "Seems like Scarlett is fine with you smoking."

"As long as it's sparingly." He lit up and released a puff of smoke to the ceiling. "So I have a cigar once a week. Sometimes twice if the kids really drive me up the wall."

"Or if Scarlett drives you up the wall."

He shook his head slightly. "She can drive me as crazy as she wants with an ass like that." He pulled the smoke into his mouth then stared at the fire as he enjoyed it, his eyes lost in a momentary glaze. "What's new with you?"

"I'm no closer to finding Draven than I was before. His distributors deal with his henchman, which is a different person every time. So I'm not sure if he rotates them or kills them after their use expires."

"Sounds like pussy shit."

"He knows I'm on to him, which means he's got eyes on me, or ears in my vicinity."

"You could ask Dante for help. He still knows people."

"I'm not asking that little bitch for anything."

"Yeah, I get it." He released the smoke from his mouth.

"I can't divide and conquer. I need to do one at a time, and Bolton is the greater threat."

"He won't be a threat after tomorrow night."

"No, probably not." I brought the cigar to my lips and pulled in the smoke.

Axel stared at the fire for a while. "So, did Astrid like her food?"

I'd known the topic was just around the corner, driving around the bend. "Yes."

"What did she order?"

"I don't remember." It was the truffle pasta with cream sauce.

Axel turned to me. "Why did you pick Scarlett's restaurant?"

"It's your restaurant too."

"I disagree. She's the one who does all the hard work. I just eat everything then fuck the chef afterward." He smirked then pulled the cigar out of his mouth to let it rest between his fingertips. A cloud of smoke erupted a moment later. "Don't dodge the question."

"It's a good restaurant."

"Or you wanted Scarlett to see you…"

"How would I know if she's working?"

"Because you know shit, Theo." His eyes pierced mine.

"I may be a mastermind at work, but I'm not a mastermind on my time off."

"But you never have time off, right? Work is life, and life is work."

I met his look with my own ferocity, quiet and sheathed. "What's your point, Axel?"

"No point." He shrugged then removed the silver dish, revealing the little soufflés underneath. "Scarlett learned how to make these from watching a video. Crazy, right?" He grabbed one along with a fork then started to eat.

I didn't take one, not having an appetite at this time of night.

"How long do you think you'll keep seeing her?"

"As long as it lasts."

"What if it always lasts?"

"Nothing lasts forever."

"I hope you're wrong about that," Axel said. "Because if Scarlett tried to leave me, I'd probably jump off the Duomo."

"It'll end," I said. "Once he realizes she's sleeping with me, he'll get angry and call a halt to their arrangement. They'll work on their marriage and do counseling and all that bullshit, and I'll be out of the picture."

"What if she leaves him? Would it end then?"

I looked away toward the fire.

"Leaves him for you?"

"She won't."

"Why are you so certain?"

"Because I'm not worth it."

He cocked his head slightly.

"I think she should leave him because she deserves better. Deserves a man who would love her the way you love Scarlett. Who would threaten to throw himself off the Duomo if she tried to walk away." Astrid was beautiful and smart and thoughtful. She was fiery and passionate. Everything a man wanted in a woman. "But I'm not that man."

"Does she know that?"

"I've told her I don't take women to dinner. I prefer to pay for sex because it's easier. I think it's clear."

"But you take her to dinner. You don't pay her for sex." Axel continued to watch me, serious now that the conversation had settled over us like a heavy fog that had rolled in from the sea. "I think it's clear she's the exception."

"Don't analyze me."

"I'm not analyzing you, Theo. I just see what you try so hard not to."

13

ASTRID

Life was a blur.

I got to work an hour early and stayed an hour late.

I did whatever I could to stay out of the house and avoid my own husband, the man whose last name appeared on my driver's license and passport. He was supposed to be my family and I should wear his surname proudly, but now he felt like a stranger.

He gave me the space I didn't ask for. We slept in the same bed and barely spoke over dinner. To the outside, it looked as if that conversation had never happened, but to us, it was as if the conversation was still going, carrying on without words.

I preferred the company of silent paintings. Preferred the colors of fog and midnight blue over the watercolors of spring. Emails from clients came in, but there wasn't enough work to keep me busy, so I stared at the paintings and tried to find new meaning that I hadn't noticed before.

Life had been hard in the past, but it had stopped being hard after Bolton. Never once had I thought I'd be standing there alone, relying on a painting made one hundred and fifty years ago for support. I never thought I'd rely on work to keep me busy enough not to cry.

I stood in front of a painting of a Macedonian ship at sea, surrounded by Persian warships trying to sink it to the bottom of the ocean and take all the supplies on board. It was a new acquisition for the gallery after an estate sale by a client. She decided to downsize her accommodations after her husband passed away. It was a collector's item, and now it was back in our hands to sell once again. Artwork was like real estate. You could sell the same painting again and again, its value only growing over time.

"This is new."

I heard his voice, would recognize it anywhere, heard it in dreams I tried so hard to remember after I woke. I turned to see him standing beside me, dressed in his usual black attire, a long-sleeved shirt snug on his arms, his height making him a skyscraper. I stared at the side of his face, my heart going from a pace so slow it almost stopped beating to a sprint. "Yeah, we just got it yesterday."

"How long will it take you to sell a painting like this?"

I was still shocked to see him there because he'd never stopped by unannounced like this. "It depends on the artist. Whenever we get something from one of the greats, it's gone in a day. For a painting like this, probably a week."

He gave a subtle nod. "What's your commission?"

"Fifteen percent."

"That's a nice payday."

I put my money in a separate account from Bolton's because he said he didn't want my money, but he always shared everything he had with me. I didn't need to earn money, so it just built up in the account over time. Sometimes I spent it on expensive clothes and shoes, splurge items I didn't need, even though Bolton was happy to pay for those things.

Just six weeks ago, I would have been so grateful to have Bolton as my husband. I would have questioned how I got so lucky to find someone like him to love me and care for me. But now, it was as if our years of bliss had never happened.

"Everything okay?"

"Yeah, I'm fine." I swallowed and cleared my voice. "I just wasn't expecting you, is all."

He turned to look at me directly, his eyes absorbing my stare the way it did over dinner. "I was driving by and saw you in the window. Looked like you were having a hard day."

He saw past the distance, saw past the glare on the windows from the sunshine, because my misery was like a beacon from a lighthouse to a ship stranded in the dark sea. I wanted to lie and reject his assumption, but I couldn't.

"If my being here crosses the line, I'll leave."

"No," I said quickly. "If I wanted you gone, I'd tell you."

The smile on his lips was so subtle it was hardly visible, remembering the words he'd said to me on our first night together. "Let me take you to lunch."

We went to a café down the block, sat outside because it was a warmer day after all the rain we'd had the last week. The restaurant was on the corner, the other tables full of people who were enjoying their lunch breaks.

I ordered a latte and a croissant, not having much of an appetite the last few days.

He ordered a coffee and a sandwich.

Conversation between us had been limited. His intuition really was borderline supernatural because he seemed to know exactly how to treat me, how to tiptoe around my misery rather than confronting it head on. He didn't hit with me a slew of questions. He just let me be. Absorbed the misery with me.

"Is that your second lunch or your first?" I asked, wanting to break the last ten minutes of silence.

"First." He took another bite and chewed with that big

mouth, looking sexy as he worked his jaw and tightened the cords in his neck.

"Where were you going when you saw me?"

"A meeting."

"If you're here, then what happened to the meeting?"

He shrugged. "I'm sure they're still waiting for me."

Guilt filled my lungs like smoke. "Theo, I don't want to keep you—"

"I'd rather be here with you." He sat there, a man too big for the little chair, sunglasses on the bridge of his nose because of how bright it was. One ankle rested on the opposite knee, and he carried himself with a relaxed posture. "I'm not asking you to talk about it. Sometimes the peaceful silence of a friend is more comforting than a heavy conversation. Whichever you prefer is fine with me."

I looked at the beautiful man across from me—and didn't see a friend.

———

When I came home, Bolton was on the phone. "Yes, I'll

bring her along. I'm sure she and Abigail will hit it off." He finished the call and hung up.

I set my purse on the counter and slipped off my heels so the arches in my feet would have a break.

Bolton exited his study and walked up to me, his eyes turning guarded once he drew near. "How was work?"

Theo appeared in my mind, across from me at the café, a silent comfort like the paintings in the gallery. "It was fine. What was that about?"

"I'm having dinner with a client. I'd like you to come with me."

"It sounds like your client wants me to come with you."

His eyes flashed with a quick look of irritation, but he pushed it away. "He's bringing one of his women, and she'd like company over dinner."

"Then why don't you two just go alone?" I didn't want to make small talk with a woman who would just be replaced by someone new in two weeks.

"Because he likes to show off his woman, and I like to show off my wife."

I felt the daggers sharpen in my eyes, felt the strain of my fury. "Do you?" I tried to keep the rage out of my tone, but it was so fucking hard.

Bolton stared at me, trying to dissolve my anger with just his stare. "I love you." His words broke through his frustration and anger, coming out like the music of a songbird, loud with truth and beautiful with sincerity. "So fucking much."

For just a flicker, my reality changed and the past was rewritten. Nothing had transpired. There were no other women. It was just us, back to our lives, back to our happiness.

"And I want you there. I don't want this distance between us when I'm home. I don't want us sleeping on opposite sides of the bed. I fucking hate this. But I've given you space because I know you well enough to know what will happen if I try to force it. But my patience has waned."

How could this man ask to sleep with other women? How could he say these beautiful things to me then stick his dick in someone else? It felt like there were two versions of him, and I didn't know which one I would get.

"Come with me," he said gently. "Please."

We left the villa and drove to the restaurant.

He moved his hand to my thigh.

Guilt shot up my spine because all I could think about was Theo. When he grabbed me like that when he took me to dinner. When his fingers gently moved up my dress but never ventured past an invisible line I didn't have to draw. For the last six weeks, I'd felt like I was betraying Bolton, but now, I felt like I was betraying Theo.

I crossed my legs in the opposite direction, and that was enough to get his hand to move.

He didn't seem to think anything of it because he needed both hands when he entered the roundabout crowded with buses and motorbikes as he navigated out of the congestion and headed onto a different road.

We arrived at the restaurant moments later, and after Bolton got me out of the car, he grabbed my hand.

I didn't fight his touch, but it didn't feel the same.

Nothing felt the same.

We entered the restaurant and were taken to an empty table because Bolton's client hadn't arrived yet. He pulled out the chair for me and immediately ordered a bottle of wine for the two of us.

His arm moved over the back of my chair, his fingers gently grazing my hair. After he surveyed his surroundings, he looked at me, his blue eyes taking in my appearance the way he used to. "You look beautiful."

I wanted to flick my eyes away, but I couldn't. They were stuck in place, remembering our wedding day, the moment he dropped to one knee and asked me to be his wife, all the good memories that looked different in hindsight...that had been irrevocably changed.

14

THEO

I was in the back seat of the SUV, parked at the curb as we waited in silence.

Octavio was in the front seat, waiting for the signal we needed to move in. "They've taken the guys on the west perimeter. No gunshots."

"Good."

Another stretch of silence passed. I looked out the window onto the dark street, seeing cars pass once the light turned green. It was never quiet, not with the sounds of motorbikes and taxis constantly passing.

Octavio spoke again. "We got the east too. We're clear."

"He'll have three guys on the corners." He wouldn't have picked that spot unless he had immediate coverage, guys who were packing from the best vantage point.

Octavio spoke into the comms. "Theo says there should be three more at the corners. Check it out."

I suspected Bolton would only be armed with a knife because a gun was too bulky for dinner, even if his dinner date was criminal enough to hire a hit man. He was exactly that arrogant, assuming he would stay at the top just because he was good enough to get there in the first place.

I had the opposite philosophy. It took ten times more work to keep a position than to attain it. You had to sleep with one eye open. Look over your shoulder twice because once wasn't enough. Even the men who were closest to me had men tailing them because I trusted no one.

Octavio spoke again. "We got 'em. But we gotta move fast because I'm sure Bolton will have a backup plan."

I hopped out of the back seat and approached the restaurant at the corner, not waiting for my men to catch up. The plan was for me to go into the restaurant by myself and confront him alone rather than cause panic among innocent people whose only crime was not wanting to cook that night.

I passed the windows and saw people dining at their tables. When I opened the glass door, I was met with the loud noises of conversations and knives scraping against plates. Uproarious laughter exploded from one corner of the restaurant, while another table sang happy birthday over a small cake lit with candles.

I already knew where he was seated, so I headed to the rear of the restaurant.

None of the waiters tried to intervene, probably because I looked like I knew exactly where I was going.

I spotted Bolton, his eyes locked on the man across from him, nodding slowly like he gave a fuck about what the guy was saying. He looked even more arrogant than I remembered, his arm draped over the chair of a beautiful woman at his side. Their table was full of bottles of wine and glasses, like they'd started to drink hard before their food arrived.

My core suddenly tightened, and dread spiked in my blood out of nowhere.

My eyes traveled back to where they'd already been— and I stared at her.

Astrid.

Her makeup was done differently, so I didn't recognize her right away. She wore a black dress with gold jewelry, her hair combed back in a way I'd never seen her wear it. The one thing that hadn't changed was her eyes.

They were dead.

I stopped walking, right next to a table with a couple enjoying their dinner. They both glanced at me but didn't ask me to move.

My eyes remained on Astrid, seeing the same broken woman in the gallery, staring at a painting as her eyes started to shine with unshed tears. "Fuck."

I had a split second to decide what to do. To walk over there and grab Bolton by the neck...or leave before either one of them noticed me. Despite the problems they were having, Astrid wouldn't want him dead. And she wouldn't want me if I was the one who killed him.

That left me with only one choice.

I walked out.

I checked in with the butler then waited for Axel in the study. My men were confused by the sudden way I'd changed my mind, but I didn't owe them an explanation, so I didn't give one. Bolton would realize someone had killed all his men, and the fact that he was spared would be the greatest mystery he would never solve. Any witness he could ask had been killed.

Axel joined me a moment later in just his sweatpants, his hair messy and his eyes tired like he'd been dead asleep when his butler woke him. "What is it, Theo?" He came up to me, the concern coming from his sleepy gaze.

"I found out who Astrid's husband is."

"Shit," he said. "Did he come at you?"

"No. I came at him."

His eyebrows rose when the story made less sense.

"I walked into the restaurant to confront Bolton, and Astrid was with him." I stepped away and sauntered toward the cold fireplace, feeling the tension in my neck because my life had become complicated.

Axel took a moment to process that before he dropped onto the couch, his hands together as his elbows rested on his knees. "Jesus."

I turned back toward him, the adrenaline still in my veins all these hours later.

"What are the odds of that?"

I fell into the armchair.

"What did you do?"

"I left."

"Didn't you kill all of his men?"

"Yes."

"Then what's he going to think when he realizes someone killed all of his men but spared him?"

"I don't fucking know, Axel." He might be able to follow the clues that led back to me, but since we were already enemies at war, it didn't make much of a difference.

"You're fucked, you know that?"

"We already want to kill each other, Axel. It doesn't change anything."

"But if he knows it was you and you chickened out, he's going to wonder why."

"Let him wonder," I said coldly.

"He's a smart guy," Axel said. "He knows his wife is sleeping with other people—"

"I don't know if he knows."

"He's got to assume his wife has fucked someone at some point in the last six weeks. And even if he doesn't, he'll figure it out eventually. Once he does, he'll piece it together. That you walked in there to kill him but saw Astrid and changed everything."

I rested my chin on my closed knuckles as I stared at him. "That's a bit of a reach."

"Not if she tells him who she's fucking."

I gave a shrug. "It's done, Axel."

"Why didn't you do it?"

"Did you hear what I said?" I snapped. "He's married to Astrid."

"What does that matter? He treats her like shit, and he's the one responsible for Killian's death. And you just let him walk away?"

I looked away, feeling the self-loathing wash over me.

"I don't understand, Theo."

"Astrid has chosen to stay in that marriage, so she still loves him." It hurt to say the words out loud, marked my tongue with acid. Sometimes I wondered if she thought about him when she was with me. I wondered if she thought about me when she was with him, and I hoped she did. "I can't kill the man she loves."

Axel sank back into the couch as he stared at me. "And you say this woman means nothing to you…"

"I never said she meant *nothing.*"

"Bolton is the only one who knows who put that hit on Killian. There is no other way, Theo. So if you're going to let him walk for Astrid, then damn, this woman means a lot to you."

"It was an impulsive decision. I had less than a second to make it."

"So, you are going to kill him."

"I don't know—"

"How do you not know?"

"Get off my neck, Axel." This had just happened hours ago, and I knew I was in deep shit. My men were utterly bewildered, and I was certain Bolton was confused-as-fuck right now. My twin brother was the only person who had known me my whole life…his whole life. Not to avenge him wasn't an option. But to kill Bolton…wasn't really an option either.

"I hope you like bullshit." Axel stared at me for a while. "Because you're ankle-deep in it now."

15

ASTRID

Bolton usually left once a week or every ten days. There was a limit to the number of contracts he would personally take on. The rest, he passed on to other guys in his crew. Sometimes his clients insisted it be him since he was the one who had started the Brotherhood and, therefore, was the best at it.

So when he didn't leave after ten days, I found that strange.

He was always home, working in his study, and when I came home from work, he had dinner waiting for me.

I'd never seen him make dinner. Didn't know he even knew how to use the oven.

But he was quiet and distant, not like he was angry with me, but like he had something else on his mind. He rarely talked about work, and I didn't ask because those were details I preferred to avoid, but I suspected that was the reason for his change of mood, for the fact that he hadn't gone to work in so long.

Theo didn't text me either. Didn't come by the gallery again. Even though it'd been the longest stretch of time we hadn't spoken, he seemed unbothered by my silence. He was probably trying to respect my boundaries, but I always assumed the worst.

I approached the dining table and saw the feast Bolton had made, roasted chicken surrounded by slow-cooked rice and potatoes. It was coated in a white sauce, something that smelled like garlic and rosemary. "This looks good." I took my usual seat and placed the napkin across my lap.

He opened a bottle of white wine and poured two glasses. "It's amazing what the internet can teach you." He sat across from me and draped his napkin across his lap, waiting for me to take the first serving.

I scooped the hot food onto my plate then watched him do the same, the house quiet with the exception of the music he'd put on the speaker under the window. Steam rose from my plate, smelling like a gourmet meal. "I didn't know you had an interest in cooking."

"You cook all the time. Thought I could help out."

I didn't mind cooking, but I didn't love it either. The responsibility had fallen to me because Bolton didn't want a chef or a housekeeper. Said he preferred to keep our home private rather than open to strangers. "That was sweet of you." Our relationship had been silently turbulent because we both dodged conversation like the plague. But he had been trying to get into my good graces in other ways, by cooking dinner, by kissing me on the shoulder when I sat on the vanity, being overly generous in bed, as if he was trying to compensate for some kind of shortcoming.

It was mental whiplash. Angry at him one moment then soft when the good memories flooded back. Then I would think about Theo, and the guilt would rush in. We owed nothing to each other, but I somehow felt like I'd stabbed him in the back. Bolton was the one I was married to, but sometimes it was easy to forget. "You haven't gone back to work. Is everything alright?"

He was just about to scoop a bite onto his fork, but he noticeably stilled at the question. His eyes remained down for several long seconds, seconds that felt like minutes because they were packed with so much tension. He eventually abandoned the fork altogether and set it on his plate.

I knew I'd asked the wrong thing.

He stared at his plate a moment longer before he straightened and met my gaze, his blue eyes suddenly angry. "You want me to leave?"

"I-I didn't say that. I've just noticed things are different. You're cooking at home, not going to work. It seems like something has changed. You said you would never quit the Brotherhood, so I'm not sure what's caused this abrupt change."

His eyes pierced mine, searching for a sign of a lie. "I want to end the arrangement I suggested, and I'm sorry I suggested it in the first place. If I could take it back, I would. You're my wife, and I love you more than words can say. I want to have a family with you, to raise children and leave them behind when it's our time to go."

My fingers gripped the handle of the fork as I processed his declaration. After our last argument, neither one of us had acknowledged our problems because that's how we'd always been. We just ignored things until they went away. But Bolton wasn't going to ignore this.

He continued to stare at me expectantly, waiting for me to appreciate his words and agree to the new terms.

But a bottomless pit opened in my stomach, and I'd been knocked off-balance. Those were words I'd wanted to hear weeks ago. I'd hoped he would realize how wrong it was and come back to me. And I would have forgiven him. But then there were more women, and it seemed like it wasn't a problem until he realized I was also taking full advantage of the arrangement.

"Astrid." He seemed to know that my mind had drifted.

My eyes darted away, unable to look at him without feeling the pain and the overwhelming resentment.

"I'm sorry," he said. "I'll say it as many times as you need to hear it—"

"No."

He stilled. "No, what?"

"No, that's not what I want."

His blue eyes shifted back and forth between mine, slow at first, but then with increased speed, like he could feel all the pieces of his life unravel.

"It's too late, Bolton." When I'd sat down to dinner tonight, I didn't think this conversation would transpire. I didn't think I would make this decision. It felt impulsive, but I knew it'd been creeping closer every day for the last two months. "I couldn't sleep with anyone, not even when you came home with lipstick on your neck after your first trip. The idea of being with anyone else but you...made me sick. But then you said there had been multiple women, and that was when I ended up in someone's bed. I hoped after the first woman, you would realize it was a big mistake and you would change your mind about the whole thing. But you didn't. And I think the only reason you're changing your mind now is because you know I have someone else—which is despicable."

His blue eyes remained angry as he listened. "I never see the same woman twice. They're just a means to an end. It's a transaction, a comfort in whatever city I'm forced to be in to fulfill my contract. I feel nothing for them. But what you're doing is completely different—because you're in a relationship."

"You never specified the terms—"

"Astrid." He kept his voice even, but his anger bubbled on the surface of his face. "An open marriage means you fuck other people, but you're emotionally committed to each other. Having a relationship with someone else is breaking that emotional commitment to me."

"It's not a relationship," I snapped. "And even if it were, that's really rich coming from you. You're gonna sit there and try to make me feel bad for all of this? You knew how I felt about this arrangement, but you wanted to fuck someone so bad, you did it anyway."

"You said you were fine with it—"

"But you knew I wasn't!" I couldn't restrain my anger the way he could restrain his, so it came pouring out. "You drove me into the arms of someone else because I've been a fucking mess since all this shit happened. Another man has been consoling me the nights you're gone, and if that makes you feel like shit, then good. I hope you feel like shit."

He straightened further, his jaw clenching as he listened to all of it. "The arrangement is over, Astrid. We'll go to couples therapy or whatever bullshit married couples do to fix their problems—"

"We had no problems until you wanted to fuck someone else. You're the problem, Bolton."

His jaw clenched even harder as he stared at me.

When I spoke again, my voice came out gentle. "I'm not going to stop seeing him."

"When we decided on our arrangement, we did it together—"

"I want a divorce." No one expected their marriage to end in divorce. Even though half of marriages failed, I'd expected to be in the other half that succeeded. "I should have asked for it in the first place." It had just taken me time to accept that my marriage was over, that I couldn't get over his infidelity, that whatever love I thought we had had died or never existed in the first place. "Now you're free, Bolton. Free to fuck all those women who mean nothing to you."

His eyes dropped. "I'm not going to let you go, Astrid."

"Too bad," I said. "Because you already did."

I grabbed a bag and threw a couple items inside, not really thinking about the essentials I needed because I was still in shock. Shock that I was packing my shit and leaving my home of two years...my husband of two years.

I wanted to cry, but once the tears were shed, I'd fall to my knees and never rise again. My anger spurred me on, made me grab my makeup and brushes off the vanity and shove them on top of the clothes I'd packed.

If Bolton cut me off from our bank accounts, I still had my money from my job, so I would be able to get by for a while. I could stay at a hotel until I figured out my next plan, until our divorce was final and I could move on.

I left my wedding ring on the nightstand and zipped up my bag before I hoisted it over my shoulder. When I turned around, I almost fell back because I'd run into a wall. He came up behind me without my noticing, either because he was that quiet or I was that distracted.

His arms were by his sides, and his eyes were full of sorrow. "Please don't go." His voice was gentle instead of angry like it'd been at dinner. The silent plea in his voice somehow made him more human, made him seem average...and not a hit man for hire.

I turned away.

He grabbed my arm. "Astrid."

I twisted out of his grasp. "I'm sorry."

He grabbed me again.

I twisted out of the hold exactly as he'd taught me years ago. "No, I'm not sorry." I stepped away so he couldn't reach me again, his body between me and the door, a barrier thicker than the Great Wall of China. "I'm not sorry because I didn't do this. You did."

"I'm sorry," he said. "I'm fucking sorry."

"An apology doesn't clean your dick, Bolton."

"You're acting like I cheated on you. You agreed—"

"The second you wanted to fuck another woman, you did cheat."

"Astrid, it's the real world. You've seen my clients with their handful of mistresses. Powerful men always cheat on their wives. It's just how it is."

"Wow. Just how it is…"

"But I've never been that way with you," he said. "Which is why I asked you. I understand it hurt you, but if you'd said no, I wouldn't have done it. Maybe that's not romantic for you, but it's a sign of my commitment to you. That has to mean something to you."

"I want a husband who doesn't want to cheat on me, Bolton," I snapped. "That's what I want."

"No man wants to fuck the same woman for the rest of his life. Sorry, but that's the truth. Monogamy is an obligation, not a privilege."

"If you feel that way, then why the fuck did you marry me?"

"Because I loved you," he insisted. "Because I still do. You need to understand, wanting to fuck a woman is very different from wanting to make love to a woman. You're the woman I want to come home to. You're the woman I want to spend time with. You're the woman I want to have my children. I want so much more from you. But yes, sometimes I want to fuck a woman I don't know just to scratch that itch. That doesn't mean everything else I've said isn't true. Again, if you had just told me you couldn't get past it, we wouldn't be here right now."

"Don't you fucking blame me—"

"I do blame you," he barked. "All you had to do was say no."

"I want a husband who doesn't want anyone else but me."

"Well, that's not going to happen. All men, at some point in time, desire someone else. It doesn't mean they love their wives less."

I thought of Axel and the way he smothered his wife in signs of his love. She was covered in diamonds and gold from his affection. I thought of Theo too, because he seemed like a man who would be the same way. "I don't believe that. I believe there are men out there who love their woman with everything that they have. And that's what I want. I'm not going to settle for less. I'm not going to let you gaslight me."

"I'm not gaslighting you—"

"You just said all of this was my fault. That I should have said no. That I shouldn't have slept with the same man more than once. That all of this is happening because of my wrongdoing—when you're the one who started all this bullshit. You know what I think?"

His anger started to rise. It was visible in his face.

"I think you assumed I was so stupidly in love with you that I would stay committed to you while you fucked half the town. That you could have your cake and eat it too. Well, joke's on you, Bolton. You saw a rock, but someone else saw the Hope Diamond." I moved into him, prepared to push him away if I had to, and I shoved him in the shoulder to force him aside.

He blocked my path and grabbed both of my arms to lock me in place. "Astrid—"

"Let me go."

"No." His hold tightened.

"You fight for me now?" The tears came out of nowhere, springing from my eyes like the water from the Alps in spring. "This is what I wanted, for you to fight for me, and now you do it when it's all said and done?"

His anger dimmed at the sight of my tears. His grip loosened too.

"I wanted you to love me, to want only me, and now you're trying to stop me from walking out that door. Bolton, I loved you...loved you so fucking much, and you knew that. You took advantage of that love, pushed me further than I could go. Why am I the one who loved so fiercely but also the one getting smashed into pieces?"

"Astrid—"

"I pestered you to have a family because I wanted a son who wears your face. I cooked you dinner every night because I wanted to make a home for you, to make you happy. I'd buy lingerie and do special things for you to keep you satisfied in the hope you'd never want to look anywhere else. I gave this relationship all of me all of the time because I never wanted to lose you. But it didn't matter. It didn't fucking matter."

His eyes developed a sheen, one so subtle, it was barely noticeable.

"I deserve better." I finally pulled free of his grasp because he let me go.

I walked around him, expecting him to grab me again when his senses came back to him.

But he didn't.

I walked down the stairs and reached the foyer. My keys were in the bowl, and my clutch was on the dresser below the mirror. I grabbed everything and stepped into the garage where my car was tucked away, still covered in raindrops because it had rained that morning on my way to work.

I stared at it and hesitated, knowing there was no going back now.

I got in the car…and left.

I booked a suite at a hotel and sat on the edge of the bed, my bag beside me. I didn't realize how long I'd been sitting there until sunlight came through the window and stretched across the floor. Then my boss called me and asked why I hadn't shown up.

I told him I was sick, so sick I wouldn't be in for the next few days.

At some point, I got so tired I couldn't keep my head up, so I lay across the bed and pulled the duvet over me, pulling it back away from the pillows so I was basically using the bed upside down. There was a crick in my neck from lying without a pillow, but I continued to lie there, dead on the inside, thankful that Bolton didn't try to call.

At some point, I fell asleep, my pain paused as I drifted away into nothingness.

Hours later, a text vibrated my phone, the movement so slight but enough to stir me.

I stared at it where I'd left it on the corner of the bed. I was afraid it was Bolton asking where I was so he could come get me. But it could also be Theo…maybe. He never texted me first, but maybe he'd stopped by the gallery and realized I wasn't there. Maybe he was worried.

I lay there a moment longer before I had the strength to grab the phone.

Are you alright, sweetheart?

My eyes crinkled when I heard his voice in my head. The moisture came a moment later, the crack in my voice because he'd been the ice pack on my bruises for months now. It had started on a rainy night when he'd changed my tire, and now we'd become something else. *No.*

He called me right away.

My eyes watered further when I realized how quickly he called me, like hearing my voice was what he desperately needed. They said the grass was always greener on the other side, but his grass really was a deep green from the spring rain and thick from the summer heat. It was an oasis, a pond with floating lilies, flowers in bloom, and birds full of song. I answered. "Hey…" I kept my voice steady because I didn't want to sob my heart out to him, not because another man had broken my heart.

He didn't say anything back. He just let the silence speak for him.

I loved that he didn't interrogate me. I loved that he didn't pry. He was a gardener, and he let me bloom at my own pace. "I left him. I'm at the Ritz." I wasn't sure why I told him the hotel, like I expected him to run straight to me.

He didn't say anything.

"He said he wanted to end the arrangement. Said he wanted it just to be us. If he had asked me that sooner, I might have done it. But it's too late now."

"I hope it's not because of me—but because you deserve better."

I wasn't sure what I'd expected him to say, but I was disappointed by his choice of words. "It's both."

He turned quiet again.

I expected more from him, expected him to comfort me the way he did when he showed up at the gallery, expected him to tell me everything would be alright. But he was dead silent, like he wasn't even there. "Is something wrong?"

Silence.

"Because—because you feel different."

He was quiet again, the stretch of time seeming to last forever. "I've had a rough week."

"Is everything okay?"

"Yes. My life just got complicated."

"Can I ask how?"

There was silence and then a heavy sigh.

"Can—can I come over?" Self-loathing rushed through me as I heard my own desperation. He purposely put distance between us, but I ignored it because I wanted him so much. Would settle for a different version of him, even though I needed all of him.

There was a long pause before he answered. "I'll come to you. What's your room number?"

"Two sixty-two."

"I'll be there soon, sweetheart."

I cleaned myself up a bit because I looked like a train wreck. Mascara stains were all over the duvet, so I washed the marks off my face and started over. I reapplied my makeup—but skipped the eyeliner and mascara in case those streaked again.

A knock sounded on the door.

My heart jumped when I heard it. The walk to the door felt like a mile rather than a couple feet. When I opened it, I saw the dark eyes that followed me everywhere in my dreams. They could be lethal, but when they looked at me with softness, they were harmless like a cup of coffee or the soil after a light rain.

He took me in before he stepped into my room and let the door shut automatically behind him. Every time I saw him, I forgot how tall he was, even taller than Bolton. But all he did was look at me. There was no embrace with his lips or his arms. There was no warmth to protect me from the cold.

If he wasn't going to comfort me, then why was he there?

I stepped farther into the room, a bed with a couple armchairs against the wall. My arms crossed over my chest because my own touch seemed to be the only comfort I would receive. "Did I do something, Theo?"

His eyes had been on the dresser when I asked the question, and they remained there.

"Because the other day, you showed up at the gallery when you saw me through the window. And now it's like you don't want to be here. You said if you wanted me gone, you would tell me, so tell me."

He slowly turned to look at me. "I told you it's been a rough week—"

"You're lying." I hadn't known him long, but I knew him well. "This isn't the man I know. I didn't expect us to fuck, but your hands would either be in my hair or on my ass by now."

His hard eyes remained on mine, giving nothing away.

"Did you only want me because I was married?" Now, the parameters of the relationship had changed. Now, there was nothing that separated us, and perhaps that made him uncomfortable.

"No."

"Then—then I don't understand."

"Astrid." It was one of the rare times he said my name, and he said it with a tone of anger I hadn't heard before. "I have some heavy shit on my plate right now. If you hadn't said you weren't okay, I probably wouldn't have come. But I care for you, so I came. I'm sorry that I'm not much comfort right now, but all the simplicity in my life just went out the window, and I don't know what the fuck to do about it."

Now, I felt guilty for only caring about myself. "You can talk to me about it."

"I can't."

"I know I'm not a part of your world, but—"

"I said I can't."

The anger in his tone made me back away. "Then maybe you should just go." My heart had already gone through one boxing match, and now it was going through another. It was battered and blue, in pieces on the floor.

He gave a quiet sigh, his eyes returning to the dresser

as he dragged his hand down across the bones of his jawline. "Yeah...maybe I should."

16

THEO

I sat alone in my study.

Like a gargoyle, I hadn't moved in two days.

The sun rose and set in the same places, but my life didn't change.

Astrid didn't text me.

I didn't text her.

I didn't know what the fuck to do.

Bolton hadn't contacted me or responded in any way. Had no idea if he knew I was the one who'd picked off his men one by one on the street. Maybe he didn't care as much as he should because he was distracted.

Distracted that his wife had left him.

The woman I'd bedded was married to my enemy. His last name was her last name. It was hard to shake, hard to look past. When I was in the same room with her, she felt like a different person. She was innocent of any crime, but I still felt betrayed by the association.

And I felt blindsided by it too.

I didn't know if she was still at the hotel. If she and Bolton had talked. If they would get back together, or she was set on her decision. I didn't prefer her married, but I preferred her with no expectations. Because while I did care for her, dinners and hookups were all I had to offer. Her shovel had gone as deep as it could before it hit rock, and she would never go deeper than that.

I hoped she hadn't left him for me, because she would be disappointed.

Axel texted me. *Just making sure you're still breathing.*

Not breathing. Smoking.

I'll take it. Figured out what to do about Bolton yet?

I didn't respond.

That's a no.

She left him.

Then you should be balls deep in her instead of talking to me.

I'm not.

That's it. I'm coming over.

I didn't shut down the offer, because I'd been sitting there alone for two days without any direction. I was a man of action. I just did shit when I felt like doing it. But now, my hands were bound by my invisible cords, and my brain had ceased to function.

———

Almost an hour passed before he dropped into the armchair across from me. I'd already put out my cigar a while ago, so he didn't light up one himself. I must have looked like shit since he didn't fire off questions or taunts. He sank into the chair and watched me.

"It's the first time in my life where I don't know what to do."

"If you torture and kill Bolton, she doesn't need to know it was you."

"But I would know."

"You're the one who told me I should just kill Dante. Now you know how complicated that would have been. But in my case, I loved Scarlett. And you...I don't know what your deal is."

"I care for her, but that's it."

"That's it?" he asked.

"I'm afraid she left him for me, even though I have nothing to offer her."

"You said it was clear you didn't want anything."

"I thought it was."

"Then why do you assume that?"

Because of the way she looked at me. The way she touched me. The way she said she wanted to be with me without something separating us. The way...the way the air felt when we stood in a room together. "I just do."

"The fact that you didn't tear Bolton's head off means your feelings for her are stronger than your need for revenge."

"It means I'm a disgrace to my brother. I know."

"Knowing Killian, he would have told you to pick the woman because he's already dead. No amount of revenge is going to change that. And it's not your fault that Killian got killed. That was the result of his own tumultuous decisions."

I wasn't sure if I could live with myself if I didn't bury my brother. If I didn't find a rightful place for his bones. Maybe Bolton didn't even have them anymore. Maybe whatever he would give me would belong to someone else. I could do a DNA test to figure out that since we were identical.

"I know you feel more for her than you say, Theo. And I know why you pretend."

I tried not to think of her because it was easier not to.

"Give it a chance with Astrid."

"She's not even divorced yet."

"Even better. You can take it slow."

"I'm not ready for a relationship."

"Asshole, I hate to break it to you, but you're in one. You're in a *very* complicated, *very* messy relationship. Just tell her you need to take it slow. Like fucking sloooooow. No pressure. No expectations. Just see where it goes."

I stared at the cold fireplace.

"Theo."

I wouldn't look at him.

"Your other choice was to torture and kill Bolton—and you've clearly decided not to do that. So this is the only choice. You've chosen it." He continued to stare at me. "Now go get your woman."

———

When I entered the Ritz, I made sure to take the back route. Slip in through the back door after one of the kitchen staff took out the trash. If she was still there, that meant Bolton had eyes on the building—especially if he knew about me.

I took the service elevator to her floor then headed down the hallway that I'd walked before. I wasn't sure if she was still there, if Bolton had dragged her back home, or if she'd moved in to an apartment once she had a second to breathe.

I knocked, unsure if she or a stranger would answer.

Footsteps made the floor creak slightly, and then the light over the peephole vanished as a shadow passed across.

Then the door opened, and Astrid was behind it.

Her eyes were hollow. Her fair skin was free of makeup. She wore a baggy shirt and pajama shorts, clearly not expecting visitors. Her reaction to me was subdued, that spark in her eyes stomped out by my boot. She pulled the door open wider so I could pass through but didn't actually say anything to me.

I entered the suite I'd visited before, and it looked exactly the same, as if time had been passing for her with the same painful slowness it'd been passing for me. Her suitcase was still in the corner, and a room service table was pushed against the wall, the plates mostly full of food she hadn't touched.

The depression filled the room like smoke.

I looked at her once again, seeing her arms crossed over her chest, completely cut off from me after I'd crushed her. "I'm sorry for the way I was before."

Her eyes were on the floor, her hands gripping the insides of her arms, her long hair beautifully placed around her shoulders. Even on her darkest night, she had a light so alluring.

"Not my best day."

She continued to avoid my stare like that apology wasn't good enough.

"Have you spoken to Bolton?"

After a pause, her eyes lifted to look at me. "He came by yesterday. We talked for hours and hours...and then he finally left."

Then she hadn't changed her mind.

"I can't go back to him, not when I feel this way."

"When you feel what way?"

"When I don't see him the same way anymore...when I have feelings for someone else. He could sleep with other people and keep it purely physical, but I'm not that way. I'm an emotional person. I connect emotionally, not just physically."

I watched the emotions move over her face as she spoke, watched her battle the tide that wanted to sweep her away.

"If he hadn't asked me to end the arrangement, I'm not sure how long I would have stayed. But I don't think I would have stayed forever. It'd been gnawing at me for a while, day and night, forming ulcers in my stomach. With every passing day, my lungs started to heave as I began to suffocate."

"Do you feel better now?" Because she looked worse than she ever had.

There was a long pause, a heavy one, full of so many things she never said. "I-I didn't expect to get divorced. I thought we would be together forever. Just a few months ago, I wanted to start a family...and now, I want to start a new life. It's hard because I really did love him. When he told me he wanted to be with other people, I still loved him. But over the last few months, that love changed. It stopped being enough." She swallowed and paused, forcing her eyes to remain dry. "He told me every man wants to fuck someone else besides his wife, but he was honest enough to tell me, and that somehow makes him better than all the rest. That he could have just cheated on me behind my back, but—"

"But he decided to cheat on you to your face," I said coldly. "Yes, very honorable." I hated Bolton for my own reasons, but the more I listened to her, the more I realized he was just an insufferable human being.

Her eyes latched on to mine.

"Some men want to fuck around. Men like him, who want a wife to fulfill a role, to hold her end of a business deal she didn't know she was making. She signed her name on the dotted line but didn't read the terms and conditions because she assumed she didn't need to. And other men..." Memories flashed across my mind, brief and sudden, bright colors and then rain clouds of gray. "Other men commit to one woman for the rest of their life because that's the only woman they want until they die. Men like Axel...and others like him."

Her eyes were locked on mine as she listened to me speak. She stopped blinking, regarding my stare intently. "And...what about you?"

I knew what she wanted from me, what she would never ask. "I'm a one-woman kind of man...when the time is right."

Her eyes flicked back and forth between mine, wanting to know more.

"I'm possessive. I'm jealous as fuck. Protective. Borderline psychotic. If someone tried to touch my woman, it would be the last thing they'd ever do. I'm too busy being into her to be interested in anyone else. I'm nothing like Bolton—but I'm sure you already figured that out."

"But you pay for sex and don't take women out."

She'd approached this topic once before, but I'd brushed her away. It was the red zone, off-limits. "Because I don't want to be in a relationship. It takes commitment, a level of commitment I'm incapable of right now."

Her eyes took me in with a hint of sadness. "Why are you incapable of it?"

I got lost in her eyes, almost tempted to tell her the truth, to share my hardship with another person besides Axel. I shared my truth with Axel, but I didn't wear my heart on my sleeve. "Because I am. After what Bolton did to you, I'm surprised you don't feel the same."

Her eyes flicked down for a second as she considered that. "I probably would feel that way...if I hadn't met you." It took her a moment to look at me again, embarrassed by what she had said.

I didn't want to hear those words, but I respected her for saying them.

"It'll be a while before I'm officially divorced because I know Bolton will make it as difficult as possible. It's not exactly the ideal conditions to start a new relationship...or deepen an existing one. Just because Bolton and I are in the process of separating doesn't mean I don't still have feelings for him, which isn't fair to you or anyone else. So, when you say you aren't ready for that level of commitment, that's okay, because I'm not either. But I would like to pursue this, at whatever pace is best for us." The hopeful burn remained in her eyes as she stared at me, openly wearing her heart on her sleeve, when I refused to do the same for her.

It was easy to get lost in her eyes when she spoke like that, with pure vulnerability, like she trusted me despite the skull diamond I wore on my hand, despite the fact that I was in the same business as the man who had betrayed her. Bolton and I were both black sheep, both dangerous, but she looked at me like I was different. "Relationships lead to commitment, and commitment leads to marriage—the type of relationship I never intend to offer. The last thing I want to do is waste your time, sweetheart. Please understand this isn't an empty warning. I say what I mean, and I mean what I say. You said you want to have a family, so you don't have much time to waste on someone who won't give that to you. With me, you get what you see, hear the truth even when you prefer the lie, so I'll never disappoint you the way Bolton has. But I also won't give you as much as he has."

She absorbed my words with a heavy stare, her eyes still locked on mine. Her gaze didn't hold disappointment. But she seemed to take my words seriously because she digested them during a long bout of silence. "I understand."

I waited for more, for her to elaborate on exactly what she wanted, but I refused to push.

"Yes, I'm aware of the constant ticking of the clock, but it's hard to imagine being in that place anytime soon. Right now, all I have is the present, and the only man I desire is you, regardless of what you have to offer."

I felt like the biggest jackass for wanting that answer, for watching her settle for less than she deserved just because it benefited me. Instead of giving her false hope to entice her, I was honest with her, even if that meant I'd lose her. She still wanted me, and I felt like shit about that because I was dangling candy in front of a kid—and the kid always ate the candy, even if they knew it would make them sick.

Now that the storm clouds had passed over our skies, it was just the two of us, staring at each other, an invisible magnetic force slowly pulling us closer together. She had the same confident stare that I possessed, just with a hint of softness like a flower in the spring sunshine. I'd been with a lot of women, but none of them wanted me the way she did, like her desire was deeper than the surface, like she wanted to dig her hands into my skin and reach my soul underneath.

My restraint broke like a stretched rubber band, and I moved to her, sliding my hand deep into her hair as I angled her chin back, preparing her mouth for my kiss. My lips met hers, and as always, there was a break in time, a pause that stopped the world from turning. It resumed a second later, and I deepened my kiss, my arm moving across the small of her back and squeezing her close.

She rose on her tiptoes as one hand found my chest, and her arm hooked halfway around my neck, as far as she could reach when she was at a serious height disadvantage while barefoot. But her kiss was passionate, like she'd been wanting this for every second of every day for years.

I scooped her into my chest so she could hook both of her arms easily around my neck, our mouths level so she wouldn't have to crane her slim neck so far to kiss me. My hands squeezed her ass in her little shorts as I guided her to the bed, my dick anxious since the moment she'd accepted my terms. Her legs were so toned and sexy, her toenails painted a pale blue like the sky. I pictured those little feet against my chest as I nailed her on the hotel bed.

I laid her back and hooked my fingers into her bottoms before I pulled back, tugging her shorts and the panties underneath with me. I dragged both down her toned legs and revealed the sex that I could taste on my tongue just by looking at it.

She watched me stare at her, her body propped on her elbows, her breathing elevated.

I yanked my shirt over my head and undressed, my knees sinking into the mattress when I returned to the bed.

She pulled off her shirt and revealed her tits underneath because she wasn't wearing a bra.

I moved on top of her then flinched.

I didn't bring anything.

My thoughts had been in a lot of places at once, not on sex, so I'd forgotten a crucial component to our reunion.

She seemed to read the hesitation in my eyes. "I'm on the pill."

I'd only been with one woman bareback…and that was a long time ago.

"And I got tested the other day," she said. "But if you're not comfortable, it's okay."

My arms scooped behind her knees, and I positioned her underneath me as my mouth sealed over hers once more. The kiss burned even hotter now that I knew where it would lead, when I would feel her with nothing in between us.

She seemed to feel the same way because her nails clawed at my back before I was even inside her. She even panted in my mouth between our kisses like we were already engaged in our sexy dance.

I directed my head to her entrance and felt the wet kiss of her body, the slickness that coated my skin at the first touch. Warm, tight, anxious…it was a whole different experience. An experience that surpassed my one-night stands and the sex I'd paid for. I pushed until I burrowed my head inside and then sank. "Fuck…" It wasn't just slick and tight–it was intimate.

The most intimate I'd been with anyone in a long time.

I pressed as far as I could, almost balls deep, listening to her suck in a deep breath when it hurt.

She gave a small wince that looked so sexy as her nails dug in like anchors on the sea floor.

I withdrew slightly so she could relax, removing myself for a moment until I slid back inside, coated in her slickness, my girth squeezed by her tightness. It was so different from the last time we were together that it felt like the first time.

She could feel it too, her breaths shaky and accompanied by sexy little whimpers.

Slow and easy was the most I could do, my face just inches above hers, turned on by her reaction alone.

Her hands squeezed my thick arms before her nails dug into my flesh again. Then she gripped my shoulders, drove her fingers into my hair, touched me everywhere as she took my thickness over and over.

The women who were paid to be with me wanted me, but Astrid touched me like she needed me. Her eyes were always affectionate. She was always desperate, like I was the only man in the world who could fix her problems.

It was so good I wasn't sure if I would ever get used to it, feeling her creamy flesh encased around my length, her grip tighter than the body of a viper. My hips started to thrust harder on their own, my dick taking the reins from my mind because he had the most blood of the two of us.

Once I was inside her, all I wanted to do was come, come like a teenage boy who was feeling a woman for the first time. The hormones were stronger, the desperation at its peak. It must be because it was skin to skin...or maybe it was another reason.

Her hand went to my ass and tugged me inside. "It's okay."

A burst of pleasure shot up my spine at her words, my dick even harder at her request to fill her. She watched my struggle and my restraint, saw the red tint in my face, the way I pushed through the sex rather than fucked her like I normally did.

I couldn't deny the invitation, not when the feel of her sex was so damn good. It was all I could think about, head high in the clouds, the desire making my dick so stiff it hurt. After a couple thrusts, I released, a heavy growl coming from my throat.

Her nails dug into my ass, and she pulled on me hard, wanting all of my dick as I came inside her like it turned her on to watch me fill her.

There was no greater pleasure than to come inside a woman, and I'd forgotten how good it was. To give my seed to a woman so anxious to receive it. To feel her warmth sheath me in gratitude.

Her nails loosened on my ass, her little body still folded with her flexibility.

I filled her with a load, but my dick was still stiff as a tree trunk. Still at attention and ready to serve. I started to rock into her again, but this time, I gave it to her hard, prepared to make up for that poor performance.

She gave the sexiest moan when she felt me blast off, her nails dragging down my chest as I fucked her just the way she liked, hitting my pelvic bone right against her clit.

Her skin glowed and her eyes watered. Her forehead shone with sweat even though she was only lying there and enjoying it. "Yes..." One hand went to my ass, and she clenched it with her sharp nails, pushing her body back into mine so our skin slapped against each other as we fucked.

The skin of her neck and face turned bright red, and her eyes started to glisten with impending tears. She was almost there, right at the edge, about to be swept away in the euphoria my dick was desperate to give her. "Theo." She whispered my name with her eyes closed, then she opened them again to lock her stare on me.

"Come on, sweetheart." I already wanted to come inside her again, her pussy the smoothest scotch I'd ever tasted, the best cigar I'd ever smoked.

She started with a quiet moan, but once the fuse was lit, her moan got louder, her clenched eyes releasing tears on each side. Her body gripped mine with an iron fist, and she came all over my dick, sheathing me in her cream and her warmth, saying my name with a voice that cracked.

Her sexy little performance pushed me over the edge, and I came with a grunt, filling her little pussy again, dumping another load of my desire in her tightness where it belonged. This time, my dick started to soften because he needed to reload.

But when I tried to pull away, she held on to my ass. "I want to do it again."

I smirked. "I need a couple minutes, sweetheart."

She grabbed my face and pulled my lips to her. "Then I'll wait."

I lay beside her in the king-sized bed, the heater kicking on and off throughout the night. It was the first time I'd slept with her somewhere else besides my home, so it was hard to relax. Bolton would have constant eyes on her, and even though the curtains had been drawn shut the entire time, I could still feel his stare.

I'd just come inside his wife—several times—and if that wasn't a form of revenge, I didn't know what was.

Killian would smirk at that.

I checked my phone on my nightstand, and it was

quiet. No messages from anyone. It was almost five in the morning.

I looked at her beside me, dead asleep with her arms around me like I was her favorite teddy bear. Her hair was a mess, but the sexiest mess I'd ever seen. And she had a little smile on her face, like she was happy even in her dreams.

I hated to leave, but I shouldn't stay. Not when her relationship with Bolton was so tumultuous, when he still struggled to let her go. I wasn't scared of him, but I preferred to be with her on my turf rather than the unknown.

I left the bed and got dressed.

She was so tired she didn't even notice.

I checked the peephole to make sure the hallway was vacant before I walked out. I took the service elevator like I did last time and snuck out the back of the hotel, quickly swallowed by the city.

I'd walked to the hotel, so I walked home, enjoying the city in the early morning, taking the alleyways between the buildings and the shortcuts only a resident would know. I entered the gates of my property and stepped inside the home that was my fortress, the one place where I could stare out the window without worrying about taking a bullet, because the glass was bulletproof. The place where I hid in plain sight, my walls impossible to pass unless you rammed it with a Hummer.

But the second I stepped inside, I knew something was amiss.

Not because of anything I could see…could only feel.

I stood in the foyer and noticed how bright the dimmers were set. There was a different smell, the scents of cider and cigarette smoke. I stared at the staircase before I reached for my gun tucked in the back of my jeans.

My butler knew when I was on the property and always came to greet me, regardless of the hour, and the fact that he wasn't there told me he physically couldn't be. "I hope you took your boots off before you came inside." I walked around the stairs with the gun at my side, unsure how they'd bypassed the security measures, how they'd infiltrated a place that couldn't be broken in to.

"My boots are propped on your coffee table as we speak." The voice came from the study, farther down past the staircase, the place where I spent most of my time.

With my gun still in hand, I came around the corner and spotted Bolton in my armchair, dirty shoes on my coffee table, drink in front of him, a lit cigar in his mouth because he really had made himself at home.

With a bomb strapped across his chest.

My gun had been pointed at his head, but I lowered it to my side.

My butler was in the other armchair, appearing still and calm except for his trembling hands.

Bolton pulled the cigar out of his mouth and rested it in his fingertips, not afraid of the ash that might land in the wrong spot on his chest. "You made yourself at home in my house." He smashed the cigar in my ashtray. "Thought I'd do the same to you." He nodded to the couch. "Take a seat, Theo."

I glanced at my butler then looked at Bolton again. "He's got nothing to do with this, Bolton."

"He has everything to do with this, Theo," he said. "Because we both know what he'll do once I cut him loose. Now take a seat." He gestured to the tray of cigars. "Help yourself. I don't mind in the least."

I took a seat on the couch across from my butler and stared at Bolton.

He stared back, lounging comfortably like the bomb didn't bother him at all. "When I think of revenge, I only think of torture and death. But you have a very different approach to it."

I assumed he meant Astrid, but I wasn't sure if he was fishing.

His stare continued to burn into my face, growing hotter and hotter.

I wasn't sure if he knew where I'd just been. What I'd just been doing. That my dick smelled like her because I hadn't showered.

His stare continued, explosive like the surface of the sun, his rage so intense he seemed to forget words.

Yep. He definitely knew.

"I'd kill you right here, right now, if I could. Luck is on your side, Theo. But I have another idea—a compromise."

He wanted to compromise with the man fucking his wife?

"You want to know who put that hit on Killian? I'll give you the contract details. But this man is a cut above the rest. If you intend to take him down with your usual means, you'll be unsuccessful. So, not only will I give you his information, I'll help you put him in the ground. But I want something in return."

To stay away from Astrid.

"You're going to hurt my wife."

My heart gave a sudden clench.

"There will be no explanation. You'll just dump her and ghost her. You got your revenge and poisoned my fucking soul. It's done."

"It was never about revenge—"

"Take the offer." He grabbed his gun and aimed it at my butler. "Or I shoot Grandpa in the head."

My butler stiffened, his breaths turning anxious.

"Bolton—"

He cocked the gun. "Take the deal, or he dies."

My brother was my other half, and to never reclaim his body was something I couldn't live with. I didn't want to hurt Astrid, but I didn't want to betray my own family and my butler for a woman I could never have. And even if I did have her, it wouldn't last. It wouldn't last because I was irrevocably broken and had nothing to offer. "Fine."

"Good." He set the gun next to the ashtray. "I want this done first thing tomorrow. She will know nothing of this conversation."

"Even with me out of the way, she won't go back to you."

"I disagree." He helped himself to a glass of scotch he poured for himself.

"If you didn't want your wife fucking other people, then you shouldn't have asked to fuck other people."

He took another drink and ignored me.

"I didn't do it out of revenge. I did it because I wanted to. Because Astrid is a beautiful woman—who deserves better than you."

"If she deserves better than me, then she deserves better than you."

I couldn't disagree with that.

"Dump her, Theo." He got to his feet and stuffed his

gun into the back of his jeans. "And I'll keep my word to you."

"What happened to your plan to kill me?"

He stared down at me for a second. "My wife is a smart woman. If you drop dead, she'll know it was me. And then she really will leave. But if you hurt her, her confidence will be crushed, and she'll run right back into my arms—where she belongs."

Sickness entered my chest, picturing her with him again now that she'd been mine, even if it was only for a couple of hours.

"Once the job is done, we'll get to work." He grabbed his scotch and finished it off before he moved toward me. "I'm a man of my word, Theo. And you better be a man of yours—otherwise, your other brother will suffer the consequences."

17

ASTRID

New beginnings were always scary.

I had to find a new apartment. Buy new furniture. Start a life very different from my old one. Despite my intense feelings for Theo, I was heartbroken that my marriage had ended so abruptly. It wasn't the slow deterioration that most people described, where life in the bedroom went cold, and inappropriate messages appeared on someone's phone in the middle of the night. It was sudden, like a car ran a red light, and I had to slam on the brakes to stop the collision.

It wasn't enough time to process how much everything had changed. That we went from discussing a family to discussing fucking other people. Then Theo walked into my life and set the whole place on fire. I didn't know men like him existed, but of course, perfection came with a caveat.

He wouldn't commit.

I just wished I knew why. Was it because he was the Skull King? An association with him would always be dangerous. Or was it for a different reason entirely?

I'd just packed up my things in preparation to leave the hotel when someone knocked on my door.

It was probably Bolton to make another attempt to bring me home. Theo would text me before he showed up unannounced. But then again, I wasn't really sure what he would do because he'd never been able to visit me until now.

I checked the peephole and was pleasantly surprised by the face on the other side. The dark beard on his jawline, the espresso eyes, the shoulders that blocked most of the hallway. I opened the door and saw him with my own eyes rather than through the distortion of the peephole.

My heart gave a flutter like it always did at the sight of him. My lungs filled with a fresh breath of air, and a slight chill ran down my fingertips. It was like a jolt of electricity, but cool to the touch.

His eyes didn't mirror my affection. His expression rarely changed, but it seemed like a cloud had blocked the sun from his skies. He entered the room and let the door swing shut by itself. There was no kiss. No ass-grab. It felt like we were about to have the same conversation we'd already had yesterday.

"I found an apartment. I was just about to head over." After I dropped off my things, I would begin the onerous task of retrieving my valuables from the house, a daunting endeavor because Bolton would make it as difficult as possible.

He glanced at my suitcase and stared at it for seconds, like he just wanted to have something to look at. Anything was preferable to me. Last time he was here, we'd made love in my bed on the verge of something new, and now, it was like that moment had never happened. "Astrid." He looked at me again. He said my name to get my attention, but it was just a filler because he already had my attention the second he knocked on the door. "It's best if we don't see each other anymore." He said it without missing a beat, eyes locked on mine with the same confidence he always exuded.

I knew something was amiss, but I hadn't expected him to say *that*. "What—what are you talking about?" I wished I could retain my composure as well as he could, but I wasn't a robot like he was.

"I've thought it over. It's best if we end it."

"Why?" I kept my voice steady, but it nearly cracked at the end.

"I don't want to waste your time."

"It's my time, Theo. I decide how I want to invest or waste it."

His eyes flicked away. "You were right. Our relationship only worked because you were married. Because there was an obstacle between us. Now that the barrier is no longer there, there's no excitement." He looked at me again when he finished, as confident as he was when he'd walked in the door, like he meant every word.

But I still couldn't believe it. "You said that wasn't the case."

"I lied."

"You wouldn't lie." I'd seen this man from surface to bone. Saw the integrity in his heart because he wore it on his sleeve.

"Then I lied to myself and, therefore, lied to you."

"Theo—"

"Astrid." For the first time, he raised his voice slightly. "I'm sorry. It's done."

He'd never been so harsh with me. Always treated me with respect. Validated my feelings. Now, he acted like I was a thorn that had pricked his thumb and left a spot of blood. "So you come over here and say you want to take things slow, fuck me without a condom and come inside me—and now you're just done?"

He flinched slightly at my choice of words. "It wasn't premeditated."

"Then you're lying. Which is it?"

His eyes narrowed slightly on my face.

"I know you. You're a good man, Theo. You wouldn't act like this—"

"You don't know me, Astrid. You know my surface and my craters, but you don't know my icebergs hidden in my depths. When I told you I had nothing to offer, I meant it. That's what I'm offering you now—nothing."

"You said you would try—"

"I said I would see where it goes."

"So you went home after you fucked me and just decided you already knew the destination before you stepped foot on the road?" I asked incredulously. "Where's the man who came into the gallery because he could see my despair through the window? Where's the man who said I deserved the world and the heavens too? Where's the man who picked me up when I could barely stand—" I stopped because my voice started to shake, my shell starting to crack and expose the geysers underneath. "You are not that man. You—you're a—"

"Changeling," he said. "Yes, that's exactly what I am."

I stared.

He stared back.

The silence stretched. The conversation seemed to be over. My heart was already broken from Bolton, but Theo seemed to step on the shards and grind them into beads of sand. I was lost, but my guiding star had vanished in the storm clouds. I'd never felt more alone than I did in that moment.

Theo continued to stare, as if he expected more from me.

It took a moment to collect my thoughts. "I feel like I'm looking at a puzzle with a missing piece. A portrait with a color removed. A story without a setting. Because you may think you're a changeling, that you don't belong where you stand, but that's not what I see when I look at you."

There was a flinch in his eyes, so subtle I wasn't sure if it really happened.

"I'm not going to convince someone to be with me. I'm not going to beg you to stay or tell you how much you mean to me, not when you already know the depth of my feelings that I've never had the courage to even whisper. But I want to know—why?"

He stared at my eyes and said nothing.

"Why won't you try?"

He didn't answer the question.

"Because Bolton broke my heart and shattered my trust, but I would try again…with you."

His eyes flicked away again.

"Because I know it would be different with you."

He continued to avoid my stare.

"Theo—"

"It's not about trust, Astrid."

"Then what is it about—"

"Let it go." Instead of raising his voice, he lowered it, like he didn't have the energy to fight my stream of questions. "I say what I mean, and I mean what I say. I can never offer you the things you want. I'm a great lover and a great friend—but that's it."

"With me, you were both."

He stared.

"That's all I want, Theo. I just want to *try*—"

"I'm done with this conversation, Astrid," he snapped. "I'm done with you. I'm done with us. Is that clear?"

His abrupt change in attitude was so harsh it felt like he'd shoved me against the wall. He lashed out, and it nearly knocked the wind out of me, left gashes in my lungs so I couldn't breathe. "Why are you acting like this—"

"Because I'm dumping you, and you lack the grace to accept it."

His claws made me bleed. I felt it ooze down my arms to my fingertips. My lungs took a harsh breath, and then I held it, my face feeling hot and my eyes suddenly tired. My snowcaps melted, and the dam in my throat struggled to hold back the water that wanted to gush from my eyes. "Alright…I accept it." I stepped away and moved toward my suitcase on the other side of the room, pretending to return to my packing as if the conversation had never happened. "You can let yourself out, Theo." I grabbed a stack of my sweaters that had been folded on the dresser and placed them on top of my jeans and skirts, focusing on the heels that I placed in the bottom of the suitcase, reading the brand of each one just so I had something to focus on until he left.

It took a moment for him to take a step. I imagined he stared at my back and watched me pack up my things. His first step was audible. And then the next one…and the next.

I hoped he would walk toward me, but he headed to the door.

Then it opened and closed. His footsteps disappeared a moment later.

I stared at the bottom of the suitcase as my eyes watered. I moved backward until the backs of my knees hit the foot of the bed. Then I sat down, alone in the quiet hotel suite, my tears breaking free and streaking down my cheeks. I held my breath in the hope it would stifle my tears, but it only made me gasp.

Made me gasp and cry.

Cry for a man who had never really been mine.

Next in the series...

Theo had no choice but to walk away. But will he be able to stay away from the only women who has mattered to him in a decade? Find out in ***It Pains Me.***

There's been a lot of questions about the special edition books for the Buttons Series as well as the Barsetti Vineyards merch, so let me explain.

I'll be launching a Kickstarter in July where you can get these sexy-as-fuck special edition, annotated paperbacks lined with foil, with monochrome chapter headings, and the things you want most of all -- bonus content. I've written 60k words of bonus content across these books. A long prologue that shows Crow's life before Vanessa died AND a new epilogue that follows Crow and Pearl when Tristan comes back for an unexpected visit. There's also my annotations, where I spill all the tea about writing these books. I know you guys have been in love with this series for almost ten years and it's time to celebrate. There'll be more than just the paperbacks, but t-shirts and hoodies, wine glasses and wrapping paper, a Crow Barsetti scented candle, wine, and sooo much more.

Printed in Great Britain
by Amazon

42864721R00212